To Jim who is

LOOKING FOR
TO
THE SEVENTIES

KU-082-314

with a fine degree
of optimism

M.Ed.

2.6.70.

Cliff

Roberts

LOOKING FORWARD
TO
THE SEVENTIES

*A Blueprint
for Education in the
Next Decade*

*

EDITED
BY
PETER BANDER

COLIN SMYTHE
Gerrards Cross 1968

Printed in Holland by n.v. Drukkerij Bosch Utrecht

CONTENTS

5

Contents

FOREWORD

Just as the full effect of the Industrial Revolution was not felt for many years after its beginning, so the first full effect of the Educational Revolution which started with this century, was not felt until the passing of the Education Act in 1944. There is no doubt that the *Butler Act* has exerted a great influence on the development of this country, because it laid the foundations for a real future to which our children can look forward. Since the Act was passed, every aspect of education has developed. We can rightly be proud of the progress which has been made, particularly the thorough investigations and recommendations of the Royal Commissions.

The thoroughness of the investigations, however, has led to much criticism of educational practices, institutions and policies, and this has aroused considerable resentment on the one hand, and depression on the other, so that the true picture of the achievements in education has become blurred. Each of the Commissions reported on only one aspect of education, *in isolation*; these reports were issued during a period of several years and when the last report was published, the recommendations and findings of the earlier Commissions had in many cases been shelved and forgotten.

One point is always present in the minds of educators, but is rarely mentioned, and that is the price we pay for our *democratic* educational system. Our society and its development is governed by majority decisions, and educational progress is often retarded in two directions: firstly, the report of a Royal Commission is a

7

majority report, so that the imaginative and constructive ideas of individual members are sacrificed to the common denominator of opinion, and therefore are unlikely to reach those who would be prepared to implement these ideas; and secondly, education of the young has become a major party political issue.

We have now reached the very dangerous situation where any suggestion concerning development in education is likely to become political controversy and little attempt is made to treat new suggestions objectively. Britain is blessed with a number of educationists of international standing, and it is a matter of deep regret that their suggestions, when put forward by Royal Commissions, have been taken over and often misinterpreted by politicians.

It would be unfair and misleading to single out any particular administration to prove my point; I should prefer to make out a case for putting education "top of the list" of national priorities. For many years now the operative slogan has been "economic growth," development and opportunity; national wealth and resources are the goals *every* government has promised and attempted to establish and develop during its term of office. Many an imaginative plan has been given the green light and millions of pounds to help it on its way, only to be abandoned after a while because the ultimate return could never justify the investment. And yet, our greatest national resource, our real wealth, has only been tapped very modestly, and not to its full capacity. Our greatest wealth, perhaps our only real wealth, is the talent which is latent in every British child. This talent has not been developed as it could have been. Some shafts in the minefields of our talent have never been allowed to go deeper in their search for wealth, others have been closed half-way. Whatever the reasons for this "industrial short sightedness", lack of money or emotional issues which have blurred the judgement, the fact remains that many attempts to increase productivity, particularly in respect of quality, have been doomed to remain ideas.

In spite of these sad facts, I have always believed that our education system has tremendous potentials and a future to look forward to. For some time I have felt that if our leading educationists could be persuaded to express their personal ideas and suggestions, independently of any Commission or other organisation, and cover the *whole* range of education, much stimulating discussion and enthusiasm would follow and we could look forward to the seventies

8

as a decade in which exciting progress might be achieved. I also believe that any suggestions and ideas thus expressed might be accepted and considered by our legislators, whatever their political persuasion, because they were made by individuals whose eminence in the field of education is unchallenged.

When I was invited to edit an educational symposium I realised the tremendous opportunity this afforded to produce a blueprint for education in the Seventies. The enthusiasm which the project aroused amongst my fellow educationists encouraged me to extend the scope of the symposium and invite contributions from our leading educationists. The ready acceptance of my invitations by eminent men and women proved to me that I had undertaken a task which in their opinion was vitally necessary.

I would like to make quite clear that the choice of contributors was mine alone; there are however technical limitations to the extend of a work of this kind, which restrict the number and length of contributions.

It would be superfluous to pay tribute individually to those who have contributed to this symposium, but I feel that some critics may wonder why certain curriculum aspects have not been included. To have done so would have exceeded my terms of reference and, the symposium might have lost its character.

The contributions by Sir Robert Mayer and Sir Herbert Read, dealing with music and the arts, are of particular significance in an age of increasing leisure time for young people. I consider it a matter of importance that the two elder statesmen in education who both have given a life time of service to the young, should have the opportunity to draw on their experience in expressing their hopes for the seventies. Likewise, I have invited T.R. Henn, the poet and literary doyen of Cambridge, to discuss the singularly important subject of English. In an age where our major problem is that of a breakdown in communication, the English Language and methods of teaching it cannot be reviewed often enough.

Whilst the names of most of the contributors are well known in the educational world, I cannot omit to mention those members of Her Majesty's Inspectorate who for the first time are making contributions under their own names, and not in the name of the

Department of Education and Science. The time has come to give acknowledgement to individual members of the "reticent corps d'elite of Curzon Street" as they were recently referred to in *The Times*.

I hope that this symposium will help to change the image of British education and present a true picture of a service which is positive and forward-looking. The fact that during the Sixties the products of our education are in great demand the world over testifies to the soundness of our system, and is a challenge in the seventies. Looking forward to the next decade is neither futurology nor crystal gazing; it is a sign that we have faith in our future and a wealth of valuable ideas to benefit the coming generations.

P.B.

ACKNOWLEDGEMENTS

The Editor wishes to express his gratitude to Sir Robert Mayer, LL.D., Sir John Newson, C.B.E., LL.D., Miss A.K. Davies, M.A., and Mr. Gordon Samson, B.A., for their advice and helpful suggestions, and Mr. Colin Smythe, M.A., his publisher, for making such a work possible.

THE 1944 EDUCATION ACT IN THE NEXT DECADE

*

LORD BUTLER OF SAFFRON WALDEN

Peter Bander: "Will the 1944 Act continue to provide a satisfactory basis for education in the Seventies?"
Lord Butler: "The first thing to get clear about the 1944 Act is that it has not needed major amendment up to date, and has survived a number of Governments, Administrations and Ministers, all of whom found that they could work under it. The only major change made by Mr. Anthony Crosland when Secretary of State for Education and Science was to render the form of secondary education so to speak compulsory. I say 'so to speak' compulsory because his circular gives directions from the centre. I always envisaged that in secondary education the experiments would come from the circumference, that is, from the Local Education Authorities. I never expected that the centre would give instructions as to a particular type of secondary education. The interpretation of Circular 10/65 will take some years to work out, but however long this takes, what is clear is that the Act does nothing to stop a Minister in his attempts to reform secondary education as he wishes.

Some critics have said that the Act really determined that there should be three separate sorts of secondary education. The Act said nothing of the sort! It was at first the practice that there were secondary modern schools, technical schools and grammar schools, but I was perfectly ready to see composite experiments at that date. Composite experiments have now become the fashion, and this just shows how under the Act things can develop in the seventies by yet doing no violence to the Act itself.

The Act lays down that there must be primary, secondary and further education, and I do not think that that does violence to any-

13

body. I think this is sensible. The only major amendment which could be made in the seventies might concern the implementation of the middle school idea, which would have to be classed under the present provisions of the Act as primary or secondary. If there were difficulty over this then there might have to be an amendment to the Act. After all, I have never discounted the possibility of amendments to the Act; there was quite an important one over grants for denominational schools. These grants have now been raised to over 80%. They have been adjusted from time to time from the original 50%.

I always referred to the Act as a huge temple into which any person could come, and its roof would cover any idea. I believe that to be the case today and looking forward to the seventies, while I shall be prepared to consider any point of view that may be expressed, I would like to say that the Act itself requires little amendment as it stands."

Peter Bander: "Where do you think that the priorities lie in the Seventies?"

Lord Butler: "The priorities in education have for many years been almost completely taken up by secondary education and the experiments in that field; secondly by the enormous school leaver problem, and thirdly by the entry to new universities (of which including the new colleges and Polytechnics there are about 44). The interest in primary education has come almost entirely from the Plowden Report, which has two major features of importance; first, it concentrates on primary education which had been forgotten, and secondly, it brings out the idea of official help to schools in backward areas. The Government has alread decided to act on the latter by making a grant to such schools and I should not like to see primary education forgotten in the seventies as it has been recently. After all, it is in primary education that we pick people out for the right secondary education. I would like to make the 'right' secondary education for *all* a reality in the seventies, whether by comprehensive or other means. I do not want to see the ancient grammar schools destroyed; I believe that they can find their place in a general arrangement of secondary education and I would like to deal with the problem of selecting the best pupils for further education in the higher spheres as Sir Geoffrey Crowther wanted to do.

I think that selection on ability for higher opportunity is *absolutely inevitable* and I fail to see how, at that stage when you have had a child under the educational lamp for so long, you can avoid such a test of ability. The vital moment really comes when you choose the children for their *right* secondary education and choose the schools to which they are going. Therefore I would like to see a good deal of attention paid to this transitional period, and I think this may well become the most important of the priorities. Elsewhere in this symposium Her Majesty's Chief Inspector Mr. L. J. Burrows describes a new form of school which forms the transition between the primary and secondary level and caters for the pupils aged nine to thirteen – the Middle School. This is precisely one of the experiments which I wish to see in the Seventies. In my pronouncements when I was Minister of Education I always said that I did not think that the choice ought to be made at eleven. I believed that there should be a much longer period, up to thirteen, in which that choice was made. There is no doubt that nursery schools and primary pupils up to the age of nine will receive further attention in the seventies; it is in this middle group, where we choose and select the young people, that I would like to see more experiments made.

I think that the Government of today has accepted the major principles of teaching our fifteen and sixteen year olds which was the main feature in the Newsom Report and I do not think that Sir John has much to grumble about!

Sir Geoffrey Crowther's report was such a colossal document that it is difficult to carry it all out. His main point was the finding and selection of talent, and then the training of this talent. I am so to speak an educationist by being. I have read and considered these reports carefully. I think that Crowther's main feeling, which he has not expressed fully in his report but which I *know* he has, is that *talent is our main quarry in Britain today*. We have no raw materials, we have no great wealth. **Unless we accept our own skills and talents, unless we use our education system to bring out our skills and talents, we shall never remain in the forefront of the nations.** That is why education is so vitally important to our economic future apart from our cultural and social future.

Although I consider primary education very important, I would first try to make some sense of the secondary experiments. I do not think that we have heard the last word about the comprehensive school, because if such a school is to be successful, it must have a very strong sixth form.

I would certainly not try the experiment of sixth form colleges, because they are not schools, but just *creations*! A school consists of both the younger and the older, the young having an influence on

15

the old and above all the old having an influence on the young.

To take the best pupils from the schools and put them together into a new "creation' means that the schools are decapitated and suffer as a result. I would like to see the secondary schools left as composite entities. If they have to become great in size like the comprehensive schools, they must have a really composite sixth form."

Peter Bander: "In his contribution to this symposium Lord Robbins has much criticism to offer on present sixth form practice and curricula. Do you feel that we are neglecting education for the sake of examinations?"

Lord Butler: "This of course is one of the great criticisms of education at all stages in Britain. It applies equally to the university where specialisation is so profound that only one subject is taken. Those reading humanities are virtually divided. It is almost impossible for anyone reading such a course to have any side-line whatever. This may be necessary because of the university curriculum, but I strongly believe that the danger in the sixth forms at present is that they are governed by examinations rather than by real educational needs. This is not the fault of the Education Act but has to do with the content of education with which the Act does not really deal. I think that the content of education is a very important thing to look to in the 1970's and it would be a great relief if not only could there be a Middle School but also if, in the upper branches, sixth forms of secondary schools, there could be less narrow standards for examinations. This would give the British people much less specialisation and much more real education."

Peter Bander: "Which other ideas would you like to see implemented in the Seventies?"

Lord Butler: "One idea is that of the county colleges, which I took from H. A. L. Fisher. This idea is no further ahead now, after fifty years, than it was at the time of Fisher during the first world war, when Fisher ended up as Minister of Education, or rather President of the Board of Education. I am very disappointed, not only that county colleges have not materialised, but also that there is not more release from industry amongst older children. The ordinary day-release from industry is disappointing in the country today and this connexion between school and industry leaves much to be desired. Day-release, in my opinion, is a part of the 1944 Act which hardly exists in our country at all. I regret this very much and I do not think that the technical departments of comprehensive schools have really made up for it. In the seventies, therefore, I would like to see closer contact between school and industry in industrial training.

During my term of office as Minister of Education my great disappointment was in what was called 'reorganisation of schools', that is, the segregation of primary and secondary pupils. It took such a very long time to carry out, and it was only just before this recent comprehensive boom, as I call it, that we finished educating children in all-age schools. The reorganisation went on for years after the Hadow Report which was a basis for the Education Act. This Report demanded that reorganisation of the all-age schools should be completed immediately. To think that the Report was made in the 1920's and we are now in the 1960's! What I would like to see in the 1970's is a little faster progress in creating a really fine form of secondary education and in selecting the right kind of school leaver for the Universities."

Peter Bander: "What is future of religious education as laid down in your Act?"

Lord Butler: "Perhaps the most controversial provisions of the 1944 Act are those dealing with religious education. It would be possible to make one major change in religious education, namely, to remove these provisions from the Act; removal would be in accord with some feeling in the country that it may not be right to give religious education in schools. In my day in 1941 to 1944 it was very strongly felt that these provisions *should* be inserted in the Act, and this was done with the full approval of the Churches. Of course, in denominational Schools the pupils are taught according to the tenets of their faith, but in the ordinary state schools the Act provides for religious education. The Agreed Syllabus for religious education prepared by the counties, notably Cambridgeshire, was a great innovation. In my opinion it is not so much the clauses of this religious instruction which have to be altered as the spirit in which they have been supported. I have been very disappointed by the manner in which the Churches have failed to rally to the idea of having religious education in schools. What I mean is that they are apt to think that it is all being done by the teachers in the schools, and that they now have simply to deal with the few children who come under the control of the church schools and with parents. In my opinion the only diocese at present which has realised the gravity of the problem is the archdiosese of York where a committee

17

has been set up under Mr. Richard Wood, M.P., to study the effect of religious teaching in school and the danger of its decline. I would of course see in a changing Britain every possibility that these clauses in the Act might be amended but I would be much more nervous that they might be taken out altogether.

I would never amend the settlement of what we call the Dual System because I could not allow a priest of the Church of England full rein in a county school; that would be going back a generation and would not be tolerated by the Free churches. I would not like to go back on the aided school control principle because the aided school is a very good idea which permits the tenets of religious denominations to be taught. What I fear could happen in the seventies is that the comprehensive system may envelope smaller denominational schools and place some of the aided schools in a very difficult situation. If for example an aided school has to amalgamate with a non-denominational school a very difficult situation will arise in the giving of religious instruction and this might well necessitate some amendment of the Act.

I want to see religious education continued in schools. There is no doubt that religious education is in danger. The statistics show that only about 5% of the children in England are actually under the control or influence of the Churches. That seems a very small figure but in relation to the child population of about eleven million the figure is about right. Almost 95% of all the children are provided for by the daily act of worship and certain periods of religious instruction. This keeps alive in the breast of the child some beginnings of religious belief upon which the Churches can work later. This is why I think it so important for the Churches to realise that these provisions of the Act are a very important feature, one which I would not like to see altered. **We should be a poorer country if we removed religious education from the children."**

Peter Bander: "Which do you think is the outstanding problem in the next decade?"

Lord Butler: "If you study education you come to the sad conclusion that the most difficult subject is teacher training and the number of teachers required for the Seventies. The fascinating and easy thing to do is to talk about different forms of curriculum, different forms of content of education, but in fact if you administer education you have to understand that the *main* problem is teachers and their supply. We are so short of teachers today that we cannot reduce the size of classes. Until we do reduce the size of classes we shall never get real education, we shall get *mob education*! The size of classes has not improved since I tried to reduce them some thirty three years ago. All attempts have foundered on this rock of teacher training. One of the greatest obstacles to teacher training is that although the Burnham scales are well conceived, they are comparatively low when you compare them with industry and its rewards. The teachers' rewards are not increasing to the same extent as in industry, commerce and other branches of public life. It is therefore difficult to attract people to the profession. If we were to increase teachers' salaries above the Burnham scales even further, we should make the cost of education even more astronomical than it is now. Therefore this problem of rewards is a very serious one and I believe that teachers' rewards will have to increase in the seventies whether the country likes it or not. If necessary the cost will have to be shared between the *taxes* and the *rates* which is the latest idea which I hope to see developed in the seventies. When I was at the Board of Education I wondered whether I could float the whole of the education expenses on either the rates or the taxes. Today I believe that it will have to be fairly distributed between them. That will and must happen in the Seventies.

Another problem is opportunity at the Colleges of Education. There I want to see an increase in size and a change in the type of training. Also we must give greater opportunities in the schools so that young teachers are not disappointed at the beginning of their career. A more varied curriculum in the schools would attract more teachers to the profession, and would abolish the specialisation which I mentioned earlier and which Lord Robbins strongly criticised. For example, a purely specialised mathematics teacher in a secondary school might not have a very wide outlook on life as a whole. There should always be some combination of subjects.

For students of education I should like to see a longer course and most important, a closer link with University teaching. **That is why Lord Robbins' original report, which was not accepted by either the Conservative or the Labour Government, should be implemented in the Seventies.** Lord Robbins had the idea that having the Colleges of Education side by side with University Colleges would make them susceptible of much closer co-operation, not amalgamation, because they do not have the same problems, but at least a much closer approximation of control. The non-acceptance of Lord Robbins' Report is a serious fault which I think should be put right in

19

the Seventies.

At this point I must mention the degree of Bachelor of Education. I regard the B. Ed. not only as an intellectual qualification but also as a social link, a cuff link, so to speak, between the Colleges of Education and the University, thereby bringing them more closely in touch. Many Colleges of Education are already so close to their Universities and participate in the University life that it is important that they should realise that they are as near to University teaching as possible."

Peter Bander: "What do you see as the main problems in university education?"

Lord Butler: "The main problem of University education is the immense crush which has suddenly come into the new Universities and the difficulty of maintaining standards. The problem of sifting the student material and coping with an increasing number of students will be overcome because there is no shortage of Dons or University teachers. There is still a great opening for them and they find avenues which they never thought existed. I hope that our University teachers will continue to be adequately paid in the seventies, as I believe they are now. What I do think wants doing is avoiding a purely specialist production, giving students' education a specialist rôle right through the course and then pushing the students straight into industry or some profession. **That is not the function of the University.** The old Universities used to cater for the learned professions, and this meant that the student had some sort of vocation. Today the University exists to send people into every branch of activity, not only into the learned or service professions but also into purely commercial openings. In the seventies we must teach our students some sort of vocation as well as training them for their degree.

In our new Universities we must overcome a great difficulty which arises from the lack of residence, the lack of corporate spirit, the fact that at weekends the University virtually dissipates until the following Monday and the lack of much tutorial supervision. Getting a degree is quite a strain on a young person. This is why we hear so often about drugs and diversions. I think most students work very hard, and I would not make it any harder for them to obtain their degree. I would rather make it more necessary to cultivate the leisure time of University students and give them a sense of vocation and useful service. I have been taking this theme – and I will continue to do so – as Chancellor of Essex and Sheffield Universities and at Cambridge as Master of Trinity. I think it is a very important theme which has not been mentioned much."

Peter Bander: "Do you consider the education of immigrant children a difficult problem?"

Lord Butler: "One major problem in the Seventies *will be* the education of immigrant children. The best thing to do is to treat them as our own relations and accept them into our educational system. However, I believe there will have to be some special move in those districts where there are large numbers of immigrants, *not to segregate* them, but to give them *educational opportunity,* because they are not capable of enduring the same education as our own boys and girls in those areas. The difficulty there would be to avoid the idea that we are doing it for the purpose of segregation. This is not my plan. My plan is to do it for the sake of the children themselves. There are a great many agencies such as transport, hospitals, hotel agencies and so forth in Britain, whether publicly owned or privately owned, which want these people to help and which need them in their services. You have only to look at British Railways or the hospitals to see how much they are needed. We cannot do without them. What we want to do is to avoid a surplus which creates housing and other problems, which renders a situation possible such as the terror we have at present in the United States of America. We do not want to reach that stage but we want to watch very carefully. If these boys and girls from abroad, the West Indies for example, are going into our public services, they must be well trained for our society. I do not believe that we need to segregate them into special schools, but I would suggest that in schools in those particular areas, where the immigrants have settled down in the housing estates, there ought to be more teachers who take care of special classes which may be predominantly coloured. These special arrangements could be made under the Education Act. That is the extraordinary feature of the Act. It is really a huge umbrella under which anything progressive can be implemented."

Peter Bander: "In conclusion, could you summarise your hopes for the next decade?"

Lord Butler: "My hopes for the Seventies depend really on belief in the growth of the national productivity and a come-back to a belief that our economy is going to expand. If we get back to an increase of growth in the expansion of our economy we shall have the wealth to pay for our social services. I take a positive outlook on the seventies! However, one thing frightens me at the present moment about education in the next decade, that is the enormous number of claimants for the purse. Some Universities are complaining that they are not able to carry out their agreed obligations to contractors because the University Grants Committee has cut the money available at the request of the Government. This is a very serious matter if a University cannot even carry out its contractual obligations! There are going to be heavy demands on the purse for the future middle school, for primary education, as not even foreseen in the Plowden report, for secondary education, particularly for comprehensive and other ideas, and of course, extra heavy demands for the very young children. Teacher training and the new Universities will also add heavy expenses on the education bill. The danger I see is that education will be starved of money in the seventies unless the national productivity grows, and with it the amount of money to spend on social services.

I am very hopeful – with the young people of this country. I think that all generations have their fads, and there will always be attempts by the student population to control the University and that sort of thing. This is a passing phase, quite natural. – As Vice-President of the National Union of Students and Master of Trinity I keep in touch with the young; I know we have the talent. The problems of discipline which arise could be solved if we were to put the discipline into the hands of young men and women on our teaching staffs; we should get on far better with the younger people.

Finally, one very important point: I think it would be a great pity if we took away the interest and control of education from the Local Education Authorities. At the time of the passing of the Education Act, there was much discussion as to what the Minister was going to do. I was criticised for saying that the Minister was going to 'take a great interest'. I believe the Minister of Education will and should always have the whip hand as far as the money goes, but I repeat, it would be a great pity to take away from the Local Education Authorities an interest in education, because it binds education to the Local Government and thereby binds it to the district and makes it the responsibility of every resident."

REVERSING THE ENGINE

*

LORD ROBBINS OF CLARE MARKET

Peter Bander: "My first question concerns your views on the expansion of colleges especially those concerned with professional training. In your Report, little was said about the training for professions other than teaching. Do you see Colleges of education expanding in the Seventies in the same way as colleges have done in the United States of America, to give training in allied professions as well? You made the following comments in Paragraph 313 of your Report:

> *'Some colleges will wish to broaden their scope by providing courses, with a measure of common studies, for entrants to various professions in the social services... the scope for such developments as these will be restricted during the next ten years or so, because the whole capacity of the colleges will be needed to match the demand for teachers.'*

> *Higher Education"*

Lord Robbins: "My hope still is that the *colleges of education* may eventually be federated with universities that are conveniently situated. I am sure that this is the right development. Whether in addition to that, colleges of education should take on supplementary tasks of giving people professional training I should not like to say without giving the problem a great deal of thought. On the whole I am in favour of professional training being combined with general higher education. There has been a very considerable move in that direction. Various long-established professions are involved, lawyers, doctors, and so on, but one has to deal with each case on its merits. There are forms of professional training

23

which are not suitably combined with degree courses but which could be suitably taught in a college of education. On the whole I would deprecate anything which tends to make the colleges of education the asylum of the residue. The important thing seems to me to be to bring the colleges of education more and more into the university ambit without infecting them with the university vice of *premature specialisation.* I think it would be good for the universities to have to cope with institutions which were firmly committed to degree courses more general in character than is commonly the fashion in the United Kingdom south of the Border."

Peter Bander: "I now quote from Paragraph 34 of your Report: 'By the middle of the 1970's we expect that a substantial number of the students will be taking four-year courses leading both to a university degree and to a professional qualification; and we hope that, long before that, the colleges in England and Wales will have been federated in University Schools of Education, that those in Scotland will have forged strong links with the universities and that both groups will be financed by the body responsible for university grants.'
This raises the following questions:
(a) Do you see the Council for National Academic Awards idea as a possible alternative in the Seventies to the four year B. Ed. course?
(b) Do you think that the universities would be willing to accept the academic standards of such a course?"

Lord Robbins: "If colleges of education could never hope to be fully integrated with the universities then the introduction of the C.N.A.A. idea would be a possible alternative in the Seventies and it is an alternative which would be pushed with very great good will by the Department of Education and Science. All I would say is: 'Watch out!' because the two things are *alternatives* as policy is conceived at the moment.

I have no doubt at all that colleges of education would have *superior status,* and leaving status apart, would be in what I would regard as the *right educational media* if they became part of federated universities, whereas if they become independent institutions subject to the examinations of the National Council, there is no doubt that they will not enjoy quite that position. The recalcitrant universities usually have a habit of coming round. This depends much more on what encouragement or discouragement they get from high quarters. It was in the Department of Education and Science that the decision was made that the recommendations of the Committee on Higher Education with regard to new colleges were not to be expected for the time being.

I do not think that the examinations now taken at the end of the three year course are so inferior to degree standard that they are unworthy of counting as such. It may be that because of the practical work, the course should last four years. I think that the habit which some educationists have of looking down their noses at the courses in colleges of education from the point of view of eligibility of degrees simply derived from the in my opinion absurd requirements which they have got into the habit of expecting by reason of the fantastically extreme specialisation in many universities."

Peter Bander: "Would it be preferable to see a small number of students taking a B.A. degree in education at a university or a greater number attempting actual degree work and a B.Ed. degree?"

Lord Robbins: "I think that this depends upon how the Bachelor of Education degree is defined. If the closer integration of colleges of education with universities meant that their courses were cut down to the Procrustean requirements of the ideas of eligibility for degrees of many university teachers, then I would say that it would be better that the colleges of education did not come so near. Colleges have an important function to perform which many are performing very well. In asking in our report that the colleges should be brought closer to the universities *we did not wish the universities to impose upon the colleges matters and requirements which were unsuitable to the discharge of this function.* We thought rather that although not all the work done in the colleges was suitable for the award of degrees, a good deal of it was, and it was unfair that a degree should not be awarded. I am not of the view that all teachers in schools should have degrees; this I think is an idea fostered by the National Union of Teachers in the interest of creating an *odious monopoly.* I see no reason at all why young women who are not capable of reaching what on the most enlightened view would be regarded as degree standard should be prevented from performing very useful and important functions in school without degrees. If I were in active politics I would resist very fiercely any attempt to impose the requirement that all teachers should have university degrees. I think that where the training has been such as to fulfill certain broad requirements it is a bad thing that a degree should not be available."

Peter Bander: "Would you consider it desirable that the next decade should see a lessening of the influence of L.E.A.'s over colleges of education?"

Lord Robbins: "Yes, I hope that the connection with the locality, which from some points of view is of great positive value, should persist, but I am not of the opinion that the L.E.A.'s are the best bodies to have ultimate power over academic bodies of this kind. That is one of the reasons why our committee suggested that not only the academic affairs of the colleges should remain connected with the University institutes, but also the actual administrative arrangements should eventually become similarly integrated.

Peter Bander: "How long can we go on expanding in Higher Education?"

Lord Robbins: "I am not afraid of the expansion of universities provided that they expand on something like a collegiate basis. That is to say, expansion is as it were cellular; it is not just a mass movement producing a vast organisation in which the students are isolated atoms without a sense of loyalty and contact. But provided that there is a collegiate or semi-collegiate structure such as at York University, or as exists at Oxford and Cambridge, I think that there can be expansion to sizes considerably greater than most of the universities in this country. When one considers the question of the optimum size of the college I would not venture an opinion without a good deal of further empirical investigation."

Peter Bander: "I quote from paragraph 71 of your Report:
 'Some seventy per cent of all students [in colleges of education] live in accommodation provided by the colleges.'
This refers indirectly to the serious problem of day students, and in particular of mature students whom you do not mention in the Report."

Lord Robbins: "I do not believe that it is necessarily the case that a college need be residential in order to have a suitable atmosphere. A residential college is all very well and has certainly some advantages, but experience the world over shows that you can have institutions where the residential facilities are very small and yet where this is deliberately aimed at, have a strong corporate life and sufficient human relations. It depends tremendously upon the complex of geography and tradition.

I think there should be special courses for mature students, but I do not see why the special courses should not take place in colleges in which there are courses for other students. I think on the whole for the mature student to mix with immature students conveys mutual benefits on each group. I would not have the training of the immature student necessarily the same as that of the mature. With mature students there are some things which can be quickly dealt with, and others which have to be spoken about at greater length. That has been my experience as a teacher at any rate.

When these courses run next to each other, they sometimes cause considerable pressure on the staff. There must be difficulties, and it may be that these difficulties are so great that there is some convenience in seperate institutions: nevertheless on the whole I would regret it if they were developed as a special set of institutions for the mature as distinct from the immature."

Peter Bander: "Is it desirable that the college or university teacher should be the agent of moral welfare of the students in an expanded and non-resident college?"

Lord Robbins: "If this means the supervision of the moral behaviour of students, I am never in favour of that. I think one teaches morals by example rather than by discipline once people have passed a certain age. I am not myself in favour of systematic attempts to teach a particular religion. I have no objection to their being taught, but on the whole in state institutions I think it better that they are left out. Needless to say, I think a most important function of higher education is to *convey* high standards of ethics and social behaviour, but I doubt very much whether this is done well by deliberate preaching. One learns much more by the example of others. Talking of the university in which I spent the greater part of my life, I am sure that what is conveyed to the student and is of value in this respect is conveyed by the example of the high standard of probity on the part of the teachers, complete candour and sincerity and frank discussion not excluding judgements of value on particular issues in different courses as they arise. To segregate moral instruction and religious instruction seems to me to be dubious. This would apply equally to universities and technical colleges, and is a very important question."

Peter Bander: "To which of the recommendations in your Report would you wish to see special priority given in the Seventies?"

Lord Robbins: "I hope to see an expansion take place, the principle of which has already been accepted. I hope to see a rather different structure with universities playing a more central part in the field of higher education instead of being kept in isolation or semi-isolation as they seem likely to be according to the conceptions of the so-called binary system. I have expressed my regrets about that in a speech I made in the House of Lords and which has been published in my book *The University in the Modern World*.

In the Report I have not strongly articulated what I would like to see happen to the texture of higher education as distinct from the institutional organisation. I would hope to see education for the first degree, whether in the colleges of education or in the universities or elsewhere, on the whole become more general and less specialised *pari passu* with the development of more extensive graduate teaching and training which in my judgement should be specialised. I am very considerably out of harmony with current educational trends in schools in so far as they tend to specialisation at an early age. I think we are out of step with almost the whole of the rest of the world in this. It seems to me to be ridiculous that a boy or girl should have to choose between the humanities and natural science at the age of thirteen or fourteen and thereafter just to have the occasional contacts in the free hours in the sixth form. I think that we make ourselves ridiculous in the eyes of the world by this evolution.

I hope therefore that the schools will reverse engines as regards specialisation. It is a most important issue in school education at the present time."

Peter Bander: "Instead of the G.C.E., would you prefer a certificate on continental lines, comprising nine or ten subjects which must be passed to gain university admission?"

Lord Robbins: "I should be sorry to take continental practices as according an exact model. I would only say that I think the continental practices follow sounder lines than those which have been developing in this country in the last twenty or thirty years with the development of sixth form specialisation. The fact is that the rest of the world does not practise this and even north of the Border in Scotland the boys and girls are not forced into this grotesque distortion of their talent. It may be that the boys and girls themselves *like* specialisation because they like some subjects better than others, but is it really kindness to them to bring them up in the modern world either ignorant of natural science beyond a certain very elementary dabbling, or ignorant of the whole field of the humanities? Is it a good thing that they should grow up not having a knowledge of two modern languages, for instances?

I think in the modern age, when so many more people are seeking higher education, that it is probably better for a much larger proportion of them to have joint or mixed degrees in the Scottish or best American mode. Don't forget that the *best* American mode is very good. The old boys who jeer at the American education are a quarter of a century behind the times. It is better that a much larger proportion of the higher-educated population should be educated in that way, than at once to have their gaze focussed on a very narrow field. If you think for instance of those who are going to pursue the vocation of school-teachers, surely it is better in most cases that they should have joint degrees so that they are able to teach with knowledge in more than one subject rather than that they should go on striving to get first class honours in a history degree which may be focussed on just one or two periods and places. On the other hand, we need greater *Specialism;* the march of knowledge makes it quite impossible to lead a student up to the frontier in three or even four years. The remedy for this is not to spoil school education or undergraduate education by premature specialisation, but to develop the great graduate schools, and this is what is being done in the U.S.A. This is what *we* shall have to do if we are to keep up with them.

I am hopeful that this is going to happen in the Seventies, with the great graduate schools. The resistance of established departments to de-specialisation of first degrees is very fierce. It seems as though there we are working against the stream, against the interests of teachers in the specialised departments! To have a flourishing honours school in one subject rather than to participate in a joint degree seems to be the ambition of most professors nowadays. This thing is comparatively new. This plague of intense specialisation has spread in my lifetime. It was not always thus. After all, at the older universities they do still exist – splendid degrees which are not of that intensely narrow nature. But whether at the level of undergraduate studies the process can be reversed or not I do not know. Good experiments are taking place in some of the newer universities and of course in the social study faculties you have or should have degrees which are less intensely narrow than many of the degrees in the pure humanities or in pure natural science. I should be sorry to think that the only remedy to the present state of affairs was the migration into the social study faculties of ever increasing numbers; I think that this swing-over, although I have taught in that faculty all my life, is being vastly overdone. I think this is partly due to the phobia of over-specialisation and partly perhaps due to the fact that the entrance requirements in a good many social study faculties are not so severe, so that people with neither Latin nor Mathematics can hope to get in more easily. This, I think is wrong."

Peter Bander: "To sum up, which, in your opinion, is the outstanding problem in the next decade; is it the training and supply of teachers or de-specialisation in the upper secondary education?"

Lord Robbins: "I do not regard the two questions as being *in pari materia.* The training and supply of teachers is a matter of man-power planning. De-specialisation in upper secondary education is a matter of policy, of deciding what the supply of trained teachers shall teach. Obviously if the supply of teachers is insufficient, the supply of educational service suffers in a quantitative sense. At the same time, if we do not mitigate the degree of specialisation in upper secondary education, we shall continue to give an education which in my judgement is far less suited to the needs of modern life and to prepare for University entrance than could otherwise be the case."

WHO ARE THE REAL
BROADCAST TEACHERS?

*

KENNETH ADAM

A friend of mine who is a senior and revered figure in Oxford, and who speaks in many ways representatively for the University (I have to specify the origin because attitudes are notably different at Cambridge), told me not long ago, when we were discussing the project of the Open University, and the problems of making it a reality: "Do you know that after all these years you could still wipe all education, sound and vision alike, off the national broadcasting slate, and after a whimper here and there, especially in Wales, nobody would mind, and inside a year, nobody would ever know. You're marginal. You always will be. And I prophesy that in ten years' time, not one single person will be wearing a TV hood". Now this is extreme, I know. But the world of professional education is still often hermetic. Here is a man who after all is an ardent viewer, and was, and still is, a constant listener. However, as an academic, who began as a schoolmaster and is still active in adult education, and that makes him a rare bird, he is deeply and trebly suspicious over the air or on the screen of direct teaching. Anyone speculating on its future in the seventies must take account of a past, from the twenties to the sixties, which is littered with such objections, and of a present where they have been by no means cleared away, even among the younger generation of educators. In schools radio, the B.B.C. was for a generation almost exclusively confined to peripheral lessons, and this was not only because the wide-ranging enthusiasms of its great founder Mary Somerville led her naturally in the direction of "enrichment", but because of the psychological objections of large numbers of in-school teachers to use the loud-speaker at all. An underdog profession, still so underpaid as to lead it into direct action over the manning of school meals in 1967, could be forgiven, in days of desperate unemployment, for not welcoming an instrument which might become a rival and a supplanter. A classroom teacher might be mediocre, he might know he was mediocre, but that was no reason, in his insecurity, for welcoming the bright and busy voices from Broadcasting House and inviting comparisons from his charges. In the colleges and universities the view of radio was, for a long time, and with honourable exceptions, that it was gimcrack staff, glib and insensitive, deflecting educational purposes rather than reinforcing them. Nowadays it is common form, one might almost say snob form in such circles, to regard radio as respectable, and to wish on to television those earlier theories. Television is even more dangerous, because it saturates the majority of homes with an appetizing irrelevancy more easily even than Radio One. So again with honourable exceptions runs the opposition today. It will undoubtedly run on into the seventies, and the path of those who are still ardent and undiscouraged, or who have been converted, is not made smoother by the "hardsell" zealots who, in this country as elsewhere, put forward television, as an earlier generation rather less importunately did radio, as the solution to all remaining needs and ills. Schoolteachers, aware of inescapable and increasing shortages in their ranks, (though these by 1970 may well turn out to have been exaggerated), have, it is true, come to terms with, for example, "Mathematics in Action", "Maths Today", "Engineering Craft and Science", "Middle School Physics" in television, and with an extensive and carefully graded system of language lessons in radio. This breaking through into the field of direct teaching will doubtless continue in the years ahead.

As my colleague, Richmond Postgate, points out, the implications of the Industrial Training Act are formidable, and as yet largely unforeseen. Yet, with the thought of needful expansion in mind, one has also to remember that there are very definite limits in terms of hours, on the networks which are currently available. Those of us who normally on weekdays only read the evening pages of the "Radio Times", can see from turning to the daytime programmes not only how broad is the strand of school instruction today, but how time-consuming.

The adult or further education agencies have also embraced with open arms the new opportunities provided by television, and both B.B.C. and I.T.A. are bound to them by representative Councils whose imprimatur is necessary for courses which will enable the broadcasting authorities to exceed the number of hours permitted by the Postmaster General for general programmes in any one day or week. Again, one has to say that both day and weekend are now filled to overflowing. What worries some of these institutions and associations is that the new-found relationships and understandings between the broadcasters and themselves, (and one must remember that they have had to struggle internally with, for instance, dons like my Oxford friend, or tutors in the field who suspect they may become obsolescent), will be disturbed, if not undermined, by the concept of an Open University, subject to different control, and differently financed. My old colleague, Stuart Hood, has recently written, forcibly, in his perceptive book, "A Survey of Television", about the inadequate character of these Councils and committees – "amateurs with little knowledge of the powers and limitations of television, and little ability to judge the professional standards of what goes out..."

From practical acquaintance with them, I can disagree. They are fast becoming, in the further education field which I know best, colleagues and allies. They have been that, for many years, in school broadcasting. When he goes on, however, to speak of the Open University as follows: "We shall have in this country – which was responsible for the creation of the freest form of broadcasting in the world – at last that monstrosity: television dominated by a Civil Service Department", there is little doubt he voices the anxieties of many practioners in further education who believe in its development through television along the co-operative lines that have been painstakingly established in the last ten years, and of many broadcasters who thrive in an atmosphere where experience and feedback are readily available through simple and straightforward contacts. Since B.B.C. 2 is to play an important – though by no means an exclusive part, since there are to be a number of other partners – in the development of the Open University, this is a question of vital concern to the Television Service and to those who are responsible for the programmes, in both B.B.C. 1 and B.B.C. 2, now and in the future, which are devoted to further education. As I have said, the methods, both of control and of financing, (at present all educational programmes are paid for out of the licence fee) these new programmes in the early evening on B.B.C. 2 will be entirely novel to administrators and producers alike, and this new requirement will undoubtedly place in the next five years, a heavy strain on departments which have been coping with expansion and experiment in large measure during the last

33

five. (In further education alone a half-hour pilot in 1961 has become a planned 6½ hours in 1967.)

There can be no built-in guarantee of success in the degree and credit areas of the latest experiment; American experience in this respect, as everyone knows, has been lamentable, Russian, we are told by Lord Bowden, the reverse. In both bases, the circumstances are so different from ours as to be little guide. The least one can say, and it is not a little, is that there will be in the seventies through this means, a very considerable increase in the overall amount of adult education readily available to all through television, diploma seekers or no, and that is something in which the ghosts of Stuart, Mansbridge, Temple and Tawney will rejoice. What has certainly much to allay the revived suspicious and potential antipathies inside the adult education movement, is the publication of the names of the Open University's Planning Committee, which are those of men as practical as they are distinguished. There will be no lack of enthusiasm in the educational broadcasters to grasp their new opportunities, or of determination to overcome a new set of growing pains. The act is still one of faith, but we are committed, as we were before.

Of course, in one way, and a very important one, we are fortunate in this country, because education and broadcasting are integrated to a remarkable if not an unique extent. One of these days it may be necessary, (if the money is available, which seems unlikely) to set up a separate educational channel. I hope not. I have said publicly, on more than one occasion in the past, and shall continue to say in the future, that to segregate education from the rest of broadcasting would be like setting education aside from the rest of life. A prime reason for the standard of educational programming in the B.B.C. (and to a lesser extent in I.T.V. where the conditions are not exactly similar) is that it is produced by men and women who are part of a very large professional organisation, and who gain enormously from being in continual touch, at every sort of level, with colleagues in other branches of output. from sport to variety. Their experience is regularly enriched in this way. They have access to the free resources of the Television Centre, as well as possession of a studio of their own. They have "design and supply" enough to produce Euripides, Shakespeare and Brecht. Their teams roam the world in search of material which is shot specially on film. They can rely on access to all developments in technique as they arise. They share in the production and distributive expertise of a great publishing house, and in the export drive of the international sales areas of the television and radio services. Not least, they are subjected from time to time, at weekly programmes reviews in television, to the frankest criticism of their programmes by their equals and seniors who are concerned with different aspects of the business of communication through the screen, but who are nevertheless skilled in many areas which are relevant to the educational product. If the future sees any weakening of this association with the main stream, that will be regrettable. If it sees a divorce, that will be a calamity. Incidentally, it is quite wrong to suggest that the educational staff "are at worst either old horses put out to grass or young men who cynically use it as a means of learning the trade" (to quote Stuart Hood again). The opposite is true. It is often difficult to prise men or women away from their educational work when a wider need seems to arise, or there is a chance of internal promotion. In any case the traffic is two-way, and there are numerous examples of gifted people who leave the general service for the greater scope, or fulfilment, as they see it, of educational broadcasting. Moreover, we are continually being faced with invitations to our best people to go into, or back to, academic life. This last movement, I believe is better described as a flow rather than a drain.

I hope, in fact, in spite of the problems it sets management in the broadcasting authorities, it will increase in the seventies because it is bound to increase at the same time the mutual understanding between the two worlds, and diminish the risk of collision.

It is very important that we should not be misled in the years ahead, as we have been in danger of being in the past, by rosy reports of what is achieved by educational television in the United States. When one hears there are 120 stations devoted to this output, it sounds impressive. When one visits them, and sees their product, it is a different story. This is not to say that they do not do some good work in offsetting the commerical system which is in the hands of Madison Avenue, the sponsor, and Hollywood. But only a gigantic revolution, such as is presaged by the new Public Broadcasting Act, and by the Ford Foundations's Public Broadcast Laboratory, and which is a very long way from taking place, can alter the present picture to a point where we should even begin to think of imitating it. Most of these stations live from hand to mouth, without continuing revenue, begging for grants to keep them alive. One or two notably in Boston, San Francisco and Pittsburgh, do manage to mount a balanced and efficiently produced

35

schedule. Even so, the audiences, by the standard, say, of our week-end or latenight further education programmes, are minute. Where we get 600,000 they will get 6,000 and they are broadcasting at peak hours, which we are not. And so one gets this kind of reaction from the American sociologists who are always at hand to comment: "The viewers and non-viewers of educational television are so clearly differentiated by social and psychological characteristics that there is no reason to expect the same kind of programme to appeal to them both".

So melancholy a conclusion but in this, alas, an accurate one and from Boston, of all places, is the direct result of the broad-casting system in the United States which has created an apart-heid. We must seek strenuously to avoid anything of the kind as we make our dispositions for the future. The Dean of Syracuse University on the other hand, is too sanguine, but in so being, adum-brates what should be for us who can afford to be more optimistic, a declaration of intent: "Co-operation between educators and show-men is vital to the development of balanced programme policies. Unfortunately, educators cling to a mysterious dignity, and the combination of entertainment skills with the transcendent aims of education is difficult to effect. But it is not impossible. The possibilities are endless. The results could be phenomenal". I believe that is true, here. Real showmanship is the art of at-tracting an audience, and then of keeping it. It is as important in a programme on "The Strength of Steel" or "Electromagnetic Waves" as it is in the Val Doonican Show or "The Troubleshooters".

Nevertheless, there is, of course, a fundamental difference be-tween the general broadcaster and the educational broadcaster, which it would be a mistake not to recognise. Indeed it could be dangerous not to do so. Variety shows, documentaries, plays, news bulletins and current affairs programmes, these do not set out to persuade. Commercials, party political broadcasts, and educa-tional programmes do. Take news and current affairs. Here the purpose is to convey a correct and unslanted understanding of what is going on in this country and in the world. (This is, of course, much less true, even in Western Europe, in countries where the broadcaster is closely geared to the government machine; O.R.T.F. does not dispute that it is managed by civil servants). An old journalist like myself will not dispute, of course, that any news-gathering or news-transmitting organisation is engaged, all the time, in acts of choice, and that this process of selection may appear partial to certain interested parties, indeed almost certainly will do so. While there can be no guarantee of objectivity, however, there can be an intention, and with the producers of such programmes in this country it is to be informative, not instructional or preceptive. Commercials and party politicals are clearly at the other end of the spectrum; they exist to persuade and have no point unless they do. (Their comparative success is not, I fear, relevant to this paper!) Now it may seem monstrous to mention the advertiser, to whom education in television means educating the public to buy, and inspiration means that the public, through that education, has bought, in the same breath as those who seek to liberate, to encourage freedom of choice. To quote one of Marshall McCluan's more lucid aphorisms: "Education is Civil Defence against media fallout".

Certainly no affront is intended. But the point needs to be underlined that what the educational broadcaster is there for is to put out programmes which are by definition didactic, and are in fact becoming more so the more they move into technical and technological areas. I see this tendency as increasing rapidly, perhaps even exclusively. The days of "enrichment", as I said earlier, are fading fast, and not only in broadcasting. I wonder how many W.E.A. dramatic societies there still exist like the one in which I worked as a student and which used to take a bill of one-act plays on to the most improbable and insecure stages of country schoolrooms and parish halls. All the emphasis is on precise targets and for narrower bands of audience.

I fancy the eavesdroppers of whom once upon a time we used to boast, the sick and the shiftworkers, the old and the housebound are beginning to quail before Pig Farming Today, Maths Today, Medicine Today, and the demands of the factories and firms tomorrow, for the teaching and reteaching of apprentices and operatives. What has already happened in schools television has begun to happen also, and quickly, in further education. Once the Open University materialises, with its emphasis on credit and degree courses, specialisation will take another step forward, All this means that the *educative* task is placed more firmly than ever in the non-educational lap of television services. For myself, I accept the teacher shortage and the learning need for what they are, pressing and urgent, and am glad that the potential for high quality instruction and production is great when the educators live in the way I have described, as part of a large institution which is a going concern, and can draw on its pooled talents and resources. All the same, the imminence of new and powerful technological aids is such that any outline that has been attempted of the present could be outdated and any prophesy about the next ten years could be entirely invalidated, before we even reach 1970. It used to be said that changing education was as difficult as moving a cemetary. On that it took fifty years for a real innovation in a teaching system to seep through to the majority of schools. Now the new tools are becoming much easier to use, and not just as gimmicks. The cost of "domestic" videotape recorders has come down in the United States in the last five years from about $30,000 to $3,000. When viable machines become comparatively inexpensive over here, a whole vista opens up of using the night hours for recording. (It could even mean that some of the daytime hours might be freed for general broadcasting. I still hanker to do something for the housewife, less beseiged now than she used to be, through the use of her own technological aids, by small duties and distractions, (but still the victim of what a French writer has called her "porous" working day). Anyway, once a school or college has acquired a videotape machine, it is freed from the straightjackets of both a three-channel television day, and of the in-school curriculum, and it can do its own scheduling, playing back the lessons when it pleases.

Another development which will undoubtedly take the heat off the broadcasters to a certain extent is local close-circuiting. Cities like Glasgow and universities like Leeds are already in full control of their audiences and their programmes. Within the limit of their budgets, and of the talent they have available or can import, they can decide what they are going to put out, the way it shall be put out, and how much of it shall be put out. If they train their teachers well, and they usually use ex-broadcasters for this; if they have management committees who will allow them a reasonable amount of freedom; and if they are more interested, to begin with anyway, in quality than quantity, then they can undoubtedly hope to make a more intensive use of their medium than those schools and colleges that rely wholly on broadcasting in its present phase. Richmond Postgate goes into more detail about what is happening already, and what may be expected. It is not a substitute, of course, for broadcasting. Only the other day after talking about C.C.T.V. at a conference of teachers, I was exhorted by several of them who represented smaller cities, and indeed, smaller universities, to remember that in the United Kingdom the number of authorities who had the means or the manpower to dispense more or less with broadcasting was extremely limited. Bad teaching, they said, becomes unbearable once it is a public performance.

Who are the real Broadcast Teachers?

Of the more massive types of "hardware" that could be pressed into service, computers and distribution satellites, for instance, it is too early yet to speak. It may be that we shall never use them; we may be too small or we may be too impoverished. The grand schemes of Fred Friendly for the use of space in American education may be grandiose in our terms. In any case, the limitations in the effective use of television in education are not primarily because the medium does not get through, not because of the inadequacy of science, but because of human fallibility. The programmes are not good enough yet, and the classroom does not know how to use them properly. It is not enough to replace a blackboard by a black-and-white board. Instead of the screen being a window on the world, it too often reflects a classroom to a classroom. Yet children are sophisticated viewers, and will put up less and less with an inferior product to the one they get at home. If we were complacent about the present it might be fatal for the future. And the teacher for his part, using television must stop thinking of it as visual radio, or an electronic version of the film strip. He must apply himself to the problem of encouraging individual learning in a class in which everybody moves at the pace of the programme. He must not seem less well prepared than the instructor on the screen, or to lack his ability (if the broadcast is a good one), to communicate, to be concrete, and to be personified. He is no longer able to escape comparison or to rely on last year's notes. Learning by television is not confined to the class.

One final word on this subject. The use made inside of schools television is one thing, and depends, as we have seen on timetables, and on the flexibility and imagination of teachers. But the use made, by way of advice and especially of discussion, of the programmes seen at home, is possibly even more important. Classwork can be related to many of these programmes. Others will add to the general education of their pupils in surprising ways. One European commentator has said: "A well done variety programme, fast moving, with finished production, quality acts, top talent, is comparably more striking as a vehicle for cultural material of educational value, than, say, a transmission of boring solemnity designed to popularize masterpieces of plastic art, and which succeeds only in destroying any interest the majority of viewers might have had in its subject. There are no stupid categories of programmes, only stupid producers, or stupid educators". Certainly the response of children to television, as to other familiar people and things, is easily stimulated but this is more likely to lead to the growth of a critical approach if it is fostered at school than if it is left to the haphazards of home. I hope there will be much more teacher interest in this readily shared activity. We need more viewer discrimination at all ages. But it is better to begin early.

Arising out of this I wrote earlier of the continuing and, it could be, the increasing responsibility of the general broadcaster towards serious programmes at a time when strictly educational broadcasts were becoming more specialised and therefore had little "spillover" appeal. I am aware that to many people still the words "serious programmes" are a contradiction in terms especially in television. I hear it commonly charged that television is promoting mental laziness because it is a looking glass which presents the viewer with only those values which are accepted ones in his surroundings. I think this will not do; a mirror, by its very nature, must reflect many ideas and sentiments which are moving in the world.

Even without satellites, it is almost impossible to live, with television, with frozen images. The very vehemence of the complaints against television often springs from the intrusion of the unfamiliar on sections of society which have been brought up in certain traditions, and in the shadow of various institutions, political, economic or religious. Is there then an invasion of privacy? It depends partly on the "filters" used by those who plan the programme. But certain experiences which will be foreign to many will percolate even the most stringent barriers. And if you believe in deliberately pushing back the frontiers of negative opinion, within the climate of an essentially curious and rapidly changing democratic society, if you believe that you have a duty to inform and enlighten that society, to take initiatives, to pick out and present situations, to observe, to report, and to discuss matters and affairs which some would prefer, through vested interest or simple apathy, to go untouched and unnoticed, then you are, in my view, (and, among others, Lord Windlesham's, whose writing on this topic is particularly clear and powerful) engaging in an educative activity, and at the same time asking for trouble. Many people have an enlarged vocabulary since they watched "Steptoe and Son" and "Till Death Us Do Part". Plays like "Up The Junction" and "Cathy Come Home" taught us that things were going on round the corner, shameful to a civilised country, of which we knew nothing. It is too easy to suppose that viewers are sealed off from shock. (At least as easy as to suppose they are susceptible to it.) But shock can be an educative process too, and it would be overstating the case to suggest that out of too much viewing of the "Wednesday Play" would come social anarchy. The future does not lie in going back on what has been done in the last seven years years. On the other hand, the immediate future may call for a consolidation of those frontiers. The viewer may have been taken far enough, for the time being. This I believe to be true as much of current affairs as of any other section of television output. Experience shows the audience here to be a pyramid. At the top are the nightly devotees, the avid, compulsive watchers who cannot bear not to know, even if knowing makes no difference one way or the other. Then comes the broad middle section, made up of fairly consistent viewers of average intelligence, who are genuinely interested in information, explanation and controversy. We know there must be a good many of them, because of the consistently good audiences for "24 Hours" and "Ten O'Clock". It is they at whom we try to aim. Then there is the largest group at the base, who, apart from times of crisis or disaster, are unaware and unconcerned. They will not easily be moved, though we shall not stop trying to reach them. Something like saturation point has been reached in the treatment. As I was saying earlier about instructional programmes, what we need to do in the months and years ahead, is not necessarily to do more, but to do what is already done, better. This is as true of I.T.V. with a fine record in this field, as of the B.B.C.

One of the ways in which this will happen will be the televising (before very long, in my opinion) of nightly edited versions of the proceedings of Parliament. This will enable us to give up what I consider an obsession with Westminster politics and politicians, and to introduce into current affairs programmes much more about industry and commerce. The two most seminal programmes of the present moment on B.B.C. television are the weekly science magazine "Tomorrow's World" and "The Money Programme" which are not merely educative but highly educational. In the sociological field I would be tempted to add B.B.C.-2's "Man Alive" except that I believe this is a programme where an unusual team produces work which it is almost impossible to imitate.

Any generalisation about the future always stumbles against the man or men who turn up out of the blue with a pocketful of gold. The most one can do is to ensure that the conditions exist which give them a reasonable chance to display it.

I hope that in this essay I have not given the impression of being dogmatic, either in dealing with educational or with general programming. Thinking about television is not a state but a process. We do not want to reach an equilibrium yet. We are continually reforming our assumptions and our judgements. If we are too cautious and conservative we shall end up in institutional servility. If we are too impetuous we shall lose our sense of public service in private exploration, and so fail to provide a satisfactory service either to the educational world or to the ordinary viewer. I will leave the last word to Francis Bacon: "a froward retention of Custom is as turbulent a thing as Innovation".

THE TRAINING OF TEACHERS

*

MONICA WINGATE

Since education in the Seventies will have to be closely geared at every level to the society of which it is a part, this chapter will begin with a list of some of the characteristics of that society which will affect most closely the training of teachers. In what follows the pattern of that training will be constantly referred to its environmental setting.

The society, then, of the late Sixties and the Seventies will be one of continual change. It will be one of unprecedented expansion of education to match the population explosion and the demands of an age which is increasingly scientific and technological. Education for nearly all will have to be life-long. People will continually return to educational institutions for vocational retraining, and also for personal education to fit them for an age of increasing leisure. It will be a world already one physically and struggling to become one in all other senses, in order to survive, but also in order to enjoy the enormous riches, cultural and material, that such a global society could provide. It will be a complex society and this will be reflected in intricate organisation. There will have to be a widespread awareness not only of the regional but of the global backgrounds and of their relation to the nation and the individual citizen.

The speed of events, the necessity for quick decision and the emergence of experts in most fields will require an entirely new kind of democracy. "Death by committee" appears to be the fate hanging over democracy in its present shape. For it will be a society which will have enlarged enormously its capacity for the good life, but which will find it even harder to apply those benefits to the individual citizen since he needs to be part of a community

43

which both nourishes his gifts and needs and uses those fully developed gifts when he offers them. The problem in the vast societies of tomorrow will be to maintain for each citizen his right to matter and his opportunity to serve, since on these the health of a democratic society must depend. The dangers of apathy, of snobbery in its different forms, and of a self-centred "suburban" outlook are looming very large already. We shall have to modify existing communities and create new ones adapted to the citizens of a democracy in the Seventies.

We are, and no doubt shall remain for some decades, a society without any consciously confessed common ethos. None the less, we do live by values.

But before pursuing this further, we need a rapid factual survey of teacher training in England and Wales in the Sixties which, for the sake of brevity, must be confined to broad general statements.

At present the professional training of teachers goes on in two kinds of establishment. Those who are going to teach primary children or the "Newsom child" at present go to one of 152 colleges of education and at the end of three years are examined by whichever of the Institutes of Education includes that college. (I have excluded from this survey the specialist colleges, e.g. in Physical Education and Domestic Science.) An increasing number of such students remain for a fourth year to take a Bachelor of Education degree. At these colleges there is a concurrent training. That is to say, students simultaneously pursue education at their own level and professional training for teaching. Others, however, who are going to teach a particular subject, especially to older and brighter children, will usually first take an honours (as opposed to a pass) degree in that field at a university and may (but at present do not have to) remain at the university for a fourth year to take a professional training, leading to a diploma, in a university department of education. Thus a student in a college of education will be following an academic and professional education concurrently, while the honours university student will divide four years between three of academic education, and one of professional given by a university department of education. These are at present training 3900 students annually. An anomaly exists in that it is possible for any graduate to proceed to teaching, after three years and without professional training. This is one of the reasons why there are markedly fewer able men than women students in the colleges of education. If a young man spends three years in a university getting a degree he can at present go to teach as a qualified teacher no less than the man who has spent those three years getting a teacher's certificate in a college of education. Moreover he will have a degree. Young men of sufficient ability naturally prefer to spend the three years getting a degree. Until, then, a fourth year becomes obligatory for all, there will remain an unfair and unprofessional route into teaching for some graduates who teach untrained. The subject-graduate teachers form an important sector of the teaching scene but I am not qualified by my experience to write about the one-year training given by university departments of education and I have so much to say of the colleges of education after twenty-one years' experience, (with which, I think, the training of graduates should and probably will be everywhere combined by the seventies), that I must leave the separate training of graduates undiscussed. Very much of what I have to say will probably apply equally to both.

The colleges of education are grouped regionally in Institutes of Education, themselves (with one lamentable exception) part of a University. In England and Wales there are at present 161 colleges (including the specialist colleges for Physical Education and Domestic Science), 28 university departments of education and 5 departments of education in technical colleges training nearly 96,000 teachers. It is proposed to increase this to 111,000 by 1973/74. The rapid and enormous expansion of the colleges is manifest when this figure is compared with 28,000 in 1957/58. There could be no more significant witness to the population explosion on the one hand and to the emergence of the educated society on the other. In 1958 there were only three over 500; in 1967/68 there were 100 over 500. 109 colleges were administered by a local education authority and 46 by a religious foundation.

What then will be the role and problems in the Seventies of these institutions which are training the teachers to educate the citizens of the society I have described? For education has to be ever more closely tied to the needs of society and its patterns and structures dictated by social necessity. The problem then is how, in such a society, to prevent the college of education from assuming many of the features of a factory and from being organised and treated as if its main purpose was simply to "increase the productivity of the plant", (to quote a recent Department of Education circular). The potentially "great" society of the Seventies will ask for something better than teachers who have been processed in bulk in dehumanised communities. Quality will be at least as important as quantity, which means that "needs" will have to be widely defined to include personal as well as social, and cultural as well as economic.

There will also be a rightful autonomy of the college to be jealously guarded since ultimately the integrity, intellectual and professional, of the teacher depends upon it and without this he cannot serve a democratic society.

Technology is converting us into a society of experts. In such a society education becomes a condition of survival. Power follows it, and so there is bound to be a steady intensification of the struggle for political control of the institutions and people who supply it. We have seen something of this in the creation of a so-called binary system of higher education. It is difficult to avoid a suspicion that the polytechnics, being directly under the control of the Department of Education and Science, are partly designed to give the State full control over at least a section of higher education, while the universities continue to assert a limited independence. Who then in the Seventies is likely to control the training of teachers? Something will depend on where this training will take place. Will it be, as now, mainly in institutions devoted to this alone or will it as in parts of the U.S.A., be merely one of a number of vocational trainings going on under the aegis of a college of technology? The absorption into the universities of the Institutes of Education with their constituent colleges means that the existing colleges are not likely to disappear for a long time. As they grow in size more of them will, no doubt, make room for allied vocational courses, e.g. for social workers. It is highly desirable that they should, more especially as sociology is becoming such an important part of the educational scene. The teacher of the Seventies will have to study and understand as never before the total environment in which his pupils are growing up. The more, therefore, he rubs shoulders during training with the social worker the better.

Colleges will also exchange courses and facilities over a much wider area than they can or do now, and especially with their nearest university.

At the same time, it seems probable that some polytechnics and regional colleges of further education may also establish teacher training departments and the appearance of the National Council for Academic Awards would in time, no doubt, enable them to offer a four-year degree course outside the universities to their own student-teachers. This would surely be very much to be deplored. It is only in the Sixties that, at last, we are seeing teachers of all sorts of pupils and at all levels beginning to come together in a profession visibly one. But if in the Seventies teachers are going to emerge from two different types of institution, there is one thing we can be quite sure of. They will look down upon each other! It is ironical that it should be a Socialist government which has introduced this possibility. What blinding light was it that simultaneously revealed to the Minister of Education that "apartheid" at 11 + was unthinkable but that at 18 + it had somehow become progressive? We can only hope that wiser counsels may prevail and that at least all professional training will be integrated with the existing Institutes of Education so that they can examine all teachers seeking the initial qualification to enter the profession.

But the question of the actual government of colleges of education in the Seventies is still unresolved. The Weaver Report on the government of colleges of education presupposed that by degrees the colleges would be transferred from the control of Local Education Authorities or of religious bodies to the universities, and that the giving of a four-year Bachelor of Education degree might well depend on this transfer. The event has proved otherwise. With one deplorable exception, all the Institutes of Education are now part of their universities while colleges continue, as of yore, to be administered by the Local Education Authorities or the religious bodies, for the Department of Education and Science. And there is much to be said for this state of affairs, where the Local Education Authority, for example, is reasonably progressive, since the colleges and the schools and those who teach in either are thus brought into close contact with one another and with their common concern, the children. Though, however, autonomy has not turned out to be a prerequisite of a B. Ed. degree, it is necessary for other reasons.

Almost the most crying need of the teaching profession is to improve its status and its public image, and this calls for the autonomy of its training institutions, in the sense that parallel institutions, e.g. for doctors, are autonomous. This might lead to a greater respect for the professional element in all education than we have today. It ought, for instance, to be unthinkable that vital decisions about matters requiring professional expertise, such as syllabuses, types and length of schooling, or the size and nature of schools should be taken by bodies, such as County Education Committees, on which there is at best a tiny minority of professionals and, therefore, presumably, of those who have the expert knowledge without which all such decisions are just shots in the dark. Why is it that everyone thinks he is an expert in education? This being so, a first step would seem to be a greater measure of self-government for colleges of education than is possible under the Local Education Authorities, and this was strongly recommended by the Weaver

Report. Unfortunately, the report also recommended a form of self-government for the emancipated colleges which is not what the times require, since it is largely government by oligarchy, i.e. by committees consisting of the academic staff. The stranglehold of this committee structure would be lethal if literally applied while so many colleges are still under the control of Local Education Authorities, themselves hampered at every turn by a pyramid of committees. Anything in this bureaucratic and immensely complex society which makes it harder to act quickly must be deemed wholly anachronistic. Colleges of the Seventies will, we hope, manage their own affairs but will retain the machinery for quick decision. The various functions, e.g. the selection of staff and students and the allocation and spending of available finances will, of course, be shared, but final responsibility for all these and for general policy decisions should be carried by the head of a college. He must be a person of stature. Status rightly demands scope and responsibility. To accept responsibility without power to discharge it is not indicative of stature, nor even of ordinary morality or common sense. The future of democracy, here and elsewhere, would seem to depend on our capacity to delegate real power and at the same time to make those who hold it strictly accountable. It ought to be far easier than it is to dismiss the principal of a college! Certainly, inefficiency should be regarded as requiring dismissal quite as much as dishonesty. The difficulty lies in deciding how the inefficiency is to be precisely measured and by whom. But to rob colleges of effective leadership will be no solution. The head of a college will still, then, we hope, in the Seventies, be able to exercise his initiative and foresight and to encourage his staff to do the same. It follows that far more of the tasks of administration than now should be carried by officers appointed for the purpose and not by the academic staff whose time and energy should be devoted as far as possible to the students, to school teaching and to educational research. One hopes, too, that by then we shall all have freed ourselves from the delusion that democracy and committees are inseparable! Telecommunication within the colleges will have made communication and consultation of every sort far easier and the wasteful tedium of much of today's committees will, in retrospect, seem like a nightmare from which we have awakened.

Will students by the Seventies have a real share in the government of colleges? This important question is being debated later in this chapter. Suffice it here to say that wide consultation with students rather than control by them is likely to be the norm.

48

The Training of Teachers

It seems almost certain, however, that colleges of education are not by the Seventies going to be free in the sense that universities are free. For, on the supply and quality of the teachers everything else in education will depend and, therefore, ultimately control must be in the hands of the nation through its elected representatives. At present the colleges of education are administered (and therefore virtually controlled) by Local Education Authorities or religious bodies for the Department of Education and Science. By the Seventies it seems likely that government of the colleges will pass directly to the Department of Education and Science and that they will delegate to the colleges as much autonomy as national policy permits.

Autonomy will certainly raise the status of colleges of education. And so will their integration with the university. Universities are "news". Colleges of education are only news if something sensational occurs in them, preferably something to do with drink or drugs. Our present image is not good. This is partly because there still hangs about colleges of education some of the unpleasant aroma of a past when they were small and sometimes narrowly introverted, from which they have, in fact, wholly emerged; partly because they are hardly known and have taken little or no pains in some cases to advertise themselves in a right way. They will surely, by the Seventies, accept and discharge a social responsibility to the neighbourhood round them. This is already being done magnificently in some places by student service to the old and the infirm and to spastic and mentally handicapped children. The use of the colleges for all in-service training would go far to improve their status, for teachers would then come to be identified with their training institutions and the status of the entire profession, including the colleges, would benefit from this. For in-service training will have to recur at regular intervals of, say, five years throughout the professional career of every teacher. The pace of change and the rapid advance of technology and science will make this inevitable. When all pedagogical training at whatever age is in the hands of the Institutes of Education and their constituent colleges, and the Department of Education and Science and the Local Education Authorities have withdrawn, the student-teacher, the practising teacher and the staff of the colleges will be in the closest contact. The colleges will be wide open to visitors of every kind, so that ordinary people will be conversant in a general way with what goes on in them. They will be places to which the entire profession will resort and of which the nation will be at least as justly proud as it is of its universities.

Once the teachers and the training institutions are in this continuous and close contact, it seems reasonable to expect that colleges will affect both the content and the method of the teaching given in the schools far more radically than they do today. This, in an age of change is desperately needed. We require that our colleges of education be centres of creative thinking, so that teachers trained in them will send out from the schools in due course citizens able to guide social evolution rather than just be led by it. As I have said elsewhere, either we give democracy a new look or we shall have to bid it goodbye. Here the role of the colleges is vital. We do not, at present, educate for democracy, though of all forms of government this perhaps makes today, as in former times, the sternest demands on its citizens for self-restraint, for responsible exercise of the vote and for a disciplined use of freedom. But there is a new element in our current situation. Life today at every level demands the expert. Our politicians, however, would be the first to admit that they, with few exceptions, know little about the areas they are called upon to administer when in power. This was practicable when the pace of events left room for experiment and therefore for mistakes, and before mass media had enabled popular outcry to overwhelm innovations, although their impact had not yet been felt or assessed. For there are plenty of experts among the demos! Small wonder, then, if an inexpert minister relies too much upon the faceless bureaucracy, with results that are painfully familiar. All this brings democracy slowly but surely into contempt. What is needed is the expert in the seat of power. But experts, as we know them in this scientific and technological age, can be most dangerous in power because they have not been trained to see their expertise in relation to a much greater whole, and the art of government to a very great extend depends on that capacity. If we are to preserve, in the Seventies and beyond, the right of every citizen to matter politically, then we must have to govern us men and women who will both be experts and know the place of their expertise in the general scheme of things.

This means that, without more delay, we must radically reform our educational system. We have to create forthwith a national system of education capable of producing politicians whose education has equipped them with the authority of specialist knowledge, (e.g. education, or in health, or economics), and the perspective and judgment to apply this to our national and global problems. This will require a radical reform of the school curriculum.

It will begin in the colleges of education and through the closer integration achieved there between teachers on the job and teachers to be, it will spread rapidly. Certain basic principles will emerge at once. Every pupil has to go far more deeply than he does at present into one field and, at the same time, in a world becoming one, reality requires that he should all the time have a background awareness of the whole and be relating his specialist study to it. He will have to learn how to make rapid surveys of whole areas of experience in order to perceive and appreciate relationships within them, and if we are told that only the cleverest can do this, we can point to the millions who watch and hear news by television, and who are in fact and at their own level doing something like this every night. First, then, we shall get rid of the dead wood, because it clutters up the time-table and there is no room for additions in our grossly overloaded syllabuses. We shall, by the Eighties, have replaced the organisation of data into "little boxes" labelled History, French, English and Geography, because these divisions are no longer appropriate to man's wider perspectives and they both prevent a school-leaver from knowing much about any one area and hamper and frustrate his endeavours to set what expert knowledge he has in a wider context. For these "little boxes" we shall be substituting everywhere, what we already find springing up spontaneously in many schools, breadth courses, variously described as Combined or Integrated or Contemporary or Modern Studies.

But if we are to make the changeover swiftly enough it will have to go on simultaneously and on a much bigger scale in schools and in colleges of education. This means that the examination systems of both must welcome and assist the changeover and colleges of education will have to carry out much needed research into the best ways of examining both "breadth" and "depth" studies. It is, for instance, unscholarly to apply "depth" criteria to "breadth" studies, but twenty-one years' experience has taught me how much easier it is for those of us who were educated in the old system to assess specialist knowledge than integrated or "breadth" studies. But the zest and enthusiasm of students for this kind of study carries its own conviction.

What will this mean for the colleges? First, that these students will get much further than now in one main study since they will already know far more about it when they arrive, since so much current overlapping and distortion now imposed on them in the schools by "subjects" will have been avoided and their energy freed for studies in depth. They will not have been hindered, as

51

now, by subject "blinkers" from moving their vision, as they need, from background to foreground. So the colleges will have the satisfaction of producing better educated teachers than they can even now, because of the shortage of time, in the sense that their students will have the enriching experience of penetrating, to the full extent of their capacity, into one field, Simultaneously, the students will have greater flexibility since they will continue to pursue at their own level those studies in relationship which we may call studies in breadth. They will continue at college to review broadly the way man lives in society, in Britain and elsewhere, his values, his economic and social problems and needs. Their in-service training will, at regular intervals, provide fresh insights into the significance of contemporary trends.

Education in the Seventies will be at three levels – the national, which will introduce the pupil of whatever age to what is worth handing on in his national culture – the international, which will teach him how to compare and contrast his national inheritance with that of others – and the supranational, which will teach him how to relate his own traditions to a larger whole, e.g. to Europe or the world.[1] And so student and in-service teacher will be equipped by the colleges to go into the schools and translate their own experience into the syllabuses needed by pupils who will have to become the citizens of what we hope may still be a liberal as well as a global society in the Eighties.

For that responsibility their pupils will need expert knowledge and a broad perspective. From among such pupils, then, there may later come the better equipped politicians required by the emerging world society of the Seventies and Eighties. Flexibility and imagination go together and in an increasingly complex society teachers and schools must possess a high degree of both. They will also need a greater understanding of social factors. This will require colleges of education to give a growing amount of time to sociology.

We have been discussing, so far, the content or the "what" of the college of education syllabus. But this will be even more closely linked to the method or "how" of teaching. By the Seventies, technology will have transformed methods, and the colleges of education will have learned to use technology to lift the intellectual burdens imposed by sheer weight of information from the shoulders of students everywhere. We may assume that by the late seventies all colleges instead of the few will be equipped with closed circuit television, programme machines, language laboratories and computers, and the many other aids which will doubtless be introduced within the next decade. The National Union of Teachers has estimated that in the 1970's we shall need at least a total of 420,000 teachers to staff colleges of education and schools with any sort of efficiency. But as we already admit to colleges of education a very high proportion of the sixth forms of the Sixties, it is hard to see whether we can claim more for teaching without crippling other professions, such as medicine, which are also essential to national well-being. Such aids as C.C.T.V. will, of course, enable us to make a far more economical use of our teachers. But this is by no means the most important use of C.C.T.V. for the teacher. The teaching profession should carry a large share of responsibility for showing how to procure and make available to mankind the ever-growing masses of relevant information. Student teachers will be taught to use C.C.T.V. and similar aids, (e.g. film-making and projection), not merely to make more information available to more people, i.e. quantitatively, but how to use it qualitatively, to enrich and enhance the content of teaching, to use it creatively for stimulus and better assimilation. Students will experience for themselves and watch the effects of audience participation, of the graphic presentation of statistics through dissolving pictograms, of drama and of high-level debate. Through closed circuit television the student will watch unobserved educational techniques hitherto known only by hearsay, such as the intelligence testing of young children. He can also, unobserved, study the behaviour of children at play or in the classroom. This will certainly cut down the period of time that during initial training will need to be spent in the classroom and save for better uses the precious hours now consumed in to-ing and fro-ing. Observation, as distinct from practice in classroom teaching, will be largely covered in the college. As far as his syllabus is concerned, the student will be helped by television to compare and contrast data in bulk and more vividly in a fraction of the time taking now in library or lecture room. This medium too is of proven value for presenting the content of combined or breadth studies and for the comparison and exchange between colleges and Institutes of group research.

If man is to be master and not slave of the educational machines, then the teacher in service will need regular retraining in their intelligent use. As C. V. van Peursen has said, "Teachers... must provide the stimulus to the younger generation, and therefore deserve to have available the latest data, the best methods, the most recent understanding of how knowledge can be integrated by educational means and a personal-moral frame of reference."[2] For, properly used, closed circuit television could give back to the teacher his proper role. No longer will we have to play the part of an inferior machine and relay information and instruction to groups. Instead, the student-teacher will find himself working in school as part of a team including lecturers and the school staff. Whether then he is helping children to use programmed machines to make their own encounter with their material or whether he is following up with a small group of children some first-class talk given through C.C.T.V. by a team-leader, always he will be learning to play his part in a concerted operation planned to use mass media to free the teacher to make that personal relationship with each child on which true education depends, and of which today's vast classes have deprived to a shocking degree both teacher and taught.

Again an intelligent use of television in college and school will help to prepare the citizen of the Seventies for the greater proportion of his time which he will spend in other than paid occupation.

A further valuable use of closed circuit television will emerge as colleges, universities and schools establish regional networks for the exchange of programmes. The availability of the best will have a galvanising effect on all teachers, and the exchange of views and techniques will facilitate and promote the continuous research demanded in an age of ceaseless change.

The links between colleges of education and their universities will get closer because the colleges need the information university research can produce and the university needs very badly the "know-how" of colleges in training teachers to use it when found. "The centre of gravity," says van Peursen, "has shifted from 'what' to 'how'."

The citizens of the Eighties must be equipped for action. They will have to be capable of discrimination and of relying on their own judgment rather than on mass opinion. This means they must, from the Seventies, have teachers capable of making effective choice and of standing apart from the herd. But effective acts of the will rely on the balanced and simultaneous use of reason and of emotion and, in the Sixties, our schools and colleges are failing, to a greater or lesser degree, to give this training. The almost automatic exclusion of emotion from fields where it is necessary if we are to discover the truth is seen in much current teaching of history and of literature. That may be due to a right respect for the part that reason plays in science, and a false transference of that approach to reality to fields where it can only conceal it. But if forced to exercise their reason without their emotion in the classroom, our pupils

54

will naturally find emotional outlets elsewhere and these will be divorced from reason. Hence much modern hysteria, and perhaps too some of the increase among the rising generation of mental and nervous disorders.

The colleges of education must and will increasingly attend to this problem. Very many primary school teachers have been trained to combine training of the reason and the emotions by what are known as activity methods. Children and teacher together explore a given theme, say, "How daddy goes to work". In groups they go outside the school to find their data and return to assemble it. They make it available to one another by discussion, by charts and diagrams, by whatever method is most appropriate. And all the time they are actively involved and are using their whole personality to make continuous small choices. Some colleges of education already expose their students to parallel experiences. Some integrated courses, in particular, lend themselves to this type of approach. But much research still needs to be done by colleges and teachers-on-the-job to discover how to introduce this combination of reason with emotion to every level and age of education and to the intellectual as well as to the less academic pupil. But we shall need, in the colleges, to guard against the insidious temptation to turn even the exploration of the emotions into an exercise of the reason! We are prone to exalt the -ologies – psychology, sociology – and then try to exclude emotion from these areas! But is this not "to wash out the baby with the bath water"? Once more, would not something more literally humane, say Modern Studies, be more likely than the "-ologies" to yield the clue to emotional deficiencies? Nor will exposing all the students to small doses of art and music separately help us, since it is the togetherness that is wanting.

But if it is education of the whole man which fits him for commitment and action, then obviously the community itself is the finest medium for this training. What sort of community will the college of education have become in the Seventies? It will be very large by today's standards. The Robbins report suggested that seven hundred and fifty was the smallest community that could be effective and already we have ten colleges with more than one thousand students.

Will effective education of the whole personality go on in these large units? First let us count their advantages. They will contain students of all ages and of both sexes. This will deliver us all from age-snobbery. Many factors contribute to this. The pace of change sweeps each generation away from its predecessor and snaps the

55

vital links. Everyone needs two yardsticks with which to measure experience. One, which we may call the vertical, is the standards and traditions received from parents and the generations behind them. This we use to judge our contemporaries. The other, which we may think of as horizontal, is the standards and opinions of our contemporaries by which we judge our predecessors. Each of us stands at the junction of his two yardsticks. But today's rising generation, through no fault of their own, have largely to do without the vertical yardstick – either because the generation immediately behind them has few worthy traditions and little or no philosophy or religion to offer, or because they have no language or communication. In ages of less rapid change the rising generation can use the support of inherited tradition and belief until they are ready to form their own, and then, in the process of furiously tearing away the supporting corset, they develop their own mental and moral muscles and find the truth for their own day. The loss of either yardstick leaves the individual of any age ill-equipped for living. Today's loss of inherited tradition forces younger students to rely far too much on their contemporaries. In an age of mass media this exposes them to the dangers of mass hysteria, and the herding together in the great "cloud cuckoolands" of the modern universities of thousands of young people between eighteen and twenty-one intensifies the risk. And, of course, once "age-snobbery" has crept into one generation it spreads rapidly through them all and is accompanied by all the narrowness, limitation and distortion of view that attend every species of snobbery. But the colleges of education are already discovering how the coming of older students and mixing of the generations brings us all much closer to reality and by the Seventies we shall have, in addition, the regular return at intervals to their colleges of in-service teachers. The colleges can then act as a solvent of age-snobbery for society as a whole.

If the age of marriage continues to fall, the colleges will also cater for young married couples. There will also be much more generous grants to married students. This will attract a still largely untapped source of older men who, often from idealistic motives, would like to change their job to teaching but whose families, with the present still meagre grants, would suffer undue hardship if they did.

There will be far more younger men[3] and of much better calibre in tomorrow's colleges of education because we shall have accepted the necessity for much higher salaries, and because we shall have made the Bachelor of Education degree into a degree recognised as of comparable status with other university degrees. This last will continue to improve the calibre of all students in our colleges.

There will also be short courses for teachers who have been away from the profession for such reasons as motherhood. There will finally be adequate provision for married lecturers and their children to live on the campus. The colleges will probably continue to be places both for residential and for day students. One hopes, however, that the percentage of young students in residence will remain high because "commuting" from home does waste a great deal of energy and time and takes away from the need to stand on one's own feet and the ability to enter fully into student activities.

The danger of large educational units is that they fairly easily succumb to a sort of suburban ethos. People then identify themselves with small cliques and lose sight of the whole. But for personal fulfilment we need to see the significance of the whole of which we are a part. The large colleges of the future will, therefore, have to explore, for the benefit of large schools as well as for themselves, the ways of making the large unit into a real community. An imaginative use of modern telecommunications will help to create this awareness of what the whole stands for and of what its other "parts" are doing.

The colleges will also be places to which serving teachers of proven ability come for longer or shorter periods, to lecture or to pursue research. Lecturers, too, will be seconded for longer or shorter periods to the schools and lecturer and teacher will co-operate in research on a far bigger scale than now to their mutual benefit and that of their students. One of the most precious assets of a good college of education is its professional keenness. I have rarely met a young student in twenty-one years (admittedly most of them have been young women) who was less than wholehearted in her attitude to anything directly involving children. This dedication (no other word will describe it) is moving and should be capitalised to the full in the years of initial training, while professional attitudes are still in the making. It will also help in the Seventies to keep alive or revive the same spirit in the serving teacher returning at periodical intervals, sometimes, no doubt, in a state of disillusionment, for refreshment and further training.

It will be important to involve students more fully and really than now in the day-to-day conduct of college life. The main obstacles are in two fields. First, they are at present a part of the college community for only three or four years and, second, they make no financial contribution either to it or to the national funds which support it. Does "No taxation without representation" apply in reverse? Students would reply that they are, in fact, contributing financially because they forego earnings considerably larger than their grants during the period of training and that their training is to enable them to make a much needed future contribution to national requirements. But both obstacles will be partially removed by the return of the student to college at regular intervals throughout his professional life. A student could thus be an increasingly valuable partner in some areas of management and ways could be found of allowing him to be more fully involved and useful when actually at college and, as it were, a sleeping partner when in school. More self-respecting financial arrangements for the younger student taking his initial training and an insistence on service to the profession for a period at least equivalent to the period covered by grant would do very much to justify his sharing in decision-making in all aspects of community life, though not in matters relating to professional competence. For if a professional qualification is to have value, then the syllabus as well as the examination must be wholly independent of those on whom it is to be conferred. Their advice, however, on preparation for the qualification should be sought and used. Probably by the Seventies there will be minority representation of students, younger and older, at college executive level and of lecturers on the executive bodies of all students' unions, instead of only some as at present. This will be very beneficial because youth is predisposed in favour of change and a lot of change is going to have to take place. In fact, by the Seventies, it will be part of the ethos of colleges of education and the young will take to this as ducks to water, which will encourage their elders to do the same.

It is almost a cliché to say that education must involve the whole personality. But that does not make it easy to achieve. This is why the training of teachers must always embrace the whole personality of the student and, as we have noted, the ethos of the community must continue to play a major part in this. But the student needs something else which is hard to find today. In spite of much that is written to the contrary, man today, as in all his yesterdays, seems to need not only an ethical system but a world view. It is the genius of the Judaeo-Christian tradition that it makes them interdependent. And, if, as a little reflection may show, we cannot for long have one without the other, where shall we find a world view, (by which I mean a coherent philosophy which attempts to give meaning to the totality of experience), when, as seems like-

58

ly to happen by the 1980's, there is no longer state sanction for the teaching of the Christian world view? Will secular humanism have succeeded by then in producing one, in spite of the declaration by many humanists that the quest is an improper one? Shall we have gone down the cul-de-sac of ethics unrelated to a philosophy of the whole? And what of man's need to exercise both reason and emotion together – a need that some religions, including Christianity, can claim to meet? Shall we have tried, by then, to depersonalise ourselves, using the various -ologies to measure behaviour as if it could be evaluated by the reason alone? There will be no question in the Seventies of youth looking up to experience in this field. In fact, youth will be more likely than age to contribute the essential prerequisite which is faith. Faith that there is purpose and destiny for every human being and that they will be revealed to him if he is willing to pay the price in adventure, in self-discipline and in devotion. Colleges of education may also find the new language in which the teacher is to communicate values in the Seventies. The final reason why the colleges must be autonomous lies in this area. Teachers, like scientists, must accept a primary loyalty – to truth of all kinds – and they must be as unhampered as possible in pursuit of it. This involves loyalty to truth in dealing with developing personalities and that means reverence for personality. In fact, if reverence for life is the first article of belief for a doctor, reverence for personality must hold the same place for the teacher.

There is only one way to preserve finally the integrity of the teacher and, therefore, of the college that trains him, and that is the recognition of that which has ultimate authority above and beyond the society on which he is so utterly dependent. It is that by which he and society must finally be judged. The teacher of the Seventies is certain, therefore, to pursue, however unconsciously, the agelong quest of man for his God.

NOTES

1 The Council of Europe can provide examples of fruitful initiative in liaison in western Europe.
2 Professor of Philosophy, University of Leiden, Netherlands. "The future of the University" is a translation by Adrienne Dixon of "De Toekomst van de Universiteit", Eltheto-brochure No. 22, January 1967, published by N.C.S.V., Netherlands.
3 The present ratio of young men to young women is 1 : 2.5.

LOOKING AHEAD IN EDUCATION

*

SIR RONALD GOULD

Prophesying is always risky, and especially so, if the prophet is likely to live to see the difference between prophecy and reality. Were I accustomed to seeing portents in tea-leaves or crystal balls, or an avid reader of "What the Stars Foretell", I might be more confident with a topic like this, but being none of these, and hoping to be alive in the 1970's, I can only examine what I regard as the potent ideas at work in education today, consider how they are likely to be applied and what will be their effects.

Schools today are vastly different from those of earlier times, and even from those of a generation ago. School buildings have vastly improved, though many are still sadly deficient. In the 1920's, Dr. Christopher Addison (afterwards Minister of Health) vigorously campaigned against the ill-lit, badly-heated, insanitary and dilapidated schools of Devon, as Dr. William Savage, Chief Medical Officer, did in a more scientific and restrained way in Somerset, and as others did in varying fashion elsewhere. But progress in grappling with the problems was incredibly slow, and the majority of councillors and the public simply did not care. Today, counties like Hertfordshire can boast that they have built well over 100 new schools since the war, and even if progress generally is hampered by inadequate manpower and finance, it is not hampered because governments, councillors and the public do not care.

The demand for education has changed considerably, too. In England thirty or forty years ago, working people generally accepted that it was right for the wealthy to be educated in schools and colleges until the age of 21 or 22, but such an education was not "for the likes of us". This, however, was not true of Wales, where

61

much more enlightened attitudes had already ensured the early development of intermediate schools and the growth of universities. But in England the number of children desiring secondary education was small, and almost all could be easily accommodated in existing grammar schools. University education was rarely desired by the poor and even more rarely achieved, for entrance was largely a question of fees and scholarships were few in number. Today all children attend secondary schools; no-one is denied access to academic education and most university students are in receipt of grants.

The content of education and the methods used have also been greatly changed. In the infant schools of a generation ago, children sat in long serried rows of desks fixed in galleries, chanting in unison to memorise the alphabet, tables and nursery rhymes. Now easily-moved tables and chairs taken the place of fixed desks. A flat floor has been substituted for the multi-levels. And children are talking and moving and apparently playing, but though they may not realise it, they are using purposeful and more efficient means of attaining real understanding.

Older children, too, no longer imbibe knowledge solely from the textbook or teacher. They, too, are encouraged to use, in addition, the learning-by-discovery methods. In some cases, too, where the L.E.A. has been enlightened and generous, the radio, T.V., films, film-strips and language laboratories supplement the textbook and the teacher, all of which quicken interest and increase confidence, and children learn more readily. Further, children are treated more and more as individuals and not as groups. Because of this, the theory of "age readiness" has been undermined. No longer is it believed that a child should not be taught a particular subject or part of a subject until he is ready for it, which in practical terms means when he has reached a particular age. Thus, whilst a few years ago many believed reading should not be taught before the age of 6 or 7, or a second language until 11 or 12, or trigonometry before the age of 14 or 15, now, given good teachers and suitable methods, some children begin reading at a much earlier age, learn a second language as a means of communication without a knowledge of grammar at a very early age, and grasp the concepts of trigonometry even before the age of 11.

Taken together, these changes can only be described as revolutionary. Older teachers, myself amongst them, will recall how in their early days progress in building or renovating schools was slow or non-existent, how textbooks and curricula remained unchanged for years, and even decades, and they realise that despite the grumbles at the slow rate of progress today, we are living in a vastly changed and improved situation. Who would not prefer an age of progress, even slow progress, to an age of complacency and inertia? As Talleyrand remarked: "Those who did not live before the revolution will never know how sweet life is."

What, then, has caused these great changes? First, the growing and now insistent demand for equal educational opportunities for all; secondly, the recent and constantly increasing demand for more skilled and qualified men in industry; and thirdly, the greater expertise of the teaching profession and their increased knowledge of the way children learn.

Belief in equal opportunities in education, or social justice in education, or the democratisation of education – the same broad ideas are described in various ways by different people – is of recent development. When in the 1920's R. H. Tawney applied these ideas to secondary education, very few accepted them and fewer still thought them realistic. For education then was organised in such a way as to provide good secondary school opportunities for about one-tenth of the children and indifferent elementary opportunities for the rest. Even working people accepted with equanimity the purchase of good quality education by those who could afford it, its achievement through scholarships by a small number of clever children, and the denial of these opportunities to all others.

The system obtaining at that time, however, was inherently unjust. Tawney aptly described it thus:

"It is possible that intelligent tadpoles reconcile themselves to the inconvenience of their position, by reflecting that, though most of them will live and die as tadpoles and nothing more, the more fortunate of the species will one day shed their tails, distend their mouths and stomachs, hop nimbly on to dry land, and croak addresses to their former friends on the virtues by means of which tadpoles of character and capacity can rise to be frogs. This conception of society may be described, perhaps, as the Tadpole Philosophy, since the consolation which it offers for social evils consists in the statement that exceptional individuals can succeed in evading them."

The war, however, caused a revolution in men's thinking. In those difficult days, Britain soon learned to accept that all men counted, that it was the duty of each to care for the other, and that the world after the war should provide a better life for the old, sick, unemployed and the aging. Roosevelt expressed the mood of the time when he included freedom from ignorance in his four war aims. It was no accident that the Education Act, the Beveridge Report and the National Health scheme, were discussed and implemented at about the same time, for they were all the products of concepts like "Each for all and all for each", born of common risks, sacrifice and suffering.

Of course, idealism tends to fade when crises are left behind, and belief in equal opportunities in education is not so intense as it was in the mid and late 1950's. Yet though no-one today can claim that in practice this country provides equal opportunities for all, irrespective of colour, race, creed, sex, home background and the financial resources of parents, the belief that we should do so is still a driving force which cannot be ignored by Councillors or M.P.'s.

The modern demands of agriculture, industry and commerce on education are also effecting attitudes profoundly. Many of our present educational troubles are directly attributable to the faulty and now discredited sociological assumptions and beliefs of the past, the effects of which live on. Stephen Leacock, the Canadian humorist, once gave some sound advice on growing asparagus. "First," said he, "dig a trench five years ago". Alas, the ground for today's education was prepared twenty, thirty or more years ago and in such a way that we cannot produce the crops we now see we need.

This is obvious in one sphere. Old school buildings intended to serve the educational needs of children fifty or even a hundred years ago are still in use, though quite unsuited to today's requirements. They hamper the internal organisation of the school, and when pressed into service as parts of comprehensive reorganisation often make real comprehensive education impossible of achievement. Less obvious, but just as important as the persistence of old buildings, is the persistence of old ideas. Thirty years or so ago, George Bernard Shaw was proclaiming that in the future the vast majority would earn their living by undertaking a few hours' brainless toil each day. Karel Capek's *Insect Play* was envisaging a world in which men would toil instinctively like insects, and his *R.U.R.* a world where men would work mechanically until they became machines. Charlie Chaplin's *Modern Times,* was portraying a world in which men would become like Charlie, armed with two spanners, spending their whole lives tightening nuts, so that even when they moved away from their machines, their arms would move compulsively to the same pattern and rhythm.

Looking Ahead in Education

The technocratic theory illustrated by Shaw, Capek and Chaplin assumed that industry and agriculture would develop in such a way that only a cadre of highly skilled people would be needed; the vast majority would require neither skill nor qualifications. True, the wood-hewer's and the water-drawer's work would be different; heavy muscular exertion would cease; they would become button-pushers and lever-pullers, engaged for a few hours daily on simple manual repetitive monotonous process, which would evoke no pride or interest and demand no thought.

In such a world, vocational education and education as an economic investment are irrelevancies. So "Education for Life" and "Education for Leisure" became the educational catch-cries. Why, it was inferred, should the mass of mankind bother about science and mathematics, or even the disciplines of learning, if in their work they were to become robots? Why not teach them fretwork, pottery, music, gardening, or how to keep pigs, hens and rabbits, which would at least enable them to get some enjoyment out of their leisure, when none was to be derived from work?

But this technocratic theory has proved a complete fallacy. Obviously manual toil is rapidly giving way to lever-pulling, but the lever-pulling is being done by machines, not men. What a modern economy now needs is not muscle-men or lever-pullers, but men who can invent better and more elaborate machines, like computers and mechanical diggers, ensure their efficient working, repair them when they go wrong, organise an uninterrupted flow from raw material to finished products, plot the paths of aeroplanes, advise on political and economic questions and improve marketing and distribution.

Thus, though thirty years ago men believed that by now society would be supported by a small highly-skilled élite and a mass of button-pushers, in the event society needs a mass of highly-skilled people and a small and declining number of button-pushers. Alas, our ideas are still affected by the past, and are not geared to the production of a mass of highly-skilled people.

But this is now being realised by industry, the Government, local authorities and teachers, and – even more important – by parents and children. People see that there is a future in high-grade craft occupations, management, advertising, communications, medicine, law, education, recording and the machinery of local and national government, but there is no future in manual occupations which require nothing but simple skills. Realising this, they demand an education fitting children to take these posts. This explains the enormous growth of universities, technical colleges and colleges of education, and the increased voluntary attendance of children at school after the age of 15.

Then, too, great educational changes have been effected because of greater knowledge of children, of their needs, and of their mental development, but their full consequences have yet to be seen.

Until recently, it was generally believed – and some believe it now – that some could learn and some could not. They were born either with the ability to learn or they were not. Not unnaturally, parents of clever children warmed to this "heredity" theory, and so did administrators, for what could be easier or cheaper than to separate the able from the less able, provide books, laboratories and equipment for the clever, and very little for the rest? But, all the same, the theory was nonsense. Intelligence is partly innate and partly acquired; partly nature and partly nurture; partly due to heredity and partly to environment. To some extent, intelligence can be acquired. Apparently dull children are not hopeless. Given the right environment, they, too, can learn.

And so today, at long last, we are beginning to grasp the truth expounded years ago by Erasmus, that "no-one is to be despaired of as long as he breathes", and that apparent dullness may be induced by an unfavourable social environment. Thus there is widespread support for providing extra assistance to those who are socially under-privileged. The campaign to raise the school entry age to six is dead. The campaign to increase nursery school and class provision has been greatly strengthened. The Government has allocated extra money to tackle the problems of the inadequate buildings in some of the under-privileged areas, and the Burnham Committee is considering financial inducements to teachers to serve where the under-privileged are found in greatest numbers. All these pressures and decisions will profoundly affect the education system and teachers.

Reference has already been made to changes that have already taken place in the content of education and the methods used in school. As ideas change, more profound changes will take place. Learning, it has been assumed, for years, is necessarily a painful process; children are wayward, limbs of Satan, affected by original sin, and don't know what is good for them, so they must be made to learn. This is the basis of the old jingle:

"Ram it in, cram it in,
Children's heads are hollow.
Reading, writing, arithmetic,
Still there's more to follow."

This is why children chanted in unison to learn tables. This is why the stick was an essential part of the school's equipment.

Now reformers like Dewey did not pretend all learning would always be painless. They believed with Plato, however, that "knowledge acquired under compulsion has no hold upon the mind". They understood Churchill's criticism – "Where my reason or imagination were not engaged I either could not or would not learn." So they tried to eliminate compulsion and unthinking repetition; they tried to engage the reason and the imagination, to make learning more interesting, enjoyable and efficient. And they were right, despite opposition from traditionalists and the muddled thinking and even more muddled and exaggerated practices of some of their followers.

Just after World War II there came a violent swing of opinion. Years earlier the Hadow Report had declared that the education of young children had to be thought of in terms of activity and experiences rather than facts to be stored. In the idealistic days following World War II, a number of educational thinkers, largely inspired by Hadow and Dewey, began to argue in favour of greater experiment, activity and involvement on the part of the pupil rather than learning solely from books or word of mouth. Their intention was clear – to use more efficient ways of imparting knowledge with less unnecessary pain and pointless drudgery. There was no repudiation of learning or the use of the brain, but rather an exaltation of both.

Unfortunately these ideas were expressed in a kind of verbal shorthand; they were called "activity methods" and all too often the stress fell on the bodily activity rather than on the purpose. After a time some discovered that activity without purpose is educationally less efficient than even painful learning by rote. But others discovered that if all the activities were carefully planned the interest evoked discussion, a desire for further knowledge from books, pictures, experts outside the school, films and the environment outside the school. Steadily there emerged the idea that the function of a teacher was not merely to teach, but rather to organise the educational environment of the child so that his interests were aroused, and he became a searcher and a discoverer. Where these ideas were intelligently applied, as they were in many infant schools, education became more efficient, so much so that in educational practice our infant schools lead the world.

Thus the demands for skilled manpower and equality of opportunity, reinforced by the ability of teachers to provide much more efficient education, have produced enormous effects, and even more will be seen in the 1970's. There will be an upward thrust, for example, in the demand for education provision. When the school leaving age is raised to 16 in 1970, more children will remain voluntarily in school beyond that age. Comprehensive education will encourage that trend. And the demand for places in universities, technical colleges and colleges of education will increase.

There will also be a downward thrust. Because of new researches which have emphasised the educational importance of the early years, because it is believed social handicaps can be overcome in part by providing a good school environment, more and more children will begin school in nursery schools or classes at the age of three or thereabouts.

And all this will cost money, and will raise in an acute form the question whether small local authorities with limited financial resources, and even big authorities with bigger resources, can provide from the rates a substantial proportion of the increased costs. In the '70's there will probably be fewer and bigger local authorities and the Government will provide an increased proportion of the costs. The employers of teachers will be changed. The importance of a strong national teachers' organisation and professional unity will become even more apparent.

But the demand for education will not be merely quantitative; it will be qualitative as well. An even more insistent demand for a reduction in the size of the teaching group to improve educational efficiency will compel reform. In particular, the Government will be forced to amend the illogical regulation which prohibits classes of more than 30 in secondary schools but allows classes of up to 40 in primary schools. This is educationally indefensible and when the supply position permits, some Government or other will be forced to limit classes to 30 or even some lower figure. Until this is done, the bitterness of the primary teachers will become more intense.

School buildings, too, will be improved. The case against some old school buildings can easily be made. They are unhygienic and a danger to health; the lavatories are insanitary, the heating and lighting are inadequate. They are uneducational; they lack libraries, gymnasia and laboratories. No doubt by the mid-1970's these major criticisms will be met by rebuilding or extension or reconstruction. But even the school buildings erected recently are hardly likely to be suited to the education teachers will wish to provide in the 1970's. Few can rapidly be adapted to the use of language laboratories, teaching machines and other modern aids, or enable children to be organised in large, medium sized or small groups, as educational needs dicate. By the mid-1970's a few of the newest junior schools, and possibly some secondary schools, will certainly have classroom walls that are easily adjusted to new shapes and sizes. And some, though not physically flexible, will contain rooms of varying sizes, not all of which will be occupied at the same time, which will allow a more flexible organisation of the school. And the criticisms of those which do not allow for flexible organisation will increase in intensity.

Perhaps, however, because of changing ideas about the nature of learning, the most important change will take place inside the schools. Almost certainly the new methods so successfully applied in infant schools will be extended and adapted for use in the junior schools, partly because they are seen to be more effective, but partly because of the disappearance of the 11 + examination, which tended to distort the education provided to meet the demands of the examination. More slowly, because some will doubt their effectiveness in producing good examination results, they will be used in the secondary schools. Experiment and discovery methods are already found in the laboratories, but they will spread to History, Geography and other subjects. They will involve the use of audiovisual aids, visits to museums, art galleries and places at home and abroad. All these changes will profoundly affect the role of the teacher. For the old view, "The duty of the teacher is to teach", will be modified. He will still teach, but in a different way. For his main task will be so to organise the work of children that their interest is aroused, and that they experience the joys of discovery, and the satisfaction of achievement. He will be concerned with creating the best learning situation, and in consequence will carry a heavier responsibility.

Another development will greatly affect the work of teachers – the belief that the education service must do what it can to counter social handicaps. Strangely enough, this idea has only had any real force since the publication of the Plowden Report. Yet there is nothing new about it. Two hundred years ago Dr. Johnson wrote: 'Slow rises worth by poverty depressed." The Jesuits have believed in the enormous educational importance of the child's early years. Blind, deaf, dumb, physically and mentally handicapped children have all received special and more expensive provision of staff and equipment than ordinary children. But now in a few months it has become generally accepted that the socially deprived child who generally appears dull, but may easily have his potentialities smothered by adverse social circumstances, must receive superior treatment in buildings, equipment and staffing.

A start has already been made in making this provision, but time will show that though the school can do something to alleviate the effects of social deprivation, changing the environment of the children outside the school is needed as well. We may well see in the 1970's the teacher regarded as a co-operating agent with housing managers, child care officers, probation officers and the like, and a determined effort by society to enrich the housing and other amenities of the so-called deprived areas. Certainly teachers will protest if they, unaided, are expected to offset the effects of social deprivation.

All the increasing demands on teachers will tend to make them focus their attention on certain major issues like the supply of teachers, their qualifications, training and in-service training. All educational and professional progress depend on those.

The decision of the Government to raise the school leaving age to 16 in 1970 will increase the strain on the teachers. In the main they will not object to the raising of the school leaving age, but they will resent a shortage of teachers at that time, and will blame the Government and Local Authorities for lack of foresight and their unwillingness to pay teachers enough to attract and hold sufficient to make reforms worth-while.

Teachers, too, will demand a review of the basis of teachers' qualifications. The principle that all qualified teachers should be trained was accepted by the Government more than 20 years ago, but untrained graduates are still recognised as qualified teachers. With the growth of comprehensive schools and teachers in them having to teach children of greatly varying abilities, the necessity for training is being revealed. Thus the pressure for a fully-trained profession will grow.

So, too, will pressure for the elimination of unqualified teachers. Today, young people of 18 with five O Levels can become teachers and can be placed fully in charge of a class. This is a scandal and will be seen to be a scandal as the facts as to their inadequacy as teachers are revealed. Equally, the employment of people without any training or education as occasional teachers will become more and more resented by teachers and may easily lead to direct action.

The training of teachers will also become a matter of greater concern, as, like doctors, teachers learn how fundamental to status is the quality of their training. The Colleges have already shown their ability to adapt themselves to changing conditions. All will emphasise the sociology of education more, and some will perhaps train other social workers besides teachers.

In-service training, too, will develop as the demands on teachers grow. Teachers' centres, the Schools Council, Universities and Colleges of Education will all play a part. A new insistent demand for in-service courses leading to a B.Ed. or similar degree will also develop.

And last, but by no means least, because of all the pressures in demanding radical changes in curriculum and method, teachers will have to choose between allowing others to dictate change, with all the loss of liberty this entails, or play a large part in shaping the changes themselves by individual and collective effort. There is no other possibility. For teachers to resist the mighty pressures forcing change is to be overwhelmed. To allow others to dictate change is professionally disastrous. Teachers will realise this and by accepting their responsibility to guide and shape change will protect their freedom, enhance their status and ensure greater professional recognition.

THE PUBLIC SCHOOLS

*

ANTHONY CHENEVIX-TRENCH

I am no prophet. Or at least I am not concerned with the prediction of the future. Like St. Paul, I am content to say "Brethren, it is not yet clear what we shall be", when the dialogue between Sir John Newsom and his team on the one hand, and the schools on the other, is completed, and when the Government has decided what to do with the resulting report. Maybe "we shall all be changed" – but I hope it will not be "in the twinkling of an eye" but in a more considered and leisurely way. Indeed, I hope that the voice will be active not passive. I hope that we shall change, rather than be changed, for in a world that is changing so fast all around us, the willingness and the ability to adapt where there are sound *educational* reasons for adapting is a necessary condition for survival for the schools, indeed for the nation. But there is an older meaning of the word "prophet" – one who "speaks out" as it is proper for a man to do where his convictions are concerned. In that sense I am a prophet. I declare in this essay my hopes and my fears for the future of the type of school in which my life as a teacher has been spent, a type in which I believe and which I love, but not (I hope) blindly.

One more thing by way of introduction. Emotive as the phrase "The Public Schools" has lately become, no-one knows exactly what schools it labels within the very large spectrum of schools which are independent of State finance, local or central, and therefore of direct State control – though all of course are liable to scrutiny by Her Majesty's Inspectors of Education who themselves enjoy the same sort of independence from Government control as do Her Majesty's Judges. Even if one excludes schools run for private profit, there are very many independent schools of all sorts and sizes, all with widely differing purposes and catering for widely different needs, schools ranging from the excellent to the very bad indeed. I intend by the phrase "Public Schools" those independent schools that are members of the Headmasters' Conference, and I shall be thinking chiefly of those that are boarding schools. Yet even within this comparatively narrow bracket, there is such a variety of structure, ethos, purpose, method and merit that the portmanteau description bursts at every seam. These schools are often presented, not least by their enemies, as uniform and homogeneous in type. The truth is that they present a picture of great variety and diversity. It is necessary to stress this, to avoid misunderstanding and rash generalisation.

Have these schools then any special contribution to make to British education in the nineteen seventies? Or are they petrified relics of a by-gone age, the educational instrument of an empire that is no more, at best irrelevant, at worst positively harmful in the context of to-day and to-morrow?

For many reasons I think that they have a most important contribution to make, perhaps a more important one than ever in their history. Let us consider these reasons one by one.

Society, and the knowledge that so powerfully affects society are in a state of flux, to which one is tempted to add the scriptural epithet. If it was true that knowledge "doesn't keep any better than fish" when Professor Whitehead said it, it is even truer now. At no time has it mattered more that our Schools should be sensitively adaptable, both as regards what is learnt and as regards how it is learnt. On the other hand, it is as important that the heady wine of mere novelty should not sweep us off our feet. An aim or a method are not good merely because they are new – or old, for that matter. While no one, as far as I know, has criticised the Public Schools for "spending their time in nothing else, but either to tell or to hear some new thing", like the Athenians as seen by the author of the Acts of the Apostles, the opposite charge of complacency and conservatism has often been made against them. Now there is no doubt that there was a time when not only Public Schools, but indeed most of our schools were to some extent open to such a charge. One remembers how distinguished Head Masters declared that Chemistry, even French, were not studies that should find a serious place in the curriculum, if they found a place at all. But those days are long past, and such residual complacency as there may be is far from confined to any one sort of school.

Indeed, the recent record of the Public Schools in this matter is far from discreditable. When the science syllabus taught in schools came under the fire of a group of distinguished scientists as being out of date, it was the Science Masters' Association that responded with proposals for change, a body of teachers from maintained and independent schools. Having gained the support for their proposals, of the Nuffield Trust (itself an independent institution), teachers from the Public Schools played a very great part in working them out in detail with the help of the Trust. The initial impetus for the School Mathematics Project came from four independent schools, and with the help of their colleagues in both sectors, in a mere three years a new "O" level course was under way. It would be possible to enumerate many more instances of the will to change and to experiment in many fields which the Public Schools have been showing.

It is also healthy that this willingness to experiment cannot be faddy or irresponsible. For unlike the maintained school, the Public School relies for its finance on the fee-paying parents who are its clientele, and whose confidence it must retain to survive. It may be argued that parents are not experts themselves, nor abreast of the thinking of experts in education, and do not know what is best for their own children. There is much truth in this: but there is also much danger in an over-readiness to adore the "expert". Pericles of Athens knew this when he said: "Though only a few may initiate a policy, we are all able to judge it." I suppose Plato would have thought of himself as an "expert" in education – but few of us would have liked to live in his ideal Republic, or under the "Laws" as outlined in his work of that name. And to whom do the children belong if not to their parents? If a parent does not like the educational policy of a Public School, he is free to judge and to make a change.

With this sensible check on theory divorced from experience, and on rash and wholesale experiment, the Public School with its flexible organisation and time advantage of boarding (of which more later) possesses to a greater degree than most maintained schools the ability to experiment and to innovate freely and quickly, a very great advantage indeed when the world around is changing so fast. It is over a hundred years since William Johnson Cory wrote in his booklet "Eton Reform": "You go to school at the age of twelve or thirteen; and for the next four or five years you are engaged not so much in acquiring knowledge as in making mental efforts under criticism. A certain amount of knowledge you can indeed with average faculties acquire so as to retain: nor need you regret the hours that you spent on much that is forgotten, for the shadow of lost knowledge at least protects you from many illusions. *But you go to a great school not for knowledge so much as for arts and habits;* for the habit of attention, for the art of expression, for the art of entering quickly into another person's thoughts, for the habit of submitting to censure and refutation, for the art of indicating assent or dissent in graduated terms, for the habit of ragarding minute points of accuracy, for taste, for discrimination, for mental courage and for mental soberness. Above all, *you go to a great school for self-knowledge.*" In 1861 Cory was of course well ahead of his time. But dare anyone say that these "arts and habits" are not even more necessary to-day? They demand a flexible curriculum, men not merely with the devotion but also the *time* to work away at instilling them (did I say "men"? I include of course women), and the Public Schools are able to provide both.

This is the first reason why I think they have their own particular contribution to make in the years ahead.

Then there is the fact that the majority of them are boarding schools. Now boarding education is only one way of education, and it is not likely to appeal to more than a comparatively small minority of parents, but we are told that there is an unsatisfied need and an unsatisfied demand (two different things) for it, and of it these schools have very great experience. If there is really such a demand and need, we say as we have said for forty years that we would like to see this education more widely available. There are of course disadvantages as well as advantages in boarding. On the one hand there is a danger always to be watched that the "totality" of a boarding school will tend to make it insular, and that children who attend such schools have little chance of putting down roots in the environment of their homes. Indeed, where a boarding school is a good and happy one, a child may put down his roots there rather than in his home, and it is perhaps for this reason that the ex-pupils of such schools revisit them so often with affection, rather than for the less worthy reasons so often attributed to them by the scoffers at the "old school tie". Again, the wrong children may be sent there for the wrong reasons. But against this must be set the advantages – for the right child – of a whole time education with the whole time (week-ends and all) of the teaching staff devoted to it – they *chose* to teach in such schools –, the opportunity for a very wide choice of extra-curricular activities, and a continuous, firm and sensible control offering both security and a training in responsibility.

Whatever their faults may have been, perhaps the greatest contribution the Public Schools have in the past made to education in this country has been their concept of the school as a place in which to grow as well as to learn. True, they are schools based firmly on the Christian religion and centred round their own place of community worship, and in an age when this faith and its values are attacked on all sides by all sorts, this is no small consideration. (As the Paul Report[1] says, instead of complaining at the high percentage of men from the Public Schools in the ministry, "we can stand the usual questions on their head and say the plight of the Church would have been poor indeed had the response to the appeal of the Church for clergy been as low from the Public Schools as it has been from the grammar schools".) But this is not all. True again that they are schools with, for the most part, high traditions of scholarship and vigorous, Sixth Forms. But this is not all. True they are schools which through play have aimed at the ideal of health of body as well as excellence of mind, but this is not all. True they are schools which through play have aimed at the ideal of health of body as well as excellence of mind, but this is not all. True they have stressed the importance of arts and crafts, of extracurricular activities through boy societies and so on, but this is not all. It is not only religion, only scholarship, only physical fitness, only the encouragement of a wide range of activity, but a fusion of all these in a common life as a common ideal that has characterised them. As a result no maintained school in this country now regards itself as *merely* a place of academic or technical learning. This is far from true of schools in general in Europe, and is something peculiarly British, and unlike some peculiarly British characteristics, it is something very good. And this, in company with the other schools of this land, the Public Schools still offer, and offer perhaps more richly in so far as boarding education gives more time and opportunity to offer it.

If then there is indeed a demand and need for boarding schools, then this type of education is a second contribution which the Public Schools have to offer in the next decade. For it seems most improbable that any government faced with the enormous expense of financing the raising of the school leaving age, the implementation of the Robbins and Plowden reports, and the replacement of makeshift and hasty arrangements by purpose built comprehensive schools, will be able to give much priority to the construction of its own boarding schools. But if the Public Schools are to help to meet the demand for boarding by the acceptance of state-financed pupils, as I believe they should, it must be on certain clear conditions, and the first and most important of these is that the prime consideration should always be the happiness and good of the child, which must override all other considerations whether social or political. It is for instance idle to believe that a maladjusted child from an environment totally alien to any boarding education and in particular to that of the Public School, is likely to be happy and have his or her problems solved by being thrown into a school community whose mores and aims and methods are all utterly strange. It is more likely that the reverse will be the case, and the greatest care will have to be taken that the wrong children are not, on the strength of some theory unsubstantiated by experience, consigned to schools which are not suited to their needs. The essential conditions of success, if a really "new" intake is to be admitted, are firstly that the parents *want* their children to go to these schools, and secondly that the children themselves should be psychologically *well* adjusted and stable. Otherwise the child's own problems combined with the novelty of the school environment are likely to be too much for him – or her.

In short, for the "difficult" child, to whom both the idea of boarding in itself, and the particular ethos of the boarding education at a Public School are alike utterly strange, I entirely agree with Dr. Royston Lambert that if a boarding education is necessary, the boarding school should be "tailor made" for the child.

This is not of course to say that the Public Schools can complacently take a sort of "lump it or leave it" attitude. There is much that they can and should do to make the kind of reform that they themselves have so long advocated workable. And indeed many of them have already started in a sober way to experiment towards this end. But there are certain hard facts to be faced. One is that most boarding Public Schools are of such a size that if they were to admit a truly comprehensive intake, one or two results must follow: either their Sixth Forms, with all the flexibility and choice they offer in terms of subjects, and their consequent value, must be destroyed, or their staffing ratio of teachers to taught must be made even more expensive than at present, and neither of these, in my view, can we as a people afford. It is true that many of our schools are more "comprehensive" than the maintained Grammar Schools, but there is a point beyond which we cannot move without vastly increased numbers, and it is at least doubtful whether a boarding school can retain its "family feeling" beyond

a certain number. I think that most Heads of co-educational boarding schools would say the same about the viability of coeducation in
such schools – indeed, I have reason to believe that they would put
the maximum number at about four hundred, and that is smaller
than *most* Public Schools which are also boarding schools. All
these are real *educational* difficulties, and when the headmasters
of the Public Schools, caring chiefly for the worth of the education
they offer, and the happiness and success of the children for which
they are responsible, draw attention to true difficulties it is surely
irresponsible to accuse them, (as did Ann Scott James in a recent
column), of "dragging their feet", and to talk of "compulsion"!

But though there is much more that might be said, for example about the educational disadvantages of turning Public Schools
into boarding Sixth Form Colleges or the difficulty of defining the
criteria on which the selection of pupils financed in some degree by
the State should be selected (and I do not think these difficulties
insuperable on the one hand, or rightly glossed over on the other),
it is time to come to the nub of the whole matter. In my view the
greatest contribution the Public Schools can make to education in
Britain for not only the next ten years but for many many more
is the retention of their independence. Just that. I believe that this
independence is good both for the Public Schools themselves, and
for education in the country as a whole. I believe that the great
independent schools have profoundly influenced the maintained sector in the past, as they have also been influenced by it, and I
am sure that were they to disappear, the maintained sector
would lose not gain. The State and the independent systems profit
one from another. You will note that I have said "the great independent schools". I do not wish to be thought either to underestimate the excellent work done by some independent schools which
are less "prestigious", nor to claim that independent schools are
per se better than maintained ones. But I *do* believe that, like it or
not, it is those schools which are justly prestigious that have influenced and will influence most our national education. To destroy
these, and permit the survival of the lesser independent schools
seems to me the ultimate in folly and illogicality.

How does independence benefit the Public Schools? Firstly, because they are communities dependent on themselves, subject to
no exterior control (except that of scrutiny by Her Majesty's Inspectors who owe no political allegiance); they are torn by no con-
flicting loyalties. Governors, parents, teachers, taught form a unity
which is responsible for its own life and its own decisions and its

own success or failure. It has the strength of an institution to which neither the teachers nor the taught have been allocated: the taught are there because their parents chose it, the teachers because *they* chose it. For the most part, the governors govern because *they* chose to. There is an internal power and magnetism in a community freely chosen by all who in any sense belong to it, and have for that reason a personal stake in it. Of course it is true that very many local authorities give the greatest freedom in practice to the headmasters of their schools: it is equally true that some are very far from so doing. But this is beside the point. In the nature of things no maintained school can in the same sense be a community freely chosen by all who belong to it. It is not that independent schools are cut off from the outside world, for they are constantly and deeply affected by it, but all *decisions* are taken within the community, and in the context of the freedom I have tried in a few words to outline. If they are foolish decisions, no outside power such as the State will come to the rescue. Independent schools are self-drive: there is no instructor in the next seat to avert disaster. Therefore such a school has to be a community not only cemented by a common choice, but bound by a common responsibility.

But it is not only the independent schools themselves that derive a peculiar benefit from their independence, but the nation as a whole. This is not, of course the view of those who, while not denying the merits of such schools, accuse them of being the main cause of the social divisions in this country. Yet surely this accusation is in itself over simple and naive? Is it really true that schools produce society? or are they produced by it? Which is the chicken, which the egg? Where do colour, race, cash, and all the ghosts of our own complex history which we must in any case suffer – where do they come in? I do not believe that schools of any sort should be held responsible for the evils of our society, which, if truth be told, schools of all sorts are trying so hard to correct. Public Schools have seldom been the schools of a *hereditary* class: far more often they have absorbed generations of "novi homines" along with their older clientele, and the same is true of the independent preparatory schools, as their recently published statistics tellingly show. Cash, not birth has decided who goes to school where. And true to their traditions, Public Schools have long asked that the central government should provide the cash for those who should be, but are not able, to go where their parents wish, if they are suitable – that is, likely to thrive.

Does this offend the feelings of an egalitarian society? But *is* a society which allows such differences between one man and another in terms of wealth so egalitarian, and would it be more so in allowing men to spend that wealth on any commodity in the world except education? I doubt it.

What I do not doubt is that we are fortunate that in this country education has *not* become the monopoly of the State. To cite an example from the ancient world may seem far fetched: yet one has only to look at the course of education in ancient Sparta to see how absurd and how terrifying can be the effects over the years of such a State monopoly, and how impossible it became for men to break free from it. And John Stuart Mill has some solemn warnings for society on this matter! Nor do I know of any country imposing such a monopoly, under whose government most of my countrymen would prefer to live to-day. Therefore, while we welcome the idea of State aided pupils, subvention must not be on such a scale as to imperil the independence which is in my view not only essential to the character of the Public Schools, but also part and parcel of the liberties that this nation has so jealously guarded through so many trials. (Have not the universities, drawing some 70% of their income from the State, found some reason to "fear the Greeks, *et dona ferentes*"?). We should do an ill service to the education of this country if we allowed the State to become as it were the sole parent of every schoolboy and schoolgirl in it. With this proviso let us hope that we may be allowed without political bias or dogma to see what we can do, in a reasoned cooperation with the State, to open our doors wider, not using children wholesale as social guineapigs, but feeling our way with that care that is *due* to the young. And let us not only seek to preserve *our* independence, but to extend it to others, believing that in all education independence is a *good*, not a bad thing. And above all, let those who make policies realise that schools and pupils cannot prosper unless they are allowed to live in an atmosphere of reasonable security, and that whatever this or any other government decides should be something acceptable to wise and moderate men of *all* parties, lest we have the sort of "stop-go" in education that we have had, for example, in the steel industry. "Maxima debetur pueris reverentia". Children are not the playthings of politicians.

At the outset of this necessarily brief essay, I disclaimed pretensions to prophecy. Yet I wonder what a historian would in the future have to say about any government which, at a time when Britain most needed all the skills and brains she could get, deliberately chose to destroy the academic structure of schools which provided sixth form education of acknowledged excellence, on the grounds that some schools could not offer the same: or which, in times of acute financial difficulty, chose to make it harder (let alone impossible) for parents who would and could both pay through their taxes for the education provided by the state, and relieve the state of the cost of educating their own children, thus making a double financial contribution, on the grounds that not all were able so to do: which permitted expenditure on all other "luxuries", yet branded expenditure by parents of their own money on their own children as immoral if spent on their education, or, worse still, which regarded such expenditure as moral only if spent on the worse education available for money rather than on the better. For if we are to believe that it is not the policy of our present government to make independent education illegal, then there can be no justification for state interference with any independent school except that it is a bad, not a good, school. Or worst of all, a government which regarded every teacher or parent who disagreed with its own views on education as wrong headed; for that way lies tyranny over the minds of children, nor is evidence lacking in the past or in the present that from there it is but a short step to tyranny over the bodies as well as the minds of men.

What would a future historian think of such an administration? Bad? or – more kindly perhaps – just mad?

NOTE

1 P. 114, "The Deployment and Pay of the Clergy". C.I.O.

THE GRAMMAR SCHOOLS

*

LORD JAMES OF RUSHOLME

I have been asked to say something about the Grammar schools in the 1970's, that is to say about the future of a kind of school about which I care very much and with which I was for very long associated. I suppose the first superficial answer that one could make is to say "have they got a future at all?" Is not the educational tide running so strongly against the Grammar schools, depending as they do and must do, on some principle of selection; that there is no future for them, except an absorption into Comprehensive schools? This, alas, is the view taken by many of those whose job it is to teach in Grammar schools, and hence there has been without doubt a lowering of morale in some of the schools. Anyway, that is the first question. Have the Grammar schools really got a future?

My own answer to that would be to say a quite definite "yes", at any rate a future into the 1970's. I wonder if I might quote here a passage that was written twelve years ago by Mr. Anthony Crosland our former Secretary of State for Education and Science, but which still, I imagine represents his point of view. He wrote in his very admirable book, The Future of Socialism[1] as follows: "Thus even within the State sector there can be no question of suddenly closing down the Grammar schools and converting the Secondary Moderns into Comprehensive schools. These latter require a quite exceptional calibre of Headmaster, of which the supply is severely limited; a high quality of staff for sixth form teaching – again a factor in limiting the supply; and buildings of adequate scale and scope, as most Secondary Modern buildings which would have to be converted are quite unsuitable. Until and unless the proper supply conditions exist it would be quite wrong to close down Grammar schools of acknowledged academic quality. The result would simply be a decline in educational standards and discredit on the whole experiment."

That is Mr. Anthony Crosland's view and one with which I entirely agree. That, I think, must mean that the Grammar schools have got a place in the 1970's, if not beyond. Because of financial reasons we cannot do what Crossland says there that we must do, that is provide purpose-built Comprehensive schools. Here of course one is very easily misunderstood. If one defends the Grammar schools, there are very many people who believe that one is opposed root and branch to every kind of Comprehensive school and every kind of comprehensive experiment. This not my position at all. In certain areas I think the Comprehensive school may well be the right answer, as in the county in which I live, the East Riding of Yorkshire, where over a number of years the whole building programme has been devoted towards some future kind of comprehensive organisation. What I think is wrong is, say, in a very large city, to create comprehensive schools simply by putting a new label on an aggregation of existing schools separated very often by considerable geographical distance, a mile or more, and feel that by changing the label in this way, by changing the title from grammar school to comprehensive high school, one is accomplishing an educational revolution. This is not the case. And in anything I say about the grammar schools, I do not want to be thought simply anti-comprehensive under all circumstances, because I am not.

If, then, I look at the 1970's, I do think that the Grammar schools will persist. The recent Inner London Education Authority's proposal gives them a very large number of Comprehensive schools but retains a certain number of Grammar schools. I think they may be fewer in number, but they will still be there. And I believe that they ought to be there for reasons that I hope will become apparent a bit later, but primarily because I think that this kind of school, however the selection is done, is a vital kind of school for the education of the ablest section of the population. They after all, to put it at its lowest, are as deserving of special education as any other section of the population, such as those who suffer from physical handicap or mental handicap. The very able top ten per cent deserves the best education we can give and deserves it not only because it is our duty under the Act to suit the education of the child – and not only under the Act but under the demands of common humanity – not only for that reason, but because of the economic future of the country. It is very often very largely from that highest group of the population that the inventiveness, the imagination, the administrative skill on which our economic future will depend and hence, of course, every other kind of advancement. And for that reason we cannot of course, neglect that section which is associated with the Grammar school. And further I would say this, that it is that group of people, the top ten per cent or whatever it may be, who I hope will go on being educated in selective schools. It is that section of the population that will be our future administrators, our future research workers, many of our future teachers, the people in short who will increasingly improve the general educational system of the country and not merely their own small sector.

The first change, then, is they may be fewer in number. The second group of changes is that they will modify their curriculum, and I will talk about this in a few moment, but they may modify their organisation in various ways. For example, I think there is a very great case for two smallish Grammar schools, one for girls and one for boys, coalescing to become a co-educational school, and over the next ten, certainly twenty years, I foresee a very considerable development of the co-educational school, not only because I believe in co-education, but in terms of hard educational economics. If the Grammar school is to make the best, as it were, of its crowning glory, the Sixth Form, then I do not believe that, either in terms of money or still more important in terms of teachers, we can in fact develop as we should unless schools are prepared to coalesce. It is absurd that a handful of children should be taught higher mathematics in one boys' school and very close a still smaller handful of girls be taught higher mathematics in a girls' school. To make Sixth Forms of viable size I think there must be coalescence.

Although there may be these changes, although there is this feeling that the Grammar schools are on the way out, I still think that some of them will persist, but above all the principles that they have made their own and with which they are so closely associated must be perpetuated not only as separate schools, but in what one might call the Grammar school streams of Comprehensive schools. What are these characteristic Grammar school attributes? The first, I think, is high academic standards and I think this is very important for the development of the country. We have the shortest university course of any country in the world. We have a university course of three years, or sometimes four. Compare that with a course of six or seven years that is common on the continent; compare it even with the United States where to reach the same standard as our graduates reach demands post-graduate work; compare the drop-out rate, as the Americans call it, the number of people who embark on a university course in most other countries and then fall out after one or two years; compare that with ours!

Here our university system has a comparatively low drop-out rate and a very short course and this whole system rests entirely on the very high standards of entry of our sixth formers. To put it in its simplest terms, the universities depend on the sixth formers knowing a good deal. That is because of the high standard of our Grammar schools. Unless we can keep this Grammar school contribution, then the whole of our university system will have to be reformed. Now this might be a good thing. You may say it is wrong that schools should be doing work which the universities do, and perhaps this is true, but the hard facts of the situation are these: under no circumstances have we the money or the buildings to envisage for many years a universal four, five, six-year course at the university for all our students. The Grammar school preparation as we know it is an economic necessity for our country as well as a cultural one. That is their first contribution – high academic standards which in turn react inevitably upon the universities.

Their second characteristic is one that sometimes is not associated with them and ought to be, and that is the immense amount of extra curricula activities that go on. The number of things that a Grammar school master feels he must do on his half-holidays or on his Saturdays or in the vacation is, of course, unique in the world. It has developed, if you like, from the public school at its best. The independent boarding school at its best regards school mastering as pretty well a full time job. To some extent that tradition has been taken over by the Grammar schools, and in some Grammar schools indeed extended. In the Grammar school in which I taught, for example, it was absolutely normal and accepted for a very high proportion of the staff to look after games on Saturdays, although Saturday was a holiday. They did so because it was part of their job. Still more significant was the fact that well over half the staff would devote anything between a fortnight and a month of their holidays to taking boys to camps, on trekking in the Alps or on walking over the hills in Scotland and camping every night, and they did this, of course, free. They did not have to be paid extra. This was part of the job, just as running school societies, the Dramatic Society, the Debating Society, or whatever they are, is part of their job. I do not say that this is peculiar to the Grammar schools because a lot of other schools are doing it too, but I think that tradition is particularly strong in the Grammar schools and this is something that they have to give to the other kinds of school which are emerging. It is this sense of pastoral obligation. It is not all that old in English education. People think it is, but it is not; but it is in fact now a vital part of it. The teacher in, say, France will come in and give a magnificent lecture to highly selected pupils in the Sixth Form, and walk out. That is the end. If you compare his attitude with that of the English Grammar school master you will see that here we have something of what I call the Grammar school tradition, the Grammar school ideal, not always realised, not always found at its best, not always found in every school, but found in the best Grammar schools, and which they must try to transmit to the comprehensive schools. Here you have something which *must* persist into the 1970's and beyond whatever the change in label of the schools. This is associated at its best, (and I am talking about the good Grammar school,) with an identification of the staff and the school. They are not employees distant or far away, they are part of the school, and a well-run school will see that their views, their opinions, and their policies carry weight. It is their school in a very close and intimate way and this is why we are in danger of losing a great deal of the goodwill if we simply move men or women around or alter the character of the school without full consultation.

The other characteristic of the Grammar schools is, of course, the very wide social range for which they cater, and this will become still wider as the years pass. In the Grammar school that I know best, we had the complete social range from the son of the artisan to the son of the company director, or the Vice-Chancellor of the local university. There is this tradition of wide social range and I believe that it will become still wider for this reason. People have sometimes criticised the Grammar schools because the lower middle class, or the middle class, are over-represented compared with the working class, and of course this is true of *any* other institution of higher education, certainly of universities. The proportion of working class children, to use the phrase that is sometimes frowned on, in a university is lower than the proportion of working class people in the population. Of course it is, because those children sometimes come from homes where through no fault of their own they do not have the conditions for homework, for working in the evenings, or above all for cultural stimulation. The child who comes from the home with books, and conversation, with pictures and good newspapers, has an undoubted advantage. We may regret it, but we cannot remove it, and this is why any selective academic institution must represent more favourably the middle class groupings. As the years pass, as we move into the 1970's, the balance will shift slowly but perceptibly, because what I am saying is that availability of a Grammar school education, the capacity to profit from that kind of hard academic work, depends a great deal on other social factors like housing. I have seen this in Manchester. When I first went there the number of children coming to Manchester Grammar school on a purely competitive examination from a very new housing area into which people living in the slums of Manchester had been moved, was very small. As the years passed the influence of better housing and more facilities had its effect on the children, and at the end of my sixteen years in that Grammar school the number of children coming from this new vast housing development had increased enormously. In other words we have to realise that the school by itself can do something for the child from the poor home, but cannot do everything. As the process of social advance goes on into the 1970's, it means that more children are going to have the chance to develop their capacities to the full, not because we relabel our schools, but because we reshape their social background. And this I believe to be a very important thing. It is related to what I was talking about earlier, the extra curricula activities of the Grammar schools. Here you have children from homes where there are few books, no music and so on. It is the duty of the schools to repair this deficiency in so far as they can. But they cannot repair it beyond a certain amount except with the very ablest children. This is why, with the general social advance in housing, health, nutrition and affluence, over the next ten years, you will find more children being capable of profiting from what we now call a Grammar school education.

So far I have been talking in fairly general terms about the sort of contribution the Grammar school has made and must continue to make to our society. Let me say a word now about a few quite definite changes that in many cases are already occuring.

The first is in curriculum. Here we owe a great debt to the Department of Education and Science, or the Ministry of Education as it used to be. We owe a great debt also to some private foundations, notably of course the Nuffield Foundation. We have had over the last few years for example a real investigation into the science curriculum of our schools. It is about to lead to something that must be called a revolution. One may criticise it, of course, but nevertheless the Nuffied Science Scheme, now associated with the Schools Council and with the Department of Education and Science, is going to change science teaching in this country in a way that I, as a science teacher, would have thought impossible 25 years ago. The same thing is happening with mathematics and with foreign languages.

Here in this university it so happens we are the centre of a very large project organised by the Schools Council with modern methods, with rational methods, if you like, of teaching foreign languages. It is not so much in the curriculum perhaps, as in the curriculum *together with methods of teaching* that we are on the edge of a revolution. We are also on the edge of a revolution in another way. We talk a very great deal about over-specialization, and a great deal that is said about over-specialization in the Grammar schools I think is wrong. There must be a hard core, particularly in the Sixth Form, of things which a person wants to learn and which they study in some depth so that they can hit difficult ideas. But increasingly, particularly in the Sixth Form, we are broadening that curriculum; we are having a hard core of perhaps two subjects studied to the Advanced Level, but we are paying much more attention to the periphery, to the subsidiary subjects, the supporting subjects. We are, in fact, investigating and are constructively at work on the basis of general studies. What should a person know at the age of 18 outside his specialist field? Here we are at work on a very difficult and very interesting field which I think by the 1970's certainly will have altered the Sixth Form curriculum in many schools.

This is particularly important because the Sixth Forms are going to get bigger. In some ways the most significant change in the Grammar schools since the end of the war has been the growth in their Sixth Forms and the reasons for that are complex, but the phenomenon is there. This process, I believe, is going on. I do not mean only that the number of university entrants is necessarily going to increase – it *is* going to increase, but it is not only those children who are going to stay for the Sixth Form. A very large number of children stay till the Sixth Form because they believe that education is a good thing. They may not have the very high intelligence necessary for university entrance, but they have the intelligence required for other kinds of higher education, continuing education, and in any case what they are there for is to be educated in the Sixth Form. They would rather be there than leaving school, and for some of those children we must devise quite new curricula, and

89

they are already being devised in the best Grammar schools; curricula for what is called the General Sixth Form.

I said something about methods, and certainly in many subjects, if not in all, we are on the edge of a real revolution. I would emphasise one thing and that is the strain which this is going to put on our supply of teachers. Suppose we say we are going to teach new mathematics, the kind of mathematics that is suggested by the Nuffield Project and has been pioneered in a number of experiments conducted in all sorts of schools; the teachers who may be required to teach that are unfamiliar with it. This is why all our educational development rests fundamentally on a new appraisal of the way in which we train our teachers. Above all, it rests on a willingness, a determination, to run refresher courses for teachers on a scale which we have never contemplated in this country, but which is common, of course, in the United States. Her Majesty's Inspectorate has done noble work in running vacation courses many of which were immensely successful, and continues to run a very large number, but I think we must envisage this on a still wider scale, if we are to provide all our schools with the kind of teachers who are aware of these new advances in method in the teaching of various subjects, and are keeping abreast of the growth of knowledge, not only of pedagogy, but of the actual subject itself. So the growth, development and prosperity of the Grammar schools in the 1970's depends upon the kind of teachers we produce and the kind of training we give them, not only initially, but at intervals during their teaching life.

Apart from these changes there is one change coming over all our education which is very difficult to define in exact terms, but which is nevertheless very real. I think the atmosphere of the schools is changing and will go on changing into the 1970's. The atmosphere as regards personal relationships between teacher and taught, the atmosphere as regards things like discipline is undergoing a continuous reappraisal. Here we know, of course, that there has been a really great revolution in the last 30 or 40 years. The atmosphere of our schools is more permissive, if you like, but it is at any rate happier. In our schools it is very rare to find children staying away from school simply because they do not like school. They still play truant, but the reasons are usually fairly difficult and complex and relate to the home background and psychological factors. Schools are happier places. We have adjusted ourselves to that extent. But as every schoolmaster and schoolmistress knows, today the age of maturity is getting lower, so the kinds of discipline which were appropriate in the 1920's or even the 1930's before the war are getting inappropriate. We must consider our Sixth Formers much more in the way of young adults, and I think Grammar schools are going to do this, but it is a very difficult problem and one of the interesting problems for the schoolmaster and the schoolmistress in the 1970's to reconcile this more liberal approach to more mature people with the necessary kind of authority which shall maintain the integrity of a certain scale of values. This is one of the problems which they are facing, and I think on the whole they are succeeding. I, like anyone associated with education, find that particular problem not only of great difficulty, but also of enormous interest. And it is related to another problem, the maintenance of high standards of intellect and culture, if you like to use that despised word, of culture and of behaviour in an environment which, in some ways, is growing steadily more diseducative. We all blame the mass media for all the sins of the world, and the plain fact is, they do have an effect on the child. They do, in fact, make it more difficult for the child to maintain the highest standards because he is being bombarded through the mass media, and particularly through television, with standards which are very often not of the highest.

This is particularly true, of course, of the child from a poor home. Here you get the job of the Grammar school at its most difficult, a job that is steadily growing more difficult, the job of, as it were, fighting the outside influences of the environment and the pull towards the pop groups and so on; fighting those in favour of something which we know to be more difficult but in the long run more rewarding for the individual. This is going to grow more difficult and much more interesting, as the mass media play an increasing part in life, and in particular as we draw into the higher parts of our education system more and more children from home backgrounds which do not support them in this particular way of standards of value.

One other change that I foresee is this: I think hitherto and to a great extent still today, we have tended to divide the educational system into water-tight compartments, and this, of course, is one of the reasons for the quite legitimate desire to have comprehensive schools. We have had universities, we have had technical colleges, we have had teacher training colleges or colleges of education as they are now called; we have had Grammar schools and Secondary Modern schools and those areas of education have been in my view much too isolated from one another. In connexion with the relationship between universities and schools, for example, something that I am particularly interested in and know something about, there has been a close link between Oxford and Cambridge and certain schools. What we are now doing and what will be one of the features of the 1970's is to bring the universities and the technical colleges and the colleges of education, into much closer contact with the schools, not least with the Grammar schools. It is important to realise that education, although comprising different schools and institutions for different purposes, is ultimately a *seamless webb*. This I believe is more than a phrase and more than rhetoric; it means something. Various people who are going to deal with different kinds of children, and children at different stages of development, will have much more to say to one another, than they have perhaps done in the past.

On the whole, as you can see, I am an optimist about the contribution which the Grammar schools can make in a world which may not be altogether friendly to them in the years ahead, either as separate institutions or as elements in other kinds of school. My anxieties centre round two main aspects of our problem. One is that the Comprehensive school may be pushed through too quickly, that we may ignore what Mr. Crosland told us ten years ago, that we may destroy something before we have built its successor adequately. I hope I have made it clear that I am not simply concerned with the clever child; I am not simply concerned to defend the Sixth Forms of great Grammar schools. I am thinking of the development of the educational system as a whole.

And the second anxiety, of course, is a fundamental one – what kind of staff, particularly Sixth Form staff, are we going to get in our Grammar schools in the 1970's and here we have a really crucial problem: **Whatever we say about organisation, (this is I know, a platitude, but no less true because of that), whatever the labels outside our schools, whatever the apparatus we put inside the schools, however advanced our techniques, ultimately our education will only be successful in so far as we get dedicated men and women in personal contact with the children.** This is what the school stands for; personal contact between teacher and taught and this is nowhere more true, I suppose, than in the Sixth Form of the Grammar school. Here you find the boy or girl for the first time wrestling with difficult ideas. Here you have the chance to introduce them to ideas that have hitherto been beyond them – ideas in science or in the arts, ideas concerning behaviour, morals, philosophy, religion – these important questions are being asked in the Sixth Forms of our Grammar schools and they will only be adequately dealt with if we get the right teachers.

In many ways we have cause for profound anxiety. If we look back to the 1920's and the 1930's one good effect of the slump, (I suppose its only good effect,) one good effect of the moderate indifference of industry to a need for scientists and mathematicians, was that we could recruit first class people into our schools. It is more difficult now, partly for financial reasons, partly because of the variety of other careers that are open to them, partly because the universities and the colleges of education, need the same sort of person, partly because there are more competitors, but partly also I fear because many of these people are, in fact, becoming disillusioned. They are afraid of these hasty comprehensive plans.

To some extent the universities are to blame because they have sometimes said "you are too good to teach, stay and do research". It is right that a man should stay and do a little research if he is very good, but that is not in any way incompatible with a career in teaching. I believe that we in the universities have to do two things; if our Grammar schools are to survive and make the contribution they should in the 1970's, we have quite positively to encourage people to go into teaching, and secondly we have to look again with the most critical eye on the kind of training courses which we give to people who wish to teach. I regard this as one of the really key problems of our educational system. There is nothing I want more than to see a committee like Crowther or Robbins or Plowden set up to consider the professional training of teachers at all levels, not only for Grammar schools.

Peter Bander: "Before you sum up, there are several questions arising from what you have said, and I would like you to answer these now. First; what role do you think parental choice plays in selection?"

Lord James: "Parental choice is a very difficult question. As far as possible I think parents *ought* to be able to choose. In fact, of course, that choice is for a very large number of parents, illusory. They haven't really got a choice. But nevertheless, in the first place I would say: because few have it, it is no argument for depriving those few of what is in effect a good thing. In the second place I would say that parents' choice must always be a *guided* choice. This is a thing where I think we have a long way to go. Once again I think the Grammar schools have probably done better than most schools in this, but I think that the co-operation between teacher and parent is something that has to be fostered so that the parent, in so far as he can make a choice and does make a choice, makes a sensible choice. I see no particular nonsense as it were in having Comprehensive schools and Grammar schools side by side. If the Comprehensive school is as good as its defenders say it is, then parents will send their children to it."

Peter Bander: "If the role of the Grammar School is of such importance, then why should their number be decreased? Also, who would be selected for them?"

Lord James: "I think that the number of Grammar schools will decrease more and more because there is no doubt that Comprehensive schools are going to develop in numbers and *should* do so. Some Grammar schoolchildren may find that the Comprehensive school gives them a greater chance of fulfilment. It will be true therefore to say that Grammar schools will diminish in numbers and probably therefore be more highly selective than they are.

Now you talk about methods of selection. I am afraid that on this I am intensely old-fashioned. I know that it is possible to select pretty able children with an extraordinarily high degree of accuracy at 10, or 11 or even earlier. I think there's an enormous amount of disingenuity about this. You see, we are prepared to select at a very early age for things like musical ability or ability to dance or athletic ability. We are *reluctant* to select very early for mathematical ability or ability to write English. Why? From my experience at Manchester Grammar school, we selected at 10 or 11 by straight examination. At the end, 75% of those we had selected were going to the university. Of the remaining 25% many could have gone to the university, but they did not; they wanted to go into father's business or they thought the way to be an accountant was to go and *be* an accountant. But I would certainly say that difficult though it is to get into a university, we were selecting with something like 90% success at 10 or 11 which is very high when you think of the temperamental difficulties that may crop up. So I *do* believe in the possibility of selection by examination.

I think we have given up that battle much too easily. We have been very superficial over this."

Peter Bander: "Should there be a rigid application of selection at eleven, and if so would there be no provision to enter a Grammar School at a later age?"

Lord James: "I would be perfectly prepared to take a child into my Sixth Form. I would take a child at any age and did take – some at 13 and some into the Sixth Form, but there is one very great danger here: the best teachers on the whole will want to teach in the Sixth Form. Some very good ones want to teach in the Primary school. But there is this terrible gap in the middle where the child may in fact be badly taught by someone who does not want to teach him. After all, in the prep. schools which as you know recruit at 8 and go on until 13, are having an appalling task in recruiting teachers of mathematics. Almost the first question that any schoolmaster will ask when you are interviewing him for a job is, 'shall I have a Sixth Form?'

If you say 'no, there is no Sixth Form', then you will not get that sort of man. The sub-stratum, the foundations of the education in the Sixth Form, will be very much weaker if you simply have Sixth Form colleges.

Now one point that I want to elaborate a little: you were talking about selection. We at Manchester Grammar school had a selection procedure of our own, but it was pure examination. I was not prepared to interview. I did interview the first year I was there, but after the first year I came to the conclusion that interviewing is wrong at that age, (10 or 11,) because the home background carried an undue weight, so we relied simply on marks. I would modify that, and to some extent did so, on recommendations from Primary school Heads. If Primary school Heads had the courage to place their children in a definite order of merit just as Grammar school Heads do for the universities, and are really honest in their statements (many of them are absolutely prepared to be,) then I think a lot of the nonsense about selection would be killed."

Peter Bander: "Do you consider the General Certificate of Education an adequate examination to terminate the Grammar School course?"

Lord James: "I think it's a reasonably good examination. I certainly think it will persist to the 1970's. What will alter, as I indicated in my comments on curriculum, is the number of Advanced Levels which a person will take. I think that we shall almost certainly by then be following the lead of the Schools Council (thought of something like 15 or 20 years ago by Headmasters), of only having two A levels at any rate in some fields with a periphery of other subjects, a broader education in some ways and a more specialised one in others. I think it not unlikely that for university entrance we may by that time know the answer to a question we are asking ourselves now, one with which I am personally connected, namely, how good are these American-type scholastic aptitude tests for diagnosis for the university. I do think, in other words, that over the next ten years a great deal of research is going on and will go on to modify examinations in the direction of being tests, not only of accumulations of knowledge, but of potentiality for advanced work. I sometimes think that we are a little naive about examinations; I think we underestimate the amount of work which does go on. An examination board like the Northern-Universities Joint Matriculation Board, for example, has a research unit; they *do* do work designed to develop the examination system. Their work on general papers, for example, is of very great interest. I think the next 10 years will certainly see modifications in the examination system, though I think that in 10 years something like the A level will still remain at the heart of it. No less important, of course, are changes that ought to take place in university examinations. In the Finals examinations we are carrying on experiments in this university over the kind of examination you set to students, which I think will be at least as revolutionary as those produced in schools.

One other thing, I have hopes that schools will take examinations a little less seriously as they gain confidence in their academic standards. A very good school academically like Manchester Grammar school or like Winchester can afford not to bother much about examinations. Sometimes when I have given prizes and a boy or girl has come up with 9 or 10 O levels, my blood runs cold because the ablest boys at Manchester Grammar school never took more than four O levels. They took the bare minimum for university entrance, because O levels you take in your stride if you're going into the Sixth Form. This attitude will spread. I think we shall move more and more towards the ideal held by the old Secondary Schools Examinations Council and its successor, the Schools Council, of not regarding the O level as a hurdle, but regarding education as much more a continuous process right through to the Sixth Form and, indeed for many people right through into university."

Peter Bander: "Which role does moral and religious education play in secondary education in the next decade?"

Lord James: "I think that to some extent we have lost our nerve over this question of moral and religious education, in this way – we are so afraid of indoctrinating the pupils that we give them the view that 'after all, your opinion is as good as another, so choose

with a pin, old boy!' We have been afraid of sticking our necks
out and saying: 'You are entitled to your opinion, but MY opinion
is this!' We are far too much afraid of giving a definite lead, and
have fallen over backwards to avoid doing so.

One of the great fields we are beginning to explore is the meaning of moral education in a really secular society. I do not think
that this is a problem which concerns the Grammar school Sixth
Form only; on the contrary. There you can tackle ethics as ethics.
For example, with clever boys you can read the first book of the
Republic and you can do so with great success. But at lower levels
and in Secondary Modern and Comprehensive Schools I fully
agree with what the Plowden Report and the Newsom Report have
to say on the subject, namely that we have to consider most carefully how to really bring in questions of morals as real issues for
the child. We must give the child real moral education.

Yet, let me stress that I am in favour of retaining one period of
religious instruction on the time table but not the kind of compulsory religious instruction most children receive at the moment. That
one lesson has absolutely no effect whatever. We live, after all,
in a Christian tradition, and if the child has never read the
Gospel of St. Mark or some chapters from the Old Testament
it is just the same as if he had never read Shakespeare or Wordsworth. But that has very little to do with moral education if it is
read and taught in the manner so common in that one compulsory lesson the children get at the moment.

We must take our coats off and say: "here is a new field!"

A few remarks in conclusion. I believe that the English
Grammar school is in some ways unique. Today there is a tendency to say, "yes, it is unique, we are the odd man out. Look at
the rest of Europe, look at America, they do not in fact have the
high degree of specialisation that we have, yet look how well they
do". I have seen Sixth Forms in the United States and in Germany. They *are* different, and in some ways they are superb. But
do not let us forget that the American educational system is increasingly attempting to modify itself so that it shall be more
like our Sixth Form. To some extent the same sort of thing is true
in Germany. I would not myself be ashamed of our record vis-à-
vis the rest of the world given the basic fact that we are not a very
rich country like America, and that we cannot afford a normal six
or seven years at the university.

And even quite apart from economic arguments, I believe

that psychologically it is good for the able child, of 16 or 17 to come up against difficult problems, to struggle with difficult ideas, provided they have the leadership of a very good teacher. In some other ways I think our Grammar schools have contributed something to education which is unique in the world: the belief that once you become a teacher you are, signing on for life, and all this extra curricula and holiday activity is far more important than we realise. It is an affirmation, in fact, that education is something a great deal more than the purveying of information, that education is concerned with the whole personality of the child.

Therefore I believe that our Grammar schools have set an example in these particular fields, an example that is being increasingly followed by other kinds of school in so far as they are given a chance, (and after all, in the 20 years since the war they have been given a very small chance indeed, and have been starved of money). In so far as the Grammar schools have set an example of what a school can be, and their particular contribution of high academic standards together with an educative community becomes ever more necessary as we extend our education, as we must if we are to survive, then I believe that though they may be fewer in number and different in character, and though they may alter their techniques, the role of the Grammar schools will be of even greater importance in the 1970's.

NOTE

1 *The Future of Socialism:* pub. Jonathan Cape, 1956.

EQUALITY & FRATERNITY

*

SIR JOHN NEWSOM

I am always suspicious of excessively simple ways of laying down the priorities of education. When people carve their way through complex topics like African explorers on safari, cutting a broad swathe through the impenetrable undergrowth at the stroke of a pen, it always seems a bit spurious to me. The complexities are part of the given situation – it always pays to distrust the person who pretends to make everything simple. Having said that let me begin by formulating a few simple propositions about the educational needs of the Seventies.

As I see its there are a number of outstanding aims which should direct educational policy. I am not putting them forward in the order of priority – they are inter-related in such a way as to make them co-equal competitors for first place, but for the sake of clarity they have to be set out separately.

First of all there is a need for a complete overhaul of the content of secondary education and the organization of the curriculum.

Second – and within this – there is a need to revalue the pupils who have been consistently undervalued – meaning the children of average and below average ability who have come to be known as Newsom children.

Third – there is a need to make a reality of the Plowden conception of the first school for children from 3 to 9, with a flexible starting age for compulsory schooling.

Fourth – there is a need for determined efforts to tackle the linked social and educational problems of schools in poor areas.

Fifth – there is the need to equip and inspire teachers capable of rising to these demands.

I have not included the Public Schools in these five top agenda items. In a very real way the public schools get a good deal too much attention. It is important to remember that 98 per cent of the under elevens are in maintained primary schools and 95 per cent of the over 11s also are within the national system. It doesn't do any good to get this out of proportion.

Many of the changes which are going to overtake secondary schools in the seventies will affect public schools and maintained schools alike – changes in curriculum and in the organization of subject matter and subject grouping.

If the links between the public schools and the maintained schools are to become closer by sharing facilities and putting the boarding resources of the public schools to wider use, this will emphasise what these schools have in common rather than their differences. Comprehensive reorganization, and the challenge which, one way or another, this is going to present to the public schools will be a further factor to reckon with.

I hope there will always be some part of our educational system which is not controlled by the State. There must be room for eccentricities. You cannot deny people, who wish to take it, the personal responsibility of sending their children to particular kinds of schools, provided the schools satisfy certain basic standards. But private education is a minority activity and is going to remain one, and it is as well to remember this.

There doesn't seem much point to me in building up the conflict between liberty and equality as ingredients in the public school controversy. Arguments based on the Universal Declaration of Human Rights seem to me to be high-flown, to say the least. The third leg of the liberty and equality trio is fraternity. I think that whether you translate this into political or theological terms, charity is another way of expressing fraternity. This may be the solvent which can help to get a broad equity within an education system – in which there is opportunity for every child, and where the differences between one institution and another do not make people feel that they are intrinsically better or inferior because they have had the chance to go to this school or that.

This is by way of a digression. I do not wish to underestimate the importance of finding ways of removing a divisive influence in the education system. But the fact remains, in my judgment, that all this is, in any case, of declining importance. What school you can say you went to is not what matters these days. The question now is not – "Where did you go to school?" but "What degree have you? Are you qualified?" The worst kind of social division in the late seventies is going to be between those who become qualified by passing exams and those who obtain no qualifications whatever. It is these people who will feel most bitterly rejected by our examination-conscious society. I should be very sorry if neurotic concern with the public schools and with higher education once again obscured the most important task which is to attend to the educational needs of ordinary people.

Turning, then, to my first proposition – that the form and content of secondary education is due for a major overhaul – this has to be taken against the background of the end of the 11 plus at one end and the expansion of higher education at the other. The overhaul is needed for the academic, university-orientated pupils and also for the Newsom children. It entails, too, a host of consequences for the universities.

Already the process of curriculum reform is going on apace through the Schools Council and the Nuffield Foundation. Once this starts it is something which has to go on – you can never hope to get the curriculum "right" once and for all and then forget about it. But not less important than the review of the content of what we call subjects is the need to reconsider the groups of subjects which together form courses.

It is obvious to anyone with half an eye that the present degree of over-specialisation is quite wrong. I once heard someone say at a conference that it did not matter what a boy learned provided he disliked doing it. This is an old fashioned view which has happily been discarded but it is going to be important to avoid the equal and opposite heresy that nobody should do anything unless he really likes doing it. The important thing is going to be to get away from the notion that after the age of 16 pupils can spend all their time on two A levels except for the odd page of scripture and the occasional football match.

Why should we not learn from European countries which show that this is entirely unnecessary? The French and the Dutch, the Germans and the Norwegians do not let their older schoolchildren live entirely in a world of mathematics and science or entirely in a literary world. The Dutch school system seems to me to have something to teach us. Students go to school till 19 and only *then* decide whether to go to a university or a technical college, and whether to read the sciences, classics or the humanities. They keep their freedom of manoeuvre to the last and can perfectly well switch from one discipline to another at 19 instead of being "doomed" as in

101

England from 15 or younger.

I would like to see the G.C.E. "O" level abolished. I would replace it with the Certificate of Secondary Education, using the opportunity this provides for the schools to devise and examine their own courses with an outside moderator. I would postpone the first external examination till seventeen and a half – at some stage it is obviously necessary to have an assessment made by someone other than the teachers who have been directly concerned. The corollary of this, of course is that this first external examination would cover a spread of subjects and do so at the appropriate standard. It would be pointless to switch over in this way if the sixth forms continued to concentrate on the same absurdly narrow front as they do now.

The comprehensive school is an important new factor in all this. What is the ending of "selection" going to mean? I have to confess to a certain scepticism about all this – depend upon it, selection is going to continue but in a different form. There is no doubt in my mind whatever that the business of dividing children up into separate schools at 11 is no longer a serious proposition – a common schooling for all up to 16 or so makes practical sense. But this doesn't mean an end to selection – teachers adapt the education which children receive to their talents and this means that in practice they tend to stream them, or at least to set them into ability groups for particular subjects.

We are not all equal in capacity, however much we may be equal in the eyes of God. Each person in his own capacity is going to make a different contribution to the economy of the country. I am only against examinations if they come too early: you cannot let a man practise as a surgeon or an engineer unless he has the tested ability which the job needs. I am not saying as a matter of dogma that this means there must be streaming. I am only observing that teachers in practice do a good deal of selection along the line and that I would be sceptical about administrative attempts to stop this.

This has a good deal to do with the kind of revolution in the education of the Newsom children which I want to see. You are not likely to get this revolution if you are forbidden to do anything which might conceivably identify which children they are. I believe that if we really paid sufficient attention to the process of education at all levels we could narrow the gulf between what we now call the clever and the stupid.

This calls for sensitive and devoted teaching. It also calls for the right kind of curriculum and the right teaching materials – a new content and new method which, linked together, constitute a new quality of education. In the Newsom report we discussed some of the ways this can be brought about – the kind of contact with the real world which is needed to keep a spark of curiosity and learning alive in youngsters who are all too ready to contract out of school long before they leave. And, of course, it calls for the raising of the school leaving age, too, and the stimulus which this challenge must bring to the schools.

Many youngsters we now call stupid are limited by their home and social environment. I am sure that education has tended to progress faster than the social environment, which is why I place so much importance on the Plowden Report's proposal to give special priority to certain areas which are pockets of bad housing, unemployment and generally slum conditions.

This clearly throws into relief the needs of the neighbourhood school. Without a concerted social policy for the educational priority areas, there is no long term answer to the neighbourhood school which brings together the biggest educational and communal problems of the worst areas and magnifies social and educational inequality. Throw in the immigrant question and the neighbourhood school is an amalgam of trouble for the Seventies. What has to be recognised is that at present the children whose needs are greatest get the rawest deal. Somehow we have got to break this closed circle. To do so we shall have to call on resources outside the schools themselves and make this a prime objective of all branches of social work.

Much of this applies just as much to the primary schools as it does to the secondary. We have the opportunity now to exploit the tremendous work which has already been done in the infants school, by consolidating it with nursery schools at one end and by extending the first school up to eight at the other. We need to get away from the rigid starting age to a much more flexible arrangement of full and half-time nursery schooling to take children through from three and a half to between five and six before nursery education merges into infants education, with the first part of the infants school between five and six also being largely on a half time basis. Nobody pretends that this can be carried out at once but it provides pattern for the future which we must work towards.

But the organisational change – the substitution of a first stage from three and a half to eight, followed by a middle school from eight to twelve – is of minor importance beside the far more fundamental need to extend and generalise the best quality of contemporary infants education. The emphasis has to be on the child discovering things under guidance rather than being instructed; on individual and group methods; on "go and find out" instead of "I'm telling you".

The abolition of the 11 plus is freeing the primary schools from the more rigid formal requirements. If nothing is put in their place standards will fall. What needs to be put in the place of formal examination requirements is a new teaching ethic and a new insight into the development of children which makes heavy demands on the teacher. But this is crucial. This is what I understand people to mean when they talk in clichés about the primary schools laying the foundation of what comes later. In this sense the re-making of primary education is the only way to do something for the Newsom children. It is the key to curriculum reform at the later stage.

I think much of our secondary education could be greatly improved if these primary methods were used to replace conventional secondary techniques. In a sense, this is what the introduction of "discovery" methods mean. But there is a long way to go, even at the primary stage. About half our primary schools still haven't come to terms with the new methods, and many old schools are too small and cramped for the freedom of movement and the busy activity which all this involves.

But the biggest task is still going to be the re-education and retraining of the teachers, implicit in these changes. There is no point in underestimating what this means – there are no unintelligent children, only unintelligent teachers. Like any other group, teachers are likely to be conservative about their profession or occupation. The methods and attitudes of the past have produced the submerged tenth of Newsom "failures" who constitute a problem in themselves in many secondary schools and for whom the raising of the school leaving age is both a necessity and a nightmare.

What is needed is that the attitudes, insights and sympathies of the gifted few who are grappling with these difficult matters, should be shared by the profession as a whole – that there should be, in fact, a change of psychology as well as of technique. The in-service training of teachers is clearly going to be one of the major pre-occupations of the Seventies. The creation of local teachers' centres is one of the most promising developments of this decade; an enormous amount depends on carrying this through and making a reality of the theory to which lip service is freely paid, that professional refreshment has to go on throughout a life-long career.

But we are still a long way from having got the initial training of teachers right. We are still struggling to weigh up the relative importance of the teacher's own personal education on the one hand and this technical training as a teacher on the other. Teachers have to know the elements of sociology, psychology, pedagogy, hygiene, as well as those disciplines generally held to constitute a general education. Primary school teachers are expected to be able to express their skill manually as well as orally. They have to know something about school administration, human relationships and the many things which can irreverently be called the tricks of the trade.

Classroom technique and teaching methods are essential parts of teacher training which we can ignore at our peril. But in the next decade we have to devise a training for teachers which neither preempts so much for personal education that nothing is left for teaching methods, nor yet concentrates so severely on the nuts and bolts that they are quite incapable of standing back and thinking about the job they are trained for.

It is not at all clear how the introduction of the B.Ed. is going to help here. There is an obvious risk of this leading to a concentration on academic standards instead of on the all round development of the class teacher. The Colleges of Education are spending too much of their time designing their new hoods and gowns – metaphorically certainly; literally, conceivably. They have been caught up in what they imagine to be a University ambience. They are wondering how near they can get to the university atmosphere. If you like, you can argue that from their point of view this is a reasonable thing to do. But its most certainly not what the Treasury is spending millions of pounds of our money for. The vocational training of teachers is what will suffer. People seldom realise that an ill-prepared teacher can do radical and lasting damage, just as an ill-prepared doctor can.

Visiting schools with the Newsom and Plowden Commissions, I saw just as many unhappy teachers as unhappy children; teachers who were unprepared for the social background against which they had to work; teachers who were at a loss to know what to do, but sensed that there was a wall between the children and themselves. It was not their intrinsic competence which was in question, only their misfortune in not having been properly prepared for the job.

One way forward may be to encourage university courses like those at Sussex and York which make it possible for students doing a four year course to take a teacher training course alongside their main academic study throughout the period. I firmly believe we should get away from the conventional pattern of a three year degree course followed by a year's Dip. Ed. This is just an ineffective way of training a teacher.

But underlying all these issues are difficult and controversial matters relating to the nature of the teaching profession. It is a matter of fact that a teacher in a nursery school does not instinctively identify herself as a professional colleague of the head of the science department at Winchester. The idea of a single unified profession is largely an achievement of public relations: the facts of the situation belie it.

Salaries and prospects re-introduce the differentials which cannot be admitted openly. There are special additions for graduates with good honours degrees and for other graduates; there are additional salary payments for posts of responsibility and it so happens that a higher proportion of teachers in secondary schools get their allowances than do primary teachers. The egalitarian notion that they are all teachers break down.

Salaries are determined in the last resort by demand and supply. There are obvious differences between men and women which equal pay fails to take into account. Teaching is a well paid job for women graduates – they get paid as much as women anywhere in industry and commerce. But for men, a graduate teacher is well enough off to start with – say up to 35 – but then he starts to drop behind his opposite number outside. So he has to leave the classroom "to better himself" by becoming a head or an inspector or a lecturer in a college of education – anything but go on teaching. And the three year trained college of education man not only starts but remains underpaid by comparison with his industrial contemporaries.

Anyone "looking forward to the Seventies" would be foolish not to link the hopes and prospects of education with those of the economy as a whole. All hopes of progress in education depend on getting for education a rising share of the Gross National Product. Because of the age structure in the population as a whole and the explosion of popular demand for education on top of this, educational spending has got to go up much faster than the most optimistic estimate of national growth. This is only going to be feasible if the economy is going ahead and there is some confidence in real prosperity. This is the shadow which is going to hang over all our plans for the seventies. But important as this is – and true as it always proves to be all economic cuts strike most harshly at the needy in schools as elsewhere – the greatest opportunities for the Seventies lie in the field of educational ideas and here what is going to count is insight and determination no less than pounds, shillings and pence.

REVOLUTION IN SECONDARY EDUCATION

*

DAVID DONNISON

"Revolution" is a threadbare word, but it is the right one to describe what is now going on in secondary education. These developments amount to a revolution because they spring from – and create – irreversible changes in human rights and relationships, because they are a product of mutually reinforcing economic and social trends, and because similar changes are taking place in many other countries. The process is a slow one, checked and diverted by all sorts of local eddies and cross-currents, and it will take a generation or more to work through it. But the directions in which we are moving are becoming increasingly clear.

I want to identify these changes and briefly explain their origins. Then I shall discuss the directions in which we are going, quietening – I hope – a number of mistaken fears but posing some of the new problems to which we should be turning our attention. Education plays too central a part in shaping the society we inhabit for anyone to resolve the disputes that continually escort its progress. My aim is only to help people argue about the right things.

The pattern of change

Since the Second World War similar developments have taken place in the educational systems of a large number of countries with predominantly urban, industrial economies. The pattern has four main features.

(a) Children stay longer at school. Rising proportions of successive age groups continue their education after the minimum leaving age (generally between fourteen and sixteen) to the ages of seventeen, eighteen and beyond. The "retentivity" of the educational system – to use the jargon – is increasing.

(b) Irrevocable, or nearly irrevocable, decisions about the educational opportunities open to children are being postponed to later ages. This can be done in many ways: by postponing transfer from comprehensive primary to selective secondary schools, by educating all children together in comprehensive secondary schools, by making transfers between different types of school or different "tracks" within schools easier, by creating new forms of further education, and by opening up new routes to existing forms of further education for pupils in schools that previously led only to the labour market.

(c) These changes call for, and are hastened by, the abandonment of systems in which most secondary schools were precluded by rule or custom from offering their pupils effective opportunities of further education, and their replacement by systems in which the retentivity of secondary schools and the opportunities of further education they offer are allowed to develop as fast as the teachers, the pupils and their parents can make them grow. The rate of growth is still restrained by scarcities of teachers, buildings and equipment and by the restricted aspirations of pupils and parents, but the development of the schools is no longer held down under a lid of legal and administrative restrictions.

(d) Children are educated for longer than hitherto in schools catering for a wide variety of social classes and intellectual capacities. The extent of social and intellectual mixing depends on the composition of the neighbourhoods served by the schools, the competition for pupils permitted between schools and the degree of segregation within them. But the possibilities of mixing increase, and in many countries deliberate attempts are being made to reduce social segregation and the inequalities of educational opportunity it produces.

These changes encourage other developments which are harder to summarise with precision and depend more heavily on local conditions. Four of them are particularly important.

(e) As secondary schools recruit and retain pupils with a wider range of abilities drawn from a greater variety of backgrounds – children who may be unaccustomed to the demands of a traditional academic curriculum – there is increasing pressure to reappraise the content and methods of teaching, the process of learning and the motives for it. In every generation there are teachers with a gift for treating each pupil as a unique individual and for inspiring each to learn at his own pace and his own way. Recent developments in the schools make their colleagues more willing to listen to these teachers and learn from them.

(f) The same pressures, coupled with an increasingly sophisticated understanding of the influences impinging on the school from outside, produce a growing willingness to make contact with parents and others in the surrounding community, and to seek their help in the work of the schools. Meanwhile parents, alerted to the importance of education as never before, take a keener interest in the schools and demand to be heard on a local and a national scale.

(g) As more children stay longer at school the secondary curriculum, the choices it offers and the specialisations it imposes, are seen to play an increasingly important part in determining the patterns of higher education and of recruitment to the labour market. Debates about the pre-university years of schooling take many forms – calling for new teaching methods, for later specialisation, or earlier specialisation, for new subjects, or new combinations of subjects – but everywhere these debates become increasingly lively.

(h) The fourth in this series of subsidiary developments is plainer to see in every country. Teachers are scarce, and those for whom there is keenest demand in other sectors of the economy – the mathematicians and scientists – are scarcest of all. These scarcities help to shape the course of many other developments now taking place.

In short, the rising tide of educational aspirations is carrying into the upper reaches of the system a greater number and variety of children with a greater variety of needs than ever before. It is submerging the embankments that used to channel and confine the flow, and pushing further back the dams and sluices that effectively control its volume and direction. Within the schools this rising tide is compelling teachers to reappraise the aims and methods of their work, and to recognise more explicitly their links with the world outside the schools – both the local world of home and neighbourhood, and the national economy, its higher education and its labour market.

Pressures for change

These patterns would not recur in so many countries if they did not reflect more fundamental economic and social changes in industrial urban societies.

The labour market helps to shape the demands made on the educational system through the opportunities it offers: few people are prepared to stay at school when others leave unless they secure some gain in income or status by doing so. The educational system in turn helps to shape the growth of the economy through the aspirations and capacities it confers on the recruits it supplies. In these countries the labour required for primary industries has declined to a very low level, and in many of them the requirements of secondary (or manufacturing) industries are also declining. But both sectors demand increasingly skilled workers. Meanwhile the tertiary industries – public and commercial services calling for a wide variety of professional, semi-professional and social skills – demand continually increasing numbers of workers. Thus the hierarchy of occupations in these economies, which in the nineteenth century had a pyramid-shaped distribution of skill, status and income, first turns pear-shaped and then egg-shaped. These changes will go a lot further, and the educational system must keep pace with them.

Economic development generates political pressures. Pretty soon, half the households in Britain will own a house and a car. The distribution of family sizes over the income range is now U-shaped: a central belt of lower middle class and skilled working class parents now have small families and plenty of time for their children. The same patterns are emerging in other countries.

People who have secured a standard of living that may be superior to that enjoyed by the middle classes when they were young resent their children being confined to an inferior working class education offering inferior opportunities later in life. The fact that the most successful professional and executives appear to have succeeded pretty well in maintaining their income differentials only sharpens the ambitions of aspiring working class parents. The skilled trades to which they used to direct their children's ambitions – the engine drivers and printers, for example – have been much less successful in maintaining their status.

The figures below, derived from interviews with a representative sample of the adult population in Britain in a survey made for *New Society* by Research Services Ltd., show there is now a majority in favour of comprehensive education, even among Conservative voters. In areas where comprehensives already exist, many of those who elsewhere voted "don't know" in answer to this question seem to have swung over to support comprehensives. Among parents with children in comprehensive schools many of the opponents, too, become supporters. These figures are particularly striking when it is remembered that most of the schools described at this time as "comprehensive" were not in fact comprehensive at all. They had grown up alongside a well established system of grammar schools and were not yet securing their full share of the brightest pupils or of the best qualified academic teachers.

"Are you in favour or against comprehensive education?"

	Total of persons in sample	Areas said to have comprehensives	Other* areas	Parents of children in comprehensives	Other adults
Base for percentages	1331	444	455	33	1298
		Percentages			
In favour	52	73	42	85	51
Against	19	17	20	12	19
Don't know	29	10	38	3	30
TOTAL	100	100	100	100	100

* Excluding those where respondent did not know.

Source: Survey of representative sample of British adult population, 1967. D.V. Donnison, "Education and Opinion", *New Society*, 27 October, 1967.

But a large majority of the same people voted against the abolition of what the interviewers described as "grammar *schooling*". This is not as contradictory as it sounds. They were not voting against academic education but against the secondary modern school — massively.

Looking forward to the Seventies

Where England stands

The stage this country has reached in this revolution and the peculiarities of our position can be glimpsed in a two-volume "International Study of Achievement in Mathematics" published last year.[1] This study deals with Australia, Israel, Japan, the U.S.A. and eight countries in Western Europe.

England, like the majority of countries in the study, had a selective system of secondary schools, but we select at a younger age than most countries. The proportion of our children going to schools from which all leave at the minimum legal age was larger than in most countries. It follows that the retentivity of our system was lower. Most English children left school as soon as they could, but a large proportion of the remainder stayed on till the age of seventeen or eighteen.[2] In England, performance in mathematics at the age of thirteen was more closely related to social characteristics of the parents (particularly the father's occupation) than it was in most of the other countries. Specialisation in the closing years of school life began earlier in England and was pursued to far greater lengths. Scotland shared most, but not all, of these characteristics.

England, in short, is still at a fairly early stage in the revolution outlined at the start of this paper.

Some characteristics of secondary education in twelve countries, 1961–63

	Age of transfer to secondary education	Percentage of children at school at age:			No. of subjects studied in pre-university year
		15	16	17	
		%	%	%	
Australia	13	66	36	16	5+
Belgium	15 *	65	62	39	9+
England	11	42	22	12	3
Finland	11	43	31	24	9+
France	11 *	—	—	—	9+
Germany	10 *	56	30	31	9
Israel	13	—	—	—	8
Japan	12	64	60	57	9
Netherlands	12	62	46	34	9+
Scotland	12	42	22	13	4
Sweden	16	58	46	35	9
U.S.A.	12	93	86	74	4

* Transfer to observation or guidance period.
Source: Husén (Ed.) *International Study of Achievement in Mathematics.*

The effects

To show that we are following a path already trod by others and that strong economic and political compulsions are likely to take us further along it will not be in the least reassuring to those who do not want to go in this direction at all. The inevitable is not necessarily desirable. Many of the anxieties these developments provoke can be summed up in the question: "Will more mean worse?"

Some fairly convincing general answers can now be given to that question. But discussion of the growing *numbers* of pupils continuing their education to higher levels is often confused with discussion of the changing *structure* of the system through which they go. The confusion is natural because the two changes tend to go together. Children in schools catering for a wide range of abilities are likely to remain longer at school because the brightest pupils must be given opportunities of staying on and others are encouraged to follow their example. Meanwhile, the longer children continue working together, the wider the range of attainments that will be found among them: the longer the race, the more spread out the runners become. Conversely, an educational policy that calls for early segregation of the brightest children will generally entail early leaving for the remainder. Nevertheless the two issues of numbers and structure can be distinguished. Let us consider numbers first.

In the final stages of a more retentive system, the spread of attainments will be wider, and the average attainment will be lower. The average mathematical attainment of the 74 per cent of Americans still in school at the age of seventeen was well below the average of the 12 per cent still in English schools at the same age. In this crude sense, "more means worse". It would be very odd if it didn't.

But when comparisons are made of the *top* performers within countries or between countries there is no evidence that they suffer from working in a system that retains a growing proportion of pupils. Indeed, in mathematics the proportion of the total age group attaining given standards is generally highest in the countries retaining the largest proportions of their young people in school. If this is true for mathematics, the subject for which there is the greatest scarcity of teachers, it is also likely to be true for other subjects. Thus for the out-and-out élitist, concerned only with the top one per cent or five per cent, "more means better".

This, too, should not be surprising. A teacher who can select his high flyers from a larger field is likely to recruit a better team. Likewise (to pose the same problem in another way) a teacher who has to select his star performers seven years before they are entered for the university stakes is unlikely to get such good results as a teacher who can wait several years longer before picking his team.

On the separate question of comprehensive schooling, a massive Swedish study[3] covering almost every aspect of education shows that the change from a differentiated to a comprehensive system had virtually no effect on standards of achievement in that country – a conclusion equally depressing to all partisans. The main benefits of "going comprehensive" are likely to appear later: standards will rise because more children will stay longer at school. For a thorough analysis of British experience we must await the outcome of studies now being made by the National Foundation for Educational Research. But the study edited by Husén already provides some information about mathematical attainments among children in different types of system. In England schools classed as "comprehensive" were creamed to greater or lesser extents by grammar and independent schools competing with them for the brightest pupils and the more experienced academic teachers – particularly maths teachers. At the age of thirteen the scores of pupils in their academic streams fell between those of the grammar and secondary modern pupils. It would have been disturbing if they had been doing as well as the grammar schools at this stage: one of the purposes of the comprehensive school is to provide opportunities for more demanding academic work for pupils who would not have been good enough to get into grammar schools. But in the last year of schooling comprehensive pupils (maths specialists and non-specialists alike) were doing as well as those in grammar schools. Despite their initial handicaps, the comprehensives had caught up. The Scottish results were similar.

For the immediate future, three conclusions about the development of secondary education deserve to be stressed.

(a) If we are to maintain the standards of our educated élite in a competitive world we must enable far more children from a wider range of social backgrounds to complete their schooling and go on to higher education. This élite is already improverished because so few young people stay in the running long enough to compete for entry to it.

(b) We cannot satisfy the rising educational aspirations of ordinary people or sustain the rate of economic growth we want un-

114

less many more young people are allowed to take their education further. For most of our children, education stops far too soon.

(c) These things will not be achieved unless we carry the majority of children forward together in the same schools well beyond the age of eleven and postpone irrevocable decision about their educational opportunities to later ages.

There is nothing new about these conclusions: they have been in circulation for a long time. But there is now a growing body of evidence to support them. There would be no need to go on repeating them if they did not conflict with academic and social prejudices that are deeply rooted among influential people.

The future

Educational thinking proceeds in cycles. From time to time the whole lumbering procession slowly turns, with contradictory shouts and a good deal of abuse, to march in some new direction. But further turning points always lie somewhere ahead. However ardent our advocacy of the new route, we should already be looking for the neglected needs and problems that will in time call for fresh changes in direction.

I only have space to touch on a few of these problems. Although I concentrate on the later stages of secondary education; the first stages deserve just as much attention. A whole chapter, for example could be devoted to the destructive shock experienced by many eleven-year-olds as they move from the lively but relatively cosy world of the primary school to the impersonality – sometimes deliberately punitive – of the secondary school. "Here you'll have to *work*", said one of my son's teachers; "this is not some crummy comprehensive." The bewildered children go to different teachers for every lesson; for weeks they do not even know their teachers' names. Neither, one suspects, do the teachers know theirs. "The teachers in my new school are not nearly so clever as those in my old school," commented the boy. "They can only teach one subject." The comprehensive schools will not succeed unless their teachers learn what the best primary schools have done so well – to arouse the interest and sustain the confidence of children from the start, and to gain the enthusiastic support of their parents.

The debate about specialisation in secondary schools is already under way. Sooner or later there must be an increase in the number of subjects studied by the average sixth former and a postponement of the point at which he drops those he abandons. There is growing evidence that early specialisation does not produce higher standards in the long run; it only enables people to attain these standards a year or two earlier – at the price of complete ignorance of large fields which they will never have another chance of exploring. Meanwhile the economists stress the costs of this ignorance: they are increasingly sceptical about their capacity to forecast the skills required by a dynamic economy and therefore ask the schools and universities to produce not specialists but adaptable people capable of doing a variety of jobs and learning new things quickly. The entry to comprehensive sixth forms of pupils from a growing variety of cultural backgrounds will make the extension of basic education in a larger number of subjects even more urgent.

But real progress towards a broader sixth form education cannot be expected until the universities take a larger entry and select it in ways that do not reimpose pressures for specialisation in concealed forms. "A" level results are a poor predictor of academic potentiality but they are generally a better guide than interviews or headmasters' reports. More objective tests are needed which do not stunt the sixth form curriculum. The tide of parental discontent which is now washing away the eleven-plus selection procedures will go on rising. It will probably strike the eighteen-plus selection procedures in less than a generation. Universities and colleges had better place these procedures on a firmer footing before then if they are to avoid chaos and recrimination. Eventually they will find that the comprehensive revolution cannot be restricted to secondary education.

While the number of subjects studied by the average sixth former remains cripplingly small, the number of options available within the average sixth form proliferates year by year. It now exceeds twenty in many schools. Since half the entries at "A" level are concentrated on only four subjects (Maths, Physics, English and Chemistry) the growing tail of additional options (Geology, Ancient History, Sociology...) taken by tiny numbers of candidates means that many "A" level classes have half a dozen pupils or less. This is a wasteful use of scarce teachers. Too often the pupils are later bored stiff by a first year at university which covers much the same ground. It will become easier to impose some discipline on this proliferation of options when the opportunities for narrow specialisation are reduced.

The wrangles of recent years have encouraged too many defenders of the grammar schools to adopt a last-ditch preservationist stance. They exaggerate the virtues of selective schools and the vices of comprehensive schools, and their opponents respond by doing the reverse. The exponents of selective academic education in maintained grammar, direct grant and independent schools have no great love for each other, and unite only in defending the status quo. Debate has therefore become focussed on banal symbols and real educational problems have been neglected.

It is not the academic virtues but the secondary modern school that is obsolete. We need more and better academic education. Discrimination of various kinds between the needs of pupils with different interests and abilities will continue in every good school. The older the pupils, and the wider the spread of their interests and abilities, the more discrimination there must be. We should be discussing how to discriminate in ways that do not create or perpetuate the differences in human capacities to be catered for.

The sixth forms will be the most rapidly growing part of the whole educational system during the next twenty years. Current anxieties about the minimum size of a viable sixth form and the "creaming" of one school's sixth form by others will soon be overshadowed by more pressing anxieties about the general shortage of resources for sixth form teaching. Any school that can do a good job of pre-university education will be badly needed. But it may have to meet the nation's needs in new ways. Entrance to Oxbridge will no longer be the sole criterion of success. In many schools curricula and teaching methods are already being developed and diversified to cater for growing numbers of pupils who stay on with no intention of going to universities. Some schools, determined to maintain high standards of traditional academic teaching, cannot provide for a comprehensive intake over the whole age range from eleven to thirteen. They may have to concentrate on the last two or three years of pre-university schooling. Provided they recognise the character of the revolution going on in secondary education and find ways of adapting their work to the situation now developing, they need have no fears that their contribution will be spurned.

The vigour, wealth and character of the society we create in the remainder of this century will depend to a considerable extent on the answer to that question.

Can we abandon the increasingly boring educational disputes of recent years and turn our attention to the more important issues now confronting us?

NOTES

1 Torsten Husén, Editor: *International Study of Achievement in Mathematics. A Comparison of Twelve Countries,* John Wiley, 1967.
2 The English start school younger than others, but the authors of the study enjoyed by those entering at 5 would appear to be of no consequence as far as progress in mathematics by the age of 13 is concerned... To make the mandatory age of entry to school earlier (for example from 6 to 5) will not in itself improve performance; it is what happens in that extra initial year that is important." (Vol. II, p. 68)
3 N. E. Svensson, *Ability Grouping and Scholastic Achievement: Report on a 5 Year Follow-Up Study in Stockholm,* Stockholm, Almqvist and Wiksell, 1962.

THE TRANSITION FROM PRIMARY
TO SECONDARY EDUCATION

*

JOHN BURROWS

The word "transition" implies a smooth, systematic, unhurried progress from one state to another. But do we in fact achieve "transition" in this sense from primary to secondary education, or merely transfer? There is much evidence that we do not. At a recent conference in one area during which primary and secondary teachers spent two days in each others' schools, the former were astonished at the variety of work and approaches to be seen in the first year of the secondary schools and the secondary teachers amazed – and in some cases ashamed – before the quality and richness of the creative, descriptive and co-operative work in the last year of the junior schools. All saw much of what they had been doing with their pupils as inappropriate, out of key, failing to offer pupils opportunities for which they were ready and from which they would have gained. Perhaps most noteworthy, not only in this one area but throughout the country, is the failure to realise on the secondary side just what breadth and quality of achievement the newer primary approaches have led to in such fields as creative writing, art and craft, reading and, increasingly, mathematics. To remedy this is no simple matter, if only because the revolution in primary method is not universal and two adjoining schools may be as different in what they do as chalk from cheese – but knowledge is the first step towards salvation from the shock or jolt which too often transfer inflicts on our pupils.

Transfer we must have, but any transfer presents hazards. Will the new school excite or bore the pupils? Will it welcome or depress them? Will they find the stimulus of novelty or the dreary round of: "Now let's find out what you know"? followed by so-called revision and the inculcation of working procedures which may clash sharply with these to which the pupils have been accustomed. It would not be fair to underrate the difficulties of the secondary school; the writer has visited schools which received pupils from more than fifty primary schools, and some uniformity of procedures no doubt must be established. But surely this should be based upon knowledge of the practices previously familiar to pupils; surely primary and secondary staffs should join to ensure that "what you know" is broadly familiar to the new staff before the pupils leave the old; surely the passage to new practices and disciplines should be gradual and adjusted to pupils' previous experience. It is true, of course, that many children benefit by the sheer excitement of change and by the challenge of new subjects, of new approaches to teaching and learning, of new faces and new teachers; no one would suggest that transfer is not a right moment for new opportunities. But these are in the main children who are already on confident terms with the world of school and who receive understanding and support at home; not all do. They are the pupils who have mastered the art of forming social relationships within the group, class, or teaching unit, are at ease both with their fellows and with the adult members of their community. They are the fortunate pupils for whom the new intellectual challenge presented by specialist teaching and new disciplines in the secondary school comes at precisely the right moment in their development – those who are eager for change and for novelty and whose minds are ready to grapple with more advanced problems, more abstract concepts, and less familiar situations. They establish themselves in the secondary school, of no matter what type, and straight-way do well. Where this happens, credit is due both to the working of the system and to the generally humane approach of the English teacher. But on the debit side – and here it may be the system rather than the individual teacher which is to blame – are the uncounted but numerous children to whom transfer comes as a severe shock and requires a difficult effort of re-adjustment before they can once again proceed serenely down the path of learning and of social and personal development. There are naturally all stages and degrees of shock; to some the effort of re-adjustment is a matter only of days or weeks, and to some it may even be salutary to have to make the effort. But there can be few secondary teachers who are not aware of the price paid for transfer by the less mature, the less confident, and the more backward children. Secondary schools are rightly concerned and anxious when they find they have received pupils whose mastery of the basic skills of reading, writing, conversation and simple mathematics is uncertain or slight; often enough the truth is that transfer has come at a point where the child was slowly and unsteadily establishing himself with the help of an understanding teacher or group of teachers in the primary school, where his history was known, his progress chartered, and his needs understood. The unfamiliarity of his new teachers with his personal situation puzzles them and not infrequently drives him back into a withdrawn state, from which all too many of our secondary youngsters never again emerge in full before they leave school for the last time. Nor are these pupils always discerned as slow, backward, or handicapped in one way or another. Many of the latter do indeed pick themselves out, and in many schools of recent years there has been a most praiseworthy upsurge of understanding remedial action; nevertheless we cannot know how many of those passive, docile, ordinary children who never seem to stand out for either good or ill are in fact under-achievers who, given transition rather than transfer, might have developed a far fuller potential. Many of them might justly exclaim, in the words of Omar Khayyam:

"What, without asking, hither hurried whence?
And, without asking, whither hurried hence?"

To many such, happily, the multiplication of imaginative fourth and fifth year integrated courses for young school leavers following the Newsom Report has brought a new dimension of experience and enabled them to know themselves and recognise their own talents; but even so one cannot but regret the years which the locust has eaten. How can transfer be made merely a part of transition, so that the maturing processes of so many pupils are not sharply halted or set back, but continue with no more disturbance than, as it were, crossing a station platform to another train which will proceed equally smoothly in the same direction?

Attention during the last twenty years came to focus more and more on the effects of selection at the age of 11. Growing discontent with these effects has led steadily to either the softening or the complete abolition of the selection process in most areas. Few of us will regret this advance, but of itself, though it may remove some of the worst features of transfer, it will not cure the basic problem. One charge justly levelled against the "eleven-plus" was its restricting and distorting effect upon the primary school curriculum, and with the drawing of its sting one can see up and down

121

the land new benefits in creative work, freer methods of learning, a wider ranging and less channelled curriculum. The content of study has broadened, the range of children's experience has widened, and the steady decline in streaming within the junior school is putting an end to the kind of segregation by ability which almost inevitably followed the older form of secondary selection. But the liberation of the primary school will be abortive for many children if it is not understood and built upon in the secondary school. The child, after all, has not the adult experience which enables him to grasp the purpose and the need of switching to different techniques and different organisational patterns; his needs change, it is true, but not overnight. Unless knowledge replaces ignorance of what is happening on the other side of the transfer gap, and unless a logical sequence of teaching, learning and social patterns is developed as a result, transfer may still shock. A second charge often levelled against selection was the state of worry which it induced in parents, especially those who were concerned and ambitious for their children, and which naturally enough was often communicated to the pupils themselves. The introduction of comprehensive schools may put an end to the worry about selection, but there are many other worries which can replace it. Parents will always be concerned for their children, and if they see them bewildered, bothered or maladjusted as a result of transfer, the worry will merely have been deferred and be of a different kind. It behoves us all to exorcise parental worry about their children's progress for good, not merely to see it spring up in a new form.

A heavy responsibility is thus laid upon both school and home, and it is one which falls with equal weight upon both primary and secondary schools. The first essential is probably that parents shall be clear and not confused about what actually is happening in the schools their children attend, and why. The Plowden Report has stressed the need for improved understanding between school and home, and this must be interpreted in the first place as a need to give parents understanding of new developments in teaching techniques, in curricular scope and content, in the organisation and pattern of the school day, and so on. Without necessarily undertaking their complete education in detail, it is urgent for schools of all types to see that parents do in fact understand what is happening inside them and why. (Are we too readily inclined to assume either that they know or that there is no advantage in their knowing?) This knowledge of what actually happens on both sides of the transfer gap should then be supplemented by knowledge of the procedures and mechanics of transfer itself, and by parents having the opportunity to make the acquaintance of the new school and of some members of its staff before pupil transfer actually takes place. Some individual schools, both primary and secondary, already do well in this respect, but we cannot rest until this is universal; and really informative publications for parents by either local education authorities or individual schools are still few and far between. The informed and understanding parent is far more likely to send to school a contented and confident child, and to be able to allay the questions and anxieties which may arise in the first weeks in the unfamiliar new school.

The second need is that all teachers who are in contact with children before and after transfer shall have at least a working knowledge of current psychological and sociological theory. Child behaviour can baffle those who have no informed idea of the main processes of development and the broad stages of physical, intellectual and emotional growth through which children must pass. Similarly, some knowledge of the home and of the social pressures which surround a child is essential if his school work is to be sympathetically and profitably related to them. In the formative years of adolescence particularly we must have no truck with the theory that a teacher is there simply to impart knowledge and that other aspects of his pupils' development are not his concern. English education has of course a fine record of beneficial concern in this field, and the need for it is greater than ever. The steady growth of counselling schemes in secondary schools is an acknowledgement of this fact, and there are certainly training needs which are far from fully met. It can be assumed today that most primary school staffs are broadly acquainted with the work of Piaget and that what happens in the schools is broadly in line with the views on child development which he and his followers have advanced and tested in practice. It cannot yet be said that this knowledge is familiar to a majority of secondary school teachers; the sources from which many come to the schools preclude this. Many secondary teachers, probably an increasing proportion, are university graduates who are well qualified in their subjects but who have spent either one short year in professional training or none at all. Is there not an urgent need for in-service training to fill this kind of gap in the knowledge of those secondary teachers (particularly those entering the profession) who have had no opportunity to do so and who may not even realise what a gap it is?

The third need is, of course, that the staffs of primary and secondary schools shall understand the different loads, disciplines and approaches of the other, shall visit each others' schools and see for themselves, and shall meet and discuss how, in the year on each side of the transfer age at least, they may co-ordinate and bring together what they are doing to the benefit of the children. This is not a process that can be accomplished in an afternoon. It requires a genuine and continuing effort to enter into the minds of one's colleagues, to learn from them, to appreciate what they say, and to be able to explain what one is doing oneself, and why a different emphasis is likely to be found in the secondary school from the primary. It is necessary not only to talk but to see pupils at work, severally and in groups, for it is observation of what they are doing which prompts the significant question of how and why. Exchange of staff for a term or a year between secondary and their contributory primary schools would be well worth trying, and certainly key members of staff ought to spend more time in each others schools than ever they do at present. The teaching profession in this country is always resourceful in meeting a situation of difficulty or challenge; the preliminary is to admit the serious nature of the problem itself.

In the fields of organisation and curriculum events are indeed hustling us forward. It is clear that by the nineteen-seventies many local education authorities will be running middle schools with an age range of 9-13 years; in them an entirely new look should be possible at the whole question of transition from childhood to adolescence and from primary to secondary modes of teaching and learning, if there are fundamentally different modes at all and not rather differences of emphasis. Much may surely be learned from these schools in which transition really can replace transfer, and an encouraging feature is the thoughtful energy with which teachers, administrators and advisers in many of these areas are now studying and conferring on both basic issues and matters of detail. Within the curricular field, the ferment created by Nuffield projects in mathematics and science and the pilot projects in French means that the curriculum itself is evolving and during the next ten years is bound to change. All three of these projects have been studying and experimenting with the development of the subjects in the 8-13 age range, one which of course overlaps and has inescapable implications for both the primary and the secondary school. No longer, for instance, will the learning of French be a mystery reserved for the secondary school; increasingly, pupils will enter secondary school with three years of French studies behind them and in many cases a remarkably effective mastery of several aspects of the language already in their possession. To neglect this challenge would be shameful and, one hopes, unthinkable, to secondary schools staffs, but the questions it poses for them go down to the very fundamentals of the language teaching – purpose, scope, and techniques. Not only has their own approach to the teaching of the language to be re-thought and adapted in the light of the achievement already recorded by their new pupils, but new possibilities are opened up for the introduction of further languages and for work of an entirely different kind in French itself within the secondary school. A detailed knowledge of what has actually taken place in the contributory primary schools will of course be essential. Mutatis mutandis, the same is true of the new approaches to mathematics and science – and no doubt will be soon in many other aspects of the curriculum also, for it is not only in those areas where the resources of the Nuffield Foundation have been brought to bear that curricular development is taking place. The links and the continuity between primary and secondary schools need to be closer than ever before.

There are many other factors to reckon with which can be only briefly mentioned. The first is that the disappearance of "eleven-plus" objective tests and of selection itself means giving serious thought and investigation to the whole subject of diagnosis and records. Are there reliable diagnostic techniques which will be of service – not just as an indication of a child's verbal ability or his powers to memorise, but of his characteristics, aptitudes, and development as a whole? What should one teacher or one school tell the next about an individual child? How are subjective opinions to be balanced against objective assessments, and what weight is to be given in individual cases to home background and other environmental factors? A second factor which can no longer be ignored is the public emergence of quite vocal groups and associations of parents, who want to know and who intend to see schools improved. Parental interest in schools and children is surely much to be welcomed, and true partnership between them and schools should be sought so that they can be a real support and strength, and not merely have to be content with the role of pressure groups on the sidelines. A third factor is likely to be the steady evolution of new types of curricular and social patterns within the secondary schools of the future, the development of ancillary services inside and outside the school, and of a changing concept of the role of the teacher as member or leader of a professional team within the school.

125

There is a good deal to encourage us in the present situation, but no cause for complacency. To sum up, the principal needs, now and in the nineteen-seventies, are fourfold. First, the problems of transfer and the need to secure genuine smooth transitions between childhood and adolescence and between primary and secondary modes of education need to be recognised and their solution set as a premier objective. If this means relinquishing some cherished traditions or hardened attitudes on both sides of the age of transfer, the price is one which should be willingly paid. Secondly, a much wider understanding of child development and a willingness to keep abreast of it, to recognise the best in it and to translate it into practical terms, should be sought and supporting training facilities, especially in in-service training, should be provided. Thirdly, a meaningful partnership must be established between primary and secondary school staffs in which visits, discussions, short term exchanges of post and team work of all kinds become a normal and not an exceptional feature of the educational scene. Research into records and the passage of information about pupils is an important accompaniment. Finally, and needless to say, in all these developments the focus should be firmly on the welfare of the individual child. The increasing stress on the child as an individual rather than as a component of the group or class to which he belongs, and the resultant flexibility of organisation which permits him to belong to different groups for different purposes, may in the long term prove the most significant educational development of the nineteen-sixties. It is a good base on which to build for the Seventies.

EDITOR'S NOTE

Bruce Kemble's contribution was not part of the original plan for this symposium, but I decided to include it because it represents sentiments which lead to disturbing conclusion. As educational reporter of a national newspaper he is intimately involved in education, and he observes and records his observations for the public. Educational reporting during the past decade has more and more influenced and formed public opinion. His contribution contains criticisms of educational practices which are emotional dynamite. Many of the contributors to this symposium have made suggestions and expressed ideas about the same practices, notably, streaming and selection. Mr. Kemble discusses the present situation but his observation can teach us much that is of value for the future.

CONDEMNED AT SEVEN:
IS STREAMING REALLY NECESSARY?

*

BRUCE KEMBLE

I've always hated rain. When I was about six, a storm or shower meant I would have to wear my sister's spare rainhat. I was certain that all the children knew it was a girl's hat – I was convinced all the teachers realised we were too poor for me to have a hat of my own.

At about the same age I remember being told off by a teacher for being "scruffy" – he said: "You are a street urchin and you'll never get anywhere in life."

I recall the humiliation of wearing old trousers with a torn seat, my bare bottom exposed to everyone, all the way up the long hill home from the swimming baths.

My father was a £4 a week policeman, and most of my relatives – on both sides of the family – left school as soon as they could. My maternal grandfather left school a good deal sooner – he was the richest man in the family. He transported horse manure to a mushroom grower, and made a small fortune out of professional punting.

My mother's first husband died of pneumonia. He was a schoolteacher, and so was my father's father. But academic achievement or success at school did not run in the family.

I was an unbearable child – convinced of my own superiority, clumsy in my movements and incurably spoilt. If my mother had not been very ambitious these character traits, my family's poverty and the middle-class prejudices of teachers, could well have made certain that I did not: "Get anywhere in life." But my mother's powerful personality conquered the Primary School Headmistress, and I was given a chance to show what I could do.

After some periods languishing around the foot of different classes, I suddenly recognised the simplicity of elementary arithmetic, and my only hobby – collecting long words and discovering their meaning – began to bring success in English lessons.

I won a place at Dulwich College, by scoring 286 marks out of 300 in the 11-plus exam. It was possible to get into Dulwich on merit alone, and to have your fees paid by the Council. My mother had not moved to the area for nothing!

Therefore, because of the accidents of birth and geography – because I was lucky to have a mother who cared about my going to Cambridge, and because one did not have to be rich to go to Dulwich – the handicap of poverty did not hold me back.

I mention these memories to give weight to my overall case. I particularly wish to stress the effect a child's personal appearance and behaviour must have on his future.

I was lucky to avoid an education at a Peckham Secondary Modern School, but it was a narrow escape. I could have been "streamed" at seven – this would almost certainly have meant that the master who called me "scruffy" could have condemned me to the "C" stream for the rest of my school days.

Research shows that only between two and six per cent of children move from a "stream" – once they have been put into it. This percentage, of children who escape their labels, is slightly higher than that of pupils who manage to transfer from one school to another, after the 11-plus exam. Less than one per cent are able to move after the 11-plus test had divided children arbitrarily into eighty per cent "goats", and twenty per cent "sheep".

Today the 11-plus and "selection" for schools are utterly discredited, and newspapers are full of stories about 11-plus "failures" who have got to University, or who have won First Class degrees.

Some people argue that the success of these so-called "failures" shows that all is right with our education system. They say it proves that talent will prevail, and that no one is handicapped by our rough-and-ready methods of selection.

But this is dangerous talk. For every child who manages to overcome the stigma of being "streamed" as a "failure" at seven, and for every pupil who is successful in spite of being deprived, at the age of eleven by some method of selection for secondary schools, there must be hundreds of talented children throughout the country whose abilities are not fully developed.

Most local education authorities throughout the country have decided to abolish selection, and to introduce some form of Comprehensive schooling.

This is in accordance with the will of Parliament which was expressed in January 1965. On that occasion M.P.'s were impressed by the convincing evidence in documents such as the Robbins Report (Appendix One, page 50, table II). This shows that the academic performance of able children, who had been sent to secondary modern schools after the 11-plus exams, declined after four years. Children were tested throughout the country for ability and achievement at 11 and again at 15. The performances of grammar school children were compared with those of equally able children at Secondary moderns.

Mr. Michael Armstrong, Chairman of the Comprehensive Schools Committee, commented recently: "These extraordinary findings have scarcely had the attention they deserve. They show just how far the academic standards of a whole generation of children have been sacrificed upon the altar of 'selection'. They made it plain that the Comprehensive schools reform is indeed one of the major social reforms of our time – and already long overdue."

But others are not persuaded that this is the right way to look at these statistics from the Robbins Report: they still refuse to accept that the result of selection at the age of 11-plus is nation-wide handicapping of the majority of children. They look at this evidence and claim it damages the case for Comprehensive schools. They say the I.Q.'s and achievement of the children in secondary moderns declined – not because of their depression at being labelled "second-class" and not because of the unfairness of the selection system – but because they were taught in the same building as less-able children.

It is possible to twist the facts in this way. But anyone who deduces this is ignoring other vital evidence. How can such a person explain that a Comprehensive school full of 11-plus "failures" in South London gets dozens of children to pass "A" level exams and some to University but in the days when it was a secondary-modern school its academic record was based on a handful of "O" level successes.

I remember the former leader of the Tories on the Inner London Education Authority, Mr. Seton Forbes Cockell, scorning the academic achievement of a school full of children who failed their 11-plus. I was able to tell him – to his amazement – this same school had that year got six children to Universities, 300 "O" level passes and 90 per cent of candidates through their "A" level exams.

During 1967 several reports were published which made the arguments and controversies over "Selection", "Comprehensive Schools" and "Streaming" a great deal clearer. The issues are emerging from a fog of emotion and prejudice, and opinion is becoming based on knowledge and fact.

The most influential sentence about education published in 1967 was in that mammoth and authoritative document the Plowden Report on Primary Schools. Opposing the division of children into "streams" it said: "Children live up to – or down to – the reputation they are given." In other words the educationists who favour streaming – and who say that the transfer of only 2-6 per cent from one stream to another, shows the accuracy of a teacher's choice – are wrong.

The small number of transfers merely shows that children who receive encouragement do as well, if not better, than expected. Children who are branded as "failures" lack encouragement, and perform below their true level of ability.

During my investigations of the "streaming" problem for the Daily Express I came across a magnificent man.

Mr. Albert Rowe, Headmaster of the David Lister School, Hull, hates streaming. He is a teacher of vast experience, and has been in charge of three schools. He told me: "I have tried to create a school flexible enough to keep the door open as long as possible – until *the pupil himself closes it*. We want to build up an environment and a system of values in which he can – and will – pursue excellence of every kind – academic and non-academic alike."

He is one of the country's most imaginative Headmasters. The sort of man who was impressed by the evidence that the I.Q. of children who failed the 11-plus *actually declined* after they had been unsuccessful.

Professor Robert Rosenthal, a social psychologist at Harvard University, produced some persuasive evidence to support men like Mr. Rowe in August 1967.

Following some tentative research with rats in 1962 – which showed they performed much better, and made more progress, when those in charge of them were told (quite falsely) they had been specially bred for intelligence – he turned to children. He conducted a series of experiments on Mexican children in San Francisco. He intruced them to teachers who were misled about their abilities.

He told the teachers that certain children – who were of only average ability – would leap ahead of their classmates, and get better results. After a year these pupils displayed a much greater I.Q. improvement than the rest of the class. Their average gain was 12.22 points, compared with an average for the remaining children of only 8.42 points.

He says: "Teachers expectations can be a powerful determinant." He plans to reveal more of his work with Dr. Leonore Jacobson, the Principal of the San Francisco School. So far they have shown that children benefit if teachers believe with or without evidence they have potential.

In Mr. Rowe's school he is the only person in the building who has seen the record cards of the children's achievement in their Primary Schools. He divides the pupils into A, B and C streams on the basis of these records and teacher's reports. Then he makes sure each class has one-third "A" children, one-third "B" and one-third "C" pupils. After 18 months, he says, he checks on their progress in relation to these arbitrary gradings based on their achievement at the age of ten – and discovers that in the majority of cases the "labels" are meaningless.

Our Education system from 1944 onwards was fairly effective as a means of selecting the obviously gifted, and the handicapped, child. But it sacrifices the interests of late-developing children, and, of those pupils who always hover around the middle of any class.

I am certain that parents want a schooling system which develops their child's individual abilities to the full. I am equally certain that the 11-plus, segregation at 10-13 into "inferior" and "superior" schools, rigid streaming as early, in many cases, as seven years old, and most other insensitive, crudities from the past – are no way to select the best brains.

The whole case against "Streaming" – selecting children inside a school on the basis of their apparent over-all ability – is that it is ineffective as a means of choosing the best.

Of course teachers who have the sensitivity and intelligence to realise the dangers of streaming, also know that certain subjects, such as mathematics, cannot be taught to pupils of all abilities at the same time. This leads to another form of division inside a school – "Setting". This is selection on the basis of ability in one subject. It has the effect that a child who is humiliated by being hopeless in the "C" Set for French, can be heartened by being in the "A" set for Maths or Woodwork.

Much more research is needed into the effects of "Streaming" and "Setting" before we can be confident that all schools are organised on a basis which brings out the best in everyone.

One fact especially impressed me throughout my whole study of the problem. An investigation by the National Foundation for Educational Research, performed at the special request of the Department of Education and Science, into 100 schools (50 streamed and 50 non-streamed) showed that *none of those schools without streaming were thinking of introducing it.*

The N.F.E.R. report[1] said: "There was some evidence to suggest that unstreaming is becoming fashionable; many of the schools contemplated introducing Non-Streaming during the next two years." It also issued this warning: "It should be emphasized that the question – to stream or not to stream? – reveals itself, as the research continues – to require a far more complex and nuanced answer than the propagandists on both sides would have one believe."

I agree. The alarming thing about most educational controversies is that they are often carried on between people who fundamentally agree – but who cannot see how much they have in common, because their vision is blurred by emotional issues.

The word "Comprehensive" is losing some of the emotive associations which once made it as inflammatory as "Nationalization". To-day the public know that it is possible for a "Nationalized" Industry to make a profit – they know some services have to be State-run in the interest of the community as a whole. The word has lost its sting.

In 1967 the term "Comprehensive" became descriptive rather than provocative when a survey of 77 "Comprehensive" schools in Inner London, some of which have been going for twenty years, received a tremendous amount of publicity. I remember the lack of emotion on faces of people on my train home to Chislehurst as they read the head-line in the "Evening News" which said: "The Verdict on Comprehensives: Success story in G.C.E., Solid Evidence of Rich Education, Triumph for 11-plus failures."

But the controversy about "Streaming" continues, and it is full of ignorance, inadequate information and prejudice. To give an example: the N.F.E.R. report revealed: "It is surprising to find that so many junior schools graded their pupils without the help of standardized tests, and without making allowances for age."

And yet the reliability and validity of the methods used for grading children, when they go to Junior school, are of the utmost importance. Mr. Brian Cane, Senior Research Officer of the N.F.E.R., showed in another article published in 1967 just how vital this time is in a child's life. Vital decisions are, as we have seen, made about

134

a child's ability, often on unreliable and insufficient evidence, at the age of seven. But Mr. Cane warns: "A child's reading attainment and progress at the age of eight years is *fundamental to his whole future*. Tested reading attainment in the junior school is a fair prediction of subsequent scholastic success."

Another piece of research work published in 1967, which confirms my point that the greatest need throughout schools is for more flexibility and attention to the needs of each child, was produced by Mr. G. E. Bookbinder[2], an Educational Psychologist. He reported: "A great deal of evidence has now accrued to show that the child born in the latter part of the school year (i.e. May, June, July and August) is penalized in terms of subsequent school placement and progress." He claimed that out of a sample group of children thirty per cent of those in classes for the Educational Sub-Normal would not have found themselves there, if they had been born about eight months earlier.

His comments, on the handicap of losing vital time at school through being born in these months, are relevant to the remarks I quoted earlier from the Plowden report, and to the evidence produced by Professor Rosenthal. He writes: "The evidence suggests that because of the time of year in which they were born, some young borderline 7-year olds who might otherwise be able to respond to the normal stimulation of an ordinary class – are placed in an E.S.N. class. If this is so, one of the effects may be to hold back such a child academically – *partly by conveying to him our low expectations of his future performance*. (my italics.) It is a short and easy step for the child to adopt these low expectations for himself, and so to view himself permanently as a backward child. Selection for E.S.N. classes at 7-plus can be viewed as a kind of inverted 11-plus, and seven is a lot earlier than eleven. Selection at the infant level for this type of class seems to involve many of the disadvantages that appear to operate in ordinary streaming – such as the separation of children with poorer, and less satisfactory, home backgrounds from those with more favourable home environments. It is also probable that transfer from E.S.N. to ordinary class and vice-versa – *like movement from one stream to another* (my italics) is not as fluid as it might be."

If discussions about Streaming are to be useful and fruitful the research done by these men must be widely-known. Judging from the enormous pile of letters from parents which I find on my desk each week, the great majority of parents think injustice in our schools ceased with the decision to end the 11-plus, and to bring in

Comprehensive Schools all over the country.

But commonsense tells us that we are aiming at the impossible, in the hope of achieving the improbable, if we attempt to bring about an education system which is perfectly based on "Equality of Opportunity".

For some the phrase "Equality of Opportunity" is alarmingly inflammatory. They translate it into: "Making everyone equal", or "Dull grey Socialist conformity". These people obviously do not realise how many barriers to children's opportunities can be removed. This question, of the handicap of being born in the Summer, is clearly soluble by a more flexible and sensitive school and class organisation.

The handicap of being placed in a "C" stream at the age of 7, without good reason, is obviously removable. Very few parents and educationists feel *passionate* about the retention of streaming in Primary schools.

It is possible to lessen injustice in the classroom, and it is possible to move slowly towards our goal of giving children an equal chance to be unequal. I do not believe that all children are equally intelligent or would perform equally well if given an equal chance. I am convinced however that the slogan: *"An equal chance to be unequal"* causes less controversy than the old chant of "Equality of Opportunity".

I have tried to convey how a child's career, marriage and whole adult existence can depend on accidents of birth, wealth and geography. I have attempted to show that a pupil can be placed in an "A" stream because he is tidily and smartly-dressed, while little Brian, in his Wellington boots and his shabby blue cardigan everyday is put in the "C" stream.

I may have got from a South-East London Primary School, taking pupils from the poorest parts of Peckham and Camberwell as well as those from the Dulwich area, to a Public School and then to a Cambridge, but that does not mean that all is right with all our schools, and schooling methods. I am concerned to alert parents to their role in their child's education. I wish to inform them of some of the latest research, and new thinking, affecting their children.

The subject of streaming is not yet a public issue, even though it has been a question of controversy among educationists for the past three years. It seems to take about twenty years for a new idea in education to become common – we have a great deal more to do to get a fair, efficient and humane education system.

Is Streaming really Necessary?

To return to Albert Rowe. He told me: "Were there no research evidence at all on streaming – I would still be utterly opposed to it. It is inhuman. It turns an assessment of a child's intelligence and academic ability – made as early as seven, and by the latest at ten – into a total judgement of him as a human being. I condemn the system as wasteful and inefficient because of its rigidity and because it depresses the performance of the great majority for the sake of a very small minority."

Mr. Rowe's indictment is, as we have seen, based on experience. The stern warnings of the Plowden report should not be ignored – and they echo his sentiments. It said: "Streaming can be wounding to children. Great care ought to be taken not to suggest that trust and responsibility or prowess in games or the ability to look after library books, are the preserve of certain classes. No more certain way could be found of alienating children from school or of creating irresponsibility."

The report also revealed the shock figure that the vast majority of schools had no Parent-Teacher Association. Since the publication of Plowden the Cambridge-based Advisory Centre for Education has set about starting groups to make up for this nation-wide lack.

I am certain that one of the top priorities is to speed up the formation of these parent-teacher groups, and to spread new information and ideas among parents through them.

I am sure that a great deal of venom would go out of the row over Comprehensive schools if parents, in areas which have not yet experienced them, could learn the results of research into these schools.

The Inner London Education Authority report – which was 75,000 words long and backed up by 40 pages of statistics – showed that, in 1965, more than 17,000 parents said they wanted their children to go to a Comprehensive school rather than a grammar school. The report also disposed of the old objection to "All-In" schools that they were too big. It revealed that several London Comprehensives had fewer than 700 pupils, and only three had more than 1900.

But in any case they said there was no evidence that a community of 2,000 made children feel any different than one of 1,200, or one of 1,500. They added: "The schools take great care by means of house systems, tutor groups etc. to give each boy and girl a sense of belonging."

A great deal of ill-founded hostility to these schools would disappear if these facts were better known.

Unfortunately the facts about Streaming have not been finally settled. David Hargreaves in his excellent book "Social Relations in a Secondary School"[3] said: "The research on streaming is far from conclusive." But he is able to say: "There is a growing body of evidence which indicates that the streaming system is self-validating in that it to some extent *manufactures* the differences on which it is justified by teachers. This evidence is supported by the claims of many teachers that de-streaming has led to enormous academic and social benefits."

He also quotes other research evidence which shows that pupils in unstreamed classes have a better attitude towards their school, that non-streamed children made gains in I.Q. and became progressively better at Arithmetic and English.

He further cites evidence which proves streaming slightly lowers the general level of attainment, slightly reduces the attainments of the "bright" pupils, and markedly retards the "slower" pupils.[4]

Mr. Hargreaves has some challenging things to say about common social prejudices among parents and teachers which hinder progress in our schools. He writes: "It was common practice for the teachers (at the school he studied) to shed the blame for many difficulties, which might be caused or re-inforced by the school itself, on to the home environment. Yet the belief that children are 'difficult' in school *because* they come from 'difficult' homes is a convenient over-simplification: the misbehaviour of low stream boys was often 'explained' by the teachers in terms of a popular psychology or sociology. A teacher once remarked to me: 'Well what can you expect? That lad's got no father' – but he failed to appreciate that the most hard-working member of the 'intellectual' clique in 4A was also fatherless."

He reminds us that our school system is a major force in creating our social class system. He stresses that our children mirror our own petty snobberies. He says: "It is tragic that often an 'A' stream boy was not on speaking terms with a 'D' stream boy – even though both may have been pupils in the same class in Junior school, and both may live in the same street."

Social differences are heightened, and class divisions deepened, by another educational evil exposed by Mr. Hargreaves. He reveals that at the school he investigated many pupils who wished to take exams – who might have passed – were prevented from sitting them because the school staff did not want to spoil their academic record!!! He writes: "The children are in fact divided into sheep and goats: those who take the examinations, and those who do not. Those who are not allowed to take the external exams will perceive, quite accurately, that their occupational aspirations must be relatively lower – since many skilled occupations are closed to those without formal education qualifications."

"Don of 4D wished to enter for the examination because he wished to obtain an apprenticeship after leaving school. Although his form-master approached the Headmaster about this, permission for Don to enter was refused. There is little doubt that the Headmaster and some of the teachers were anxious to be near as possible to the top of the 'league table' of local schools taking this examination by maintaining a high proportion of successful entrants. Yet this percentage of passes is in part a function of the number of entries... (The School) could not achieve a high rank in the 'league table' *unless boys whose chances of success in the examination were small were excluded from entry*. In this way the school could maintain an apparently good academic record by depriving low stream pupils of the opportunity to enter for an external examination."

He suggests, quite sensibly, that the "league table" should be abolished and points out that if it is retained it would be healthier if it were based on a comparison between the number of successes and the number of children in the age-group – and not a comparison between those who pass, and those who enter.

I have attempted to relate the subject of Streaming with the problems of Class, snobbery and prejudice. My opening memories were intended to point the relation between class and the classroom. Every teacher who makes a judgement about a child is affected by both his own, and the pupil's, class background. This judgement, as we have seen, can be of crucial importance to the child, and yet it can be based on emotion and whim.

Mr. Hargreaves discovered some aspects of this disturbing problem – for which there is no easy solution. He writes: "The school must provide greater opportunities for members of different streams to interact, preferably in a co-operative enterprise. It would be a comparatively simple task to organise the school time table in such a way that members of upper and lower streams could take some subjects together especially in the case of Games, Art, Handicraft and possibly Music and Religious Education... Participation in the social life of the school, in such activities as sport, music and school holidays, is... a reflection of the academic hierarchy of the streams... the staff tend to favour the upper stream pupils in the process of selections for these activities. The tendency of the teachers to delete the 'undesirables' from the lists of holiday applicants deprives these boys not only of the holiday and its educational value, but also of the opportunity of extended and less formal relationships with teachers which these holidays accord."

It is often thought that the brainiest boys tend to be also the better sportsmen. But this can be a misleading impression. Boys who have been "rejected" by the school, and placed in low streams, often appear to be less interested in sport than they really are. One major factor which drives a boy on in sport is the "glory" of representing his school. But if you feel, however unjustly, that the school has treated you with contempt, you are hardly likely to get a feeling of pride from representing it.

Mr. Hargreaves quotes an experienced teacher's successful method of getting through to boys whom other teachers found "difficult" in the low streams. This teacher made sure he did two things, when first confronting a class. He asserted his authority, and he made friends with the boys who were the class's natural "leaders". He praised them even when they were hardly trying at all and he gave them tasks which he fully expected them to complete successfully. The rest of the class tended to follow the example of these boys once they began to co-operate with the teacher.

Most truths – when expressed simply and in the form of a generalisation – sound naive or banal. But it cannot be stated too often that it is vitally important for teachers to aim higher.

They must search into their deepest impulses and make sure that in all honesty they are not failing to communicate with pupils because of laziness or self-indulgent social prejudice.

Teachers who gain the co-operation of both pupils and parents are badly needed during the coming years of strain and stress caused by the raising of the school-leaving age to 16, and by the re-organisation of secondary schools along comprehensive lines. I have already urged parents to form a flourishing association with teachers. Teachers must also make greater efforts to meet parents and pupils half-way – if we are to make the minimum of mistakes in the decade to come.

There is one piece of evidence which I must mention though it appears to outweigh much of the anti-streaming opinion and research. The N.F.E.R. report contained the results of an opinion survey among parents and teachers. It alleged that most parents and teachers were in *favour* of streaming. But it is my contention that if parents and teachers were fully aware of all the evidence, they would *not* favour it.

Is Streaming really Necessary?

The N.F.E.R. report says: "The first point to be noted is that substantial proportions of teachers are in favour of streaming. Since of all junior schools in the country which are large enough to do so at least 65 per cent stream, and only 11 per cent clearly do not, it seems reasonable to suppose that the majority of junior school teachers in England and Wales are in favour of the practice, that a substantial proportion are undecided and that only relatively few are firmly committed to the opposing view. This finding must be stressed at a time when some writers suggest that the death knell of streaming has already sounded. Coupled with the finding concerning parents' views it suggests that any universal change recommended may meet with considerable opposition."

Their findings on parental opinion were : "There appears to be an association between the child's ability and his parents' attitudes to streaming. Parents of children with above average ability definitely tended to favour streaming: parents with less gifted children were much more likely to favour non-streaming. *But even in the latter group 'streamers' out-numbered 'non-streamers' by almost two to one.*" (my italics)

Without wishing to reflect upon the competence of those in charge of this opinion poll, and while admitting my own amateur status as a sociologist, I wish to criticize the wording of the questions used in this survey. It must be remembered that the word "streaming" requires clear definition. Parents must first be told, the difference between streaming, setting, selection and specialization, all of which have their opponents. It also ought to be remembered that most parents have not discussed the subject, or in any depth. So it is not surprising that those interviewed in the survey gave unsophisticated answers to elementary questions.

The queries were unsubtle, dull and unhelpful – and at odds with crucial paragraphs elsewhere in the report. For example the warning I quoted above on page 134 contained the words "complex" and "nuanced" – the authors were urging us not to take up polarised black-and-white positions over Streaming.

Another key paragraph in the report says wisely: "A mere change in organisation – the abandonment of streaming for example – unaccompanied by a serious attempt to change teachers' attitudes, beliefs and methods of teaching is unlikely to make much difference either to attainments or... to the quality of teacher-pupil relationships."

But despite these pleas for more flexibility, more sensitivity, and more imagination in our schools, the questions force parents to make black-and-white answers to black-and-white queries. Here is a sample "For children of --'s age could you tell me: Which of these you think is better? For the quicker and slower children to be mixed together in one class, or for the quicker children to be put in one class, and the slower in another?"

The latter option was chosen by 79 per cent of parents in streamed schools, and by 65 per cent in non-streamed. Less than one-third of the parents of children in non-streamed schools approved of non-streaming.

Are you surprised? It must be pointed out that these parents who seem so sure that they disapprove of non-streaming, include many who do not even know if their own children are streamed or not!!! The same report reveals that 15 per cent of parents, with children in streamed schools, did not know what methods were used, and thirty-one per cent of those, with children in non-streamed schools, could not say if they were streamed, or not, with any certainty.

The above query begs the question: "What is a 'quick' and what is a 'slow' child?" We have already seen that the same N.F.E.R. report exposes those schools which divide children into streams, as using unreliable, inconsistent methods.

This question not only allows parents to assume, quite falsely, that selection methods are infallible, but it also ignores the fact that most parents over-estimate their own children's intelligence! I recently wrote a feature on the 140,000 children in our schools who have an I.Q. of 140 or over – the "gifted" children. My phone rang incessantly, and my secretary was working for weeks, as we tried to cope with queries from parents who believed their children were "Super Brains"! Furthermore the number of parents involved in this survey was less than 120 – I would be more willing to be persuaded they were representative if the sample were ten times the size.

I would further stress that the report discovered that those who favoured streaming also tended to support the new utterly-discredited 11-plus exam!!!

To support my statement here, and earlier, that this exam is now out of favour I quote a survey by the Assistant Masters Association which was published by the Cambridge University Press in 1967. It said: "The current feeling is against starting children of eleven in a separate school because someone somehow decided they were not good enough to go to a different separate school. The battle has ceased to be about the form the 11 plus should take... to quote our

Is Streaming really Necessary?

Chairman: 'In plain unvarnished fact the margin of error in selection is now known to be so wide that the nation has lost much of its earlier faith in the whole process.'"

If we cannot accept the opinion of the teachers in the N.F.E.R. survey about the 11-plus – how can we believe that their views on streaming are representative?

Peter Ustinov once said: "When faced with a problem the Germans add, the French subtract and the English change the subject." And yet in the education field we seem to have a remarkable predilection for definition.

We are constantly trying to label our children, or to divide them, or to force them to say what they will be doing in twenty years time, or to pressure them to stop studying one subject, and to start another. Rather than our vice being one of evasion of issues, we seem in education to have a prejudice for creating unnecessary problems. Lord Bowden has said we have placed the destiny of the country in "the hands of fourteen year old schoolboys". He was referring to our peculiar emphasis on forcing children to specialize in school subjects at an age much earlier than in other countries.

Other writers in this book (Looking forward to the '70's) will comment in detail about the folly of early specialisation. Suffice it to say that it seems to me that public opinion ought to demand the end of streaming and early-specialisation as it has 11-plus selection. Leslie Hale M.P. once remarked: "The English vice is not buggery, but humbuggery." But are we incurable?

In a modern, scientific, classless Britain I would expect the custom of dividing our children into streams to disappear along with "Shamateurism" in Tennis, and corporal punishment in Primary and Approved Schools.

Our passion for social divisions, our system of classroom segregations, and our national snobberies are all related. Let us hope that a soundly-based set-up of Comprehensive schools throughout the nation will in time, with our national genius for compromise, help us to erode these barriers of the past.

Our central aim is a schooling system which helps all children to develop to the full. Such a system must benefit the nation as a whole, and must bring a truce to the class war which has made us the object of jokes and pity throughout the world.

NOTES

1 In New Research in Education, Volume I, June 1967, pub. Newnes Educational Publishing Co. Ltd.
2 In Educational Research, Volume XI no. 3 ,June 1967, pub. Newnes.
3 Routledge & Kegan Paul, 1967.
4 This research was published by J. C. Daniels in the British Journal of Educational Psychology, Volume 31, 1961 and by J. W. B. Douglas in *The Home and the School,* Macgibbon & Kee, 1964.

PRIMARY EDUCATION

*

JOHN BLACKIE

Everyone must hope that primary education will receive a larger share of the national income in the 1970's than it had to make do with in the 1960's, that the size of classes will be reduced and obsolete buildings be replaced. These are matters of money and manpower. Without ample supplies of both, education will be hindered and our hopes for it deferred, but neither will ensure a good education for young children. They will only make it rather easier to achieve whatever objectives we have chosen. Those objectives must take account of what we know about children and of what we can foresee of the world in which they will live.

To take the latter first, we can foresee the likelihood, probably the inevitability, of rapid and upsetting change. We shall have to grow accustomed to the fact that an increasing proportion of people will be unemployable and somehow learn to regard this as a blessing. We shall have to accept the real differences between people which will stand out more starkly as the artificial ones are eliminated. We shall have to endure all sorts of restrictions on our liberty, imposed by the increasing population of our islands, without, as we must hope, at the same time, losing our essential liberties of free speech and association and of protection from violence and the threat of violence. Other branches of education and other national institutions will have to contribute to the successful carrying out of change, but primary education and the home, working closely together, will have a critical part to play. If they fail, everything else, secondary school, university, trade union, industry, parliament and local government, fails with them. Already the proportion of our resources devoted to remedial work, to child guidance, to children

145

in care, to maladjustment, to broken homes, to prisons and Borstals etc. is alarmingly high and in almost every instance the trouble began at a very early age in life. If the home has the first responsibility the primary school, nursery, infant and junior, has the second, and both must co-operate.

That is the first, and probably the most important of all needs, a much closer partnership between school and home than has yet been achieved or even imagined. The organisation through which the partnership is to work will have to be thought out. The weekly report which passes backwards and forwards between school and parent in the U.S.S.R. is not, I think, the answer, though one can admire the intention behind it. Occasional open days and meetings of Parent-Teacher Associations are quite inadequate. Probably the bringing of parents into active partnership inside the school is the most promising line to follow up, but this is most difficult where it is most needed. I can think of a school where a third of the mothers are known by the Head Teacher to be practising prostitutes and I have seen the look on the faces of prostitutes' children. What sort of a partnership is possible there? There is a lot of hard thinking and hard work to be done and the most that I can hope is that it will be done and done quickly.

In the changing world two paramount needs will be adaptability and guiding principles. Adaptability, so far as we know, is learned by practice, by being faced constantly with the necessity of choice, by having to think out situations, by interchange of thought, by opportunities for inventing and exploring. All this fits in well with what is known about how children learn and with the practices of a growing proportion of English primary schools, where the emphasis is on learning rather than on being taught, on finding out rather than on being told, on invention rather than on copying, on self discipline rather than on "jumping to it". I hope that this trend will grow, but it will only grow if teachers are trained to understand it and to assist its growth. We put a heavy responsibility upon our teachers in this country. In every other country in the world, so far as I know, to a greater or lesser extent, the teacher carries out a programme or scheme of work that somebody else has drawn up. We alone leave the responsibility to the individual school and even, to a large extent, to the individual teacher. I hope this will go on and that we shall never be tempted or persuaded to adopt the American programme, or any other centrally devised curriculum. At the same time, the responsibilities of initiative are great and I do not think that the 3 year course of training, however good, can, unsupported, equip teachers to carry them. I therefore hope to see an immense development of refresher courses for teachers, not courses of lectures followed by a little discussion, but workshop courses and seminars, in which the same methods are used as those in the best primary schools and, be it added, in the best universities. I hope that the Department of Education, the Schools Council and the Local Education Authorities will play their part in the generous and imaginative provision of such courses, and that, increasingly, the teaching profession will adopt the view that regular attendances at them is a professional obligation, if not a condition of increment.

So far then, in the training of adaptability in children and in the training of teachers to educate for adaptability, my hopes are founded on an increase and an acceleration of what is already happening. But adaptability, though it will achieve much, is not enough. An adaptable mind will tend to be interested, lively, closely observant and keenly critical and will have learned how to look at evidence. These powers will be valuable, not only in intellectual situations but also in moral ones, but, though moral situations demand adaptability they also demand fibre, a capacity for making or sticking to a difficult or unpleasant or unpopular decision or choice and thus principles on which choices and decisions are made. It has been generally supposed that guiding principles are acquired partly from parental upbringing, partly from religious education and partly from membership of school communities which set an example and observe certain principles in their daily life. It is undeniable that these three sources of moral principle can all operate either separately or in concert and have so operated in many instances. The parental source is powerful but unreliable in the sense that the principles may be bad or non-existent. The religious source is much less powerful than it was and for many children almost non-existent, while the school community remains the most stable and the most reliable. Where the three work more or less in harmony the effect will be considerable, but where there is conflict the effect may be harmful where it is not feeble.

I have no doubt that the Christian insistence on unconditional love as the most important guiding principle is valid, but that this need not necessarily involve any metaphysical belief is shown by Dr. Ian Suttie in his *Origins of Love and Hate*. The need for love is even more fundamental than the need for sex and the ability to give (or withhold love) an immensely powerful influence. The influence of a good school is incalculable. The children feel that they

147

belong, that they are secure, that the adults are to be trusted, that everybody matters, that in no circumstances whatever will anyone be rejected and that anyone who harms the community by his conduct must be brought back into it. Moral precept, moral pressure and rules of conduct are feeble indeed compared with the influence of a community which is "rooted and grounded in love". Moral precepts can be delivered without sincerity, moral pressure can be cruel and guilt-making, rules of conduct can be mechanical and pointless, but love, when it is unconditional, is liberating and life-giving.

I am aware that this has a somewhat idealistic sound. It may not be difficult for Christians and non-believers alike to give a vague general assent to it, but to translate it into day-to-day action in an educationally underprivileged area is another matter. Yet it is in such areas that I have seen it more clearly and convincingly demonstrated. Here the teachers, because of the way in which they see their duties or because of what they believe about the nature of man or for some reason which has developed in them a conviction and a devotion, create a community in which all the problems of discipline, problems which have their origins in parental neglect, rejection, incompetence, or disharmony, are tackled on the basis of unconditional love. I remember a Headmaster whose school I knew over thirty years ago who unquestionably made this the basis of all he did, but he was no sentimentalist. He was a tough rather craggy character, a man's man in fact. He once said to me: "I never thrash them. Their fathers do that and do it far more brutally than I could or would. It is the fact that *I don't* thrash them which makes them pay attention to me."

I do not myself agree with the Plowden council that corporal punishment should be abolished by regulation. I regard this as interference with professional judgment and I do not want to see teachers deprived of a sanction which, in certain circumstances, some may feel is necessary. But I hope to see more and more schools in which the relationship is one of unconditional love and in which corporal punishment, indeed any punishment is rare or non-existent or even inconceivable. Only in such schools can be developed the balanced combination of adaptability and guiding principle which the future will demand.

Schools undoubtedly exist to educate children to take their place in adult society, not in blind accordance with a party line, but in a spirit at once critical and respectful. That last word is now much out of fashion, because of its associations with class, with kow-towing, with "touching the cap", and its disrepute has been accompanied by a habit of debunking, embodied in the sentence: "If you can find anything which has been treated with respect in the past and has not yet been held up to ridicule, knock it as soon as possible!" As a reaction against excessive traditionalism this is understandable and healthy, but it could easily undermine the structure of society without establishing a workable system to take the place of the old. Besides, it can and does focus critical attention too exclusively upon the past and the long-established, to the exclusion of the new and the present. Being "with it" is at least as likely to be a sign of unintelligence as of lively thinking.

Here, or elsewhere, the primary school must try to encourage and to train criticalness and tolerance, respect for what is different, whether new or old, an understanding of the merits of custom and the convenience of convention, a readiness to ask questions and to look critically at the answers, while conceding that they may be right because they come from older and more experienced people. This it will do mainly by being a society in which these things happen, thus giving to the children the opportunity of enjoying the benefits of belonging to such a society, instead of one in which authority is always right or always wrong, where the majority must always be followed or always opposed, where you grab as much as you can get and beat up those whom you dislike or fear, or always pay up or lie to avoid trouble.

It is important that our society of the future should look on primary schools not only as places for preparing children to take a part in adult life, but also as places in which they can be and live as, children, where the present is its own justification. Probably most people *think* that they agree with that statement, but it is clear from the correspondence column of the press and from general public debate that they do not. They agree with it as long as the behaviour of the children fits in with what they think it ought to be. Primary teachers increasingly agree with it and try to put their agreement into practice. Secondary teachers still have a long way to go, parents even further and the general public, which of course, includes parents whose children have grown up, further still. One of my keenest hopes for the '70's is that our society will enormously increase its understanding of children. In this respect I think both the Italians and the Russians have something to teach us. There has never been any need for a Society for the Prevention of Cruelty to Children in Italy (animals are a different matter) and, although Russian children are regimented and

149

disciplined in a manner which is surprising if not shocking to English liberalism, Russian adult society is, I think, fonder of children than ours, more ready to take individual personal trouble with them, more companionable with them, less inclined to treat them, as we do on too many occasions, as nuisances, and more aware of them as the future of the nation.

I hope that we shall hear less and less hostile criticism of primary schools because "the children play all the time" and because "they're allowed to talk as much as they like". It is now 142 years since Froebel published his *Education of Man* and subsequent experience and research have confirmed his view that play is an essential means of learning in young children. The recent researches of Jean Piaget, of Luria and many others have demonstrated that talking about learning and experience is equally essential. This is not the place to argue the matter, and it will not need arguing if teachers in primary schools have the courage of their convictions and the skill to translate the convictions into action.

It would not be in accordance with the needs or nature of children, or of society, if primary schools did not oblige them to learn the necessity and the satisfaction of taking trouble, of doing things well, of high standards. I believe that the sort of school I have been thinking about, the sort which is coming to birth at the present time is far more likely to do this than the school in which authority is based on power instead of on love. I hope we shall come to a better understanding than we have at present of the nature of authority, of the authority which is creative and which breeds creativeness as distinct from the kind of authority that Wordsworth meant when he wrote:

> "Blind Authority beating with the rod
> The child that might have led him."

It will be seen that almost every one of my hopes for primary education in the 1970's depends for its realisation upon the teachers, and upon their quality as much as or more than upon their numbers. I mentioned this in the context of in-service training and now return to it in the larger context of national education as a whole. It is inevitable that public opinion and teacher opinion should have been most vocal on the subjects of buildings, supply of teachers and teachers' salaries. These are the things that can be most easily expressed in terms of money and can be summarised statistically either to impress or dismay according to the summariser's purpose. But the first priority is the quality of the teachers, how well-educated they are in themselves, how well informed about the growth and nature of children, how well trained in their art as teachers and what they are like as human beings. All of that must depend partly upon the standards that they set themselves, upon how they look upon the role that they fill. This again depends partly upon their initial training, partly upon the outlook of the teaching profession and partly upon the way in which the nation as a whole regards them.

I hope to see, in the 1970's an improvement in all these three. The three-year course at colleges of education is still a young growth and many of those who tend it have themselves had only brief experience as teacher-trainers, since the huge expansion of the teacher-force in training has necessarily brought many new recruits onto the staffs of the colleges. Moreover, it has not hitherto been easy for the colleges to find trainers who combine first-hand classroom experience of primary school teaching with the academic qualifications and qualities of mind that are proper to institutions which are in close association with universities, and which the job of teaching at all stages requires. Now there is an increasing flow of graduates into primary schools and there is every reason to expect that the initial training of primary school teachers will improve steadily in the next decade.

The outlook of the teaching profession has been and, to some extent still is, class-ridden. The order of precedence has been something like Oxbridge, Redbrick, large public school, small public school, technical college, grammar school, secondary modern school, junior school, infant school, nursery school. This order reflects not only public opinion but to a considerable degree teacher opinion, and it is re-inforced by salary scales and allowances. There is an element of justice in some of it. People capable of teaching physics in a university are scarcer, and always likely to be scarcer, than people capable of teaching science to 10 years old. The teaching skill required is greater for the latter but the scientific knowledge and learning is not. But the only outlook that will do is that every teacher should regard all teaching as of supreme importance because all pupils matter equally and supremely. That, of course, is a matter of morals and convictions, but we need not leave it exclusively as a moral issue. I hope that every branch of the teaching profession will look at its customs and regulations as well as its prejudices and inhibitions very critically and see if there anything that it can do, professionally and internally, to create among all teachers a feeling of solidarity and fundamental equality.

What about the nation's regard? This has not in the past been high. Socially and economically the teachers of young children have occupied a humble place in society. In both respects it has greatly improved in the last decade and it has improved because the public face of the teacher has improved. I hope this will continue and am sure that it will, in proportion as the teachers are seen to put the children first, are seen to be well-qualified, efficient and attractive people, are seen to co-operate with the home and to have the sort of relationship with the children described earlier. Of course the labourer is worthy of his hire and of course I hope that the nation's regard will be exhibited in the form of good salaries and, so long as the Honours system continues, of a much more generous allocation of honours to primary school teachers than the occasional M.B.E. to which they have been treated. If better salaries could, instead of being wrung from the nation by demands and threats of strikes, be granted unasked, in recognition of good work done, my hopes for the '70's would be more than fulfilled, but we may have to wait a little longer for that!

THE COMMUNITY: THE TENSIONS AND DELINQUENCIES OF YOUTH

*

E. PARKINSON

The educator and the community

Many of those who work to the broad and encouraging terms of the Education Act of 1944 enjoy in particular its emphasis on promoting and securing effort as well as on providing facilities. They have a particular regard for Section 7 of the Act which defines the duty of the Local Education Authorities to secure efficient primary, secondary and further education to meet the needs of the population of their areas and thus contribute to the spiritual, moral, mental and physical welfare of the community. Every educator has his own interpretation of the nature of this duty and of the practical terms in which it should be expressed. It is a very relevant context within which to look forward to the problems of the adolescent and the community in the Seventies.

Section 7 of the Act is often said to have no teeth. It has been described as a general statement of intent, too broad and imprecise to ensure specific obligations undertaken within a defined period. This may be true, though the adjectives are precise and relevant, and taken together comprise a comprehensive obligation. As regards two of them – the moral and spiritual – each educator, whatever his situation has an inescapable duty to clarify his own position, a task which seems unlikely to be easier in the next decade. In a divided and confused community, he will need to call in much oftener than hitherto the assistance of the sociologist, of the psychologist, and, not least, of the philosopher, whose capacity to examine the propositions of official policy and the values expounded in the classroom has been consistently under-used.

One way of looking forward to the Seventies is perhaps first to look backwards to the Forties. It is interesting to note that the first

153

publication of the newly-established Ministry of Education in 1945 was on Community Centres and Associations. Generally known as "The Red Book" it was for years regarded with affection as well as respect in many parts of the country. Its emphasis was on vigorous local community activity, on the benefits to social health and personal education which could be enjoyed by citizens coming together in their local communities, on caring for others in an individual as well as an organised way, on identifying needs and on promoting action to meet them through voluntary effort as well as through statutory powers and public resources. A great opportunity was lost, during two decades of disillusionment and shattered hopes, when these ideals foundered on the geographically limited impact of the settlements and community associations and on the comparative unattractiveness of existing concepts of the community centre. Despite some remarkably successful achievements these institutions remained relatively few in number and it has taken the combined Crowther, Newsom and Plowden reports to restore belatedly to the forefront of educational discussion an interest in the community as the conditioning background of educational effort.

The term "community development" is now used "to denote the processes by which the efforts of the people themselves are united with those of governmental authorities to improve the economic, cultural and social conditions of communities". It is a concept particularly appropriate to this country in that community work has been regarded as an educational as well as a social process in which personal commitment and activity are seen as part of adult education. Further, the promotion of educational aims has rested on securing a supplementation of voluntary activities and resources as well as a provision from public funds. A policy of community development posits, first, active recipients of whatever is publicly provided; second, co-operation between statutory authorities, between voluntary organisations and individuals, and between both; third, economic use of resources; fourth, greater flexibility in occupational attitudes, leading to inter-professional mobility; and lastly, the involvement of as large a part of the community as possible in its own improvement. The problem for educational policy is to decide in what way, by what instruments and agencies, by what combination of provided and secured resources and at what points its efforts are to be directed. Above all, schemes must match the capacities of practitioners and the realities of situations. It is necessary to know what forms have already emerged of inter-departmental co-operation and of integration of effort between different individuals, institutions and phases of education, before a sound estimate can be made of the prospects for a flexible inter-professional relationship in future.

Everybody knows what community means, yet few care to define the term. Every human being is perforce a member of many communities related to work, welfare, recreation, neighbourhood, race, nationality, outlook and conviction. Community policy at the national level obviously covers a myriad activities, ranging from agencies assisting the rudimentary efforts of the inhabitants of poor countries to improve their material lot to complex institutions and activities designed to enhance a high-level technological civilisation in a well-developed society, to stimulate learning processes among individuals and groups as they adjust themselves to the complexities of technological and social change at sophisticated levels, and to organise, on behalf of the community, care for the infirm, the inadequate and the delinquent.

In these situations education must, in co-operation with other agencies, make its appropriate contribution. In simpler communities it will not be the most important contribution; the more advanced the community the more will its effort predominate. In England educational policy is now being implemented in a society which is more developed and affluent than most. "Affluent", like so many of the fashionable adjectives pretending to a total description of society, is a clumsy term; it is even more inaccurate than its boon companion "permissive". English society is essentially a disciplined society, the members of which accept, with varying degrees of enthusiasm, co-operation, resignation and dissent, institutions and practices designed and controlled by an élite minority. The discipline is accepted, in general, because it suits the economic interest and the comparatively mature social and political development of a free people, not all of whom are either as affluent or as free as they would like to be. Among the indubitably affluent there is a growing recognition that they are still too few in comparison with most of the people in the world to remain comfortable about an indefensible situation. Two main tasks of the educator in England are to protect and expand the inventive and inspirational forces which help maximise the affluence on which the effective expression of compassion in practical terms at home and abroad mainly rests, and through educational policy to induce the élite minority and the predominantly conforming majority to communicate and co-operate with each other over a wider area of work and leisure.

155

Many community workers in this country (e.g. child-care officers, probation officers, psychologists and psychiatric social workers, welfare officers, etc.) function within a general framework of control from other departments of government than education; many others are employed by voluntary societies. There are also within the educational system, in the three phases of primary, secondary and further education, a large number of practitioners who might be surprised and perhaps not particularly flattered to hear themselves described in future as community workers; yet many situations within the educational service are now calling for an increasing interest, not merely in the practices and influences of communities, but also in the relevance of theories of community development to the organisation and financing of educational policies. Teachers in schools and colleges can see community needs and can influence community standards at many different points and from many different angles. It is at school that the point of contact between the educational influences and the adult as parent begins in a mutual concern for the child and it is good to note the occasions when it does not end there. Teachers are being encouraged to look up from their books and away from their blackboards and to concentrate more of their attention on the outside community. The study of the community is occupying a bigger place in the curriculum; teachers are increasingly thrown into contact with specialists in employment, health, housing and welfare. Administrators, too, at all levels are realising that to plan, however efficiently, within the statutory limitations of departments is to miss opportunities of a better use of scarce resources. One consequence of the lack of general principles of community development is a reluctance of administrators to act at all in some fields, except within well-defined areas of departmental duty. Everybody's responsibility often becomes nobody's.

It is now clear that no phase of education can ignore the interaction of educational institutions with the community and its built-in tendency to undermine with the one hand what it has supported with the other. To tackle these problems through the continuous educational process envisaged in the 1944 Act will be a long-term effort if it is hampered by avoidable rigidities of professional attitudes, or if it has to be financed wholly from public sources. So far, education authorities have limited their main effort to the primary and secondary phases and to the vocational and higher sections of further education. Work with adolescents and adults has suffered by comparison. It has been argued, not unreasonably in view of the resources available, that until the primary and secondary stages of education were well established and successful, expenditure on a wider area of development, including general and informal education, was unlikely to produce a satisfactory return. But it is now recognised that too many children are being educated in schools without noticeable improvement in their capacity to enjoy or profit from the school programme, and that too many adolescents are not being educated at all. Educators are therefore driven to reconsider the whole situation and to search for remedies. Some of these will take the form of first-aid or piecemeal improvisation, but what is also required is a synoptic look at the whole situation and particularly at the application of educational policy to the development of the community on a wider basis of agreement among the different practitioners.

School and college

The consequences of raising the school-leaving age will be an important feature of the next decade. Sixteen will have a new significance in the lives of young people. To many pupils under sixteen, it will seem that their childhood and dependence are being prolonged unnecessarily and to many of those over sixteen continued association with a school may not be wholly congenial in its present form. If all schooling were deemed to end at sixteen, if the student replaced the schoolboy and schoolgirl and if all education after sixteen wherever conducted were officially described as further education, the gain could outweigh the resulting administrative problems. If, in addition, their new status was clearly visible in the rights and recognition given to them by society, both in symbols and in hard reality, young people could have practical assurance that their independence and initiative as young adults, whether at work or in full-time education, were valued elements in society.

The most serious problems in their last year at school will be presented by those who are often called the Newsom children. The Newsom Report drew a sober picture of "the contrast between those who are successful and those who are not ... Too many at present seem to sit through lessons with information and exhortation washing over them and leaving very little deposit. Too many appear to be bored and apathetic in school, as some will be in their jobs also. Others are openly impatient ... These girls and boys must somehow be made much more active partners in their own education. Whatever their natural endowments they all need to attain self-respect and a reason for wanting to work well..."

It is for these young people above all others that the original County College proposals were put in the Education Act. It was for their welfare that the Crowther proposals to implement County College provision shortly after the raising of the school leaving age were designed. If the Seventies do not see this reform, the majority of these inadequately educated young people will depend for much of their further education on the breadth and imagination with which their industrial training is handled and on their participation, if any, in youth and community activities. No single person or institution in any area will be able to keep a statutory grip on them. If educators are to influence this situation, they will need new allies, new ideas, and private as well as public resources. They will do less than is required unless they can secure the support of employers, training officers, supervisors and shop stewards inside the places of employment, as well as that of the providers of leisure and recreational activities.

For the least adequate and the deviant adolescents and for those organisations concerned with their welfare, the Seventies will be welcome for one reason at least. No young person, unless he be a spectacular criminal, will go to prison, nor will he be put in an institution whose name will accompany him back into normal life with the unfortunate associations of borstal or detention centre. Neither of these labels at present offer an easy passport into employment or into association with ordinary households. It is hoped that young offenders will be sent to Youth Training Centres intended to replace the traditional custodial institutions. Educators have a long association with the penal treatment of offenders in this country, which is described later, and their work with the Prison Department of the Home Office is an interesting example of inter-departmental co-operation in testing circumstances.

Any synoptic look at the educational provision for adolescents, some of whom, as full-time or part-time students, are under the continuous and often protracted attentions of specific educational institutions, some of whom are in circumstances or institutions which educators can influence, and many of whom appear at present not to be exposed to any form of educational effort on their behalf, must begin with the Crowther Report. This Report on the vocational and personal education of adolescents for the technological community of the future was above all its other merits of expertise and insight, essentially a practical document. It tackled what might be admitted to be the most complex area of educational policy and went to the heart of the problem in its opening sentences

– "This Report is about the education of English boys and girls aged from 15 to 18. Most of them are not being educated." Apart from the pejorative reference to "boys and girls", the implicit challenge of these words succinctly describes the situation at the beginning of the Sixties. The Report's main proposals were to implement the original aim of the 1944 Act to raise the school leaving age to sixteen between 1966 and 1969 and thereafter at the earliest possible date to make part-time education compulsory for all young persons of 16 and 17 not in full-time education. The latter reform was to be introduced in three stages, first by an increase in day-release secured voluntarily, second, by an experimental period in which compulsory County College attendance would be tried in a few suitable areas, and third, by the extension, phased over three or four years, of County Colleges throughout the country.

It will not be until the early Seventies that Crowther's first priority will be met. The encouragement of voluntary extension of day-release has had disappointing results, and there is now little prospect that County Colleges will be established. The community's disinterested influence on young workers is likely to be exercised largely through cooperation between further education establishments and the Industrial Training Boards, which have brought the complications and the, as yet, narrower conceptions of training into what was previously conceived as a broad educational approach, and through the efforts of individuals and voluntary organisations.

Despite these frustrations, there have been far-reaching consequences of other recommendations in the report. The suggestions on the content of the curriculum of County Colleges were the basis of the official advice given to colleges of further education on the methods and principles by which technical courses could be broadened through the addition of general studies. In the secondary schools, the concepts of "literacy" and "numeracy" and the use of minority time have promoted a radical examination of the elements and balance of the curriculum, which extends from the Schools Council to the universities. Increasing attention is being given to the practical possibilities of integration of courses and activities in secondary and further educaton, both before and after the school leaving age, to the references to the "adult atmosphere" of the local technical colleges and the implication for schools of its characteristic elements of permissive behaviour and vocational relevance of studies and to the emphasis on the need for flexible arrangements for deploying staffs. The concepts of "literacy" and "numeracy" go to the heart of the curricular planning. In greater or less degree, they are essential elements in the education of both the élite and the least able student. So far, with most of them, in secondary or further institutions, more success seems so far to have been achieved with "literacy" than with "numeracy".

There were many other fruitful suggestions, including the necessity for research, on which much quiet progress has taken place. The whole range of recommendations, major and minor, were presented as a coherent phased plan of integrated development. But even if it were completed at the end of the Seventies, half the young people in the country would be leaving full-time education at 16. The problem of devising some form of educational influence and community care for them, especially for the least able and delinquent section would remain. Crowther noted that the peak-age for juvenile delinquency was the last year at school and emphasised the need in these circumstances for teachers who were as much social workers as pedagogues.

Crowther argued cogently that it was within the country's resources to raise in twenty years the proportion of young people aged 16 to 18 in full-time education from one in eight to one in two and to cover the rest by part-time attendance at County Colleges. In these colleges the students would participate in courses and activities based on their vocational needs, yet giving insights into the adult world and into moral and aesthetic standards. Pending the opening of the County Colleges, a strong youth service would act as an interim stop-gap and ultimately as a complement to the colleges. The youth service has been strengthened and enlarged, but despite the Albemarle and Bessey reports it remains a thing of shreds and patches still on the periphery of the educational services. In its present form and with its existing aims and sphere of influence it is no substitute for County Colleges. The country has probably paid dearly for the naive extravagance of the original County College proposals and the failure of the programme recommended by Crowther.

The prospect then, at the beginning of the Seventies, is that many young persons will be retained in the schools at least a year longer than they wish, within the grip of institutions which are energetically devising new objectives and courses to make the compulsion more acceptable and effective. Others, uncertain about their careers, and inadequately advised on their ambitions and their potentialities, will be ready to postpone vocational decisions and to stay beyond 16 within the protection of the school. Even the ambitious minority, who know where they are going, will be remaining largely out of vocational interest in institutions many of which persist in concepts of curriculum and personal education which were critically and searchingly examined in Crowther and have been under increasing scrutiny since. Many of the pupils endure the methods and ethos of the schools because their eyes are on the positions of affluence and privilege to which the schools hold the vocational key. In general, they have the supporting background influences and the will voluntarily, and often with financial sacrifice, to continue their education instead of taking the earliest opportunity to abandon full-time studies and to begin the cruder and more haphazard processes of self-education as independent wage-earners. They may symbolise those forces within the educational system which help to perpetuate the economic and social obstacles to the building of a community with some claim to ethical as well as technological quality; but they also contribute, along with the full-time advanced students in further education, to the academic and technological élite without which both the material, intellectual and possibly the spiritual basis of society would be impaired.

This division, which the Seventies will highlight, of young people into two main streams at 16, of full-time learners on the one hand and full-time earners on the other, seems inescapable, but some of its adverse consequences could be reduced. For those who are proposing to continue full-time attendance at school, skilled attention will no doubt be given to their intellectual capacity, their aesthetic sensitivity, and their social poise and capacity to communicate with people who talk their language. If equally expert attention is given, while they are at school, to strengthening their understanding and sympathy towards the whole community, and their links with the unexciting and under-privileged sectors of the world of earning, with opportunities of practical compassion towards the aged, the desperate and the defeated, they could be given a real acquaintance with situations outside their educational and social background. A mere reading of sociological or political weeklies is a poor substitute for regular intimate involvement in the life and work of contrasting communities. These processes could be facilitated by a far more ambitious programme of extra-mural activities in clubs and settlements and by a more flexible interchange of staff between school and further education institutions of all kinds, (including in the latter not only colleges but also youth and community work, sports and art activities). It should be possible on a much bigger scale than at present to plan parts of a common curriculum and programme of activities for schools and institutions of further education to undertake jointly. The general studies would offer a good initial basis in many situations, though this approach would have limitations in those areas where schools are plentiful and colleges of further education are few. Crowther was emphatic that further and secondary institutions should come to closer co-operation. They have so much to learn from each other. There are elements in the ethos of schools which are often sadly lacking in the "adult atmosphere" of technical colleges.

In further education institutions the outstanding problems are to guide students into suitable courses, to broaden the vocational approach and to add general studies and corporate activities to the programmes of all students, including the part-timers who constitute easily the majority of those attending. Colleges will need to become unmistakably places of further education, so that all students will feel that they are coming to a community and not just to a course. Many students enter a college with a reasonably clear, if sometimes mistaken, notion of the jobs they want; some of them know the training and qualifications required if they are to achieve their ambition, and many of them are single-minded in their desire to pursue their courses with the minimum of distraction. The college's diagnosis of the student's needs may differ widely from his idea of his wants. The student's conception of the college as a service station may be irritating for the college, but the treatment of the students' wishes is a test of its liberality. The student is entitled to his point of view and, though limited, it is not an unworthy one. He is ready to make special efforts to prepare himself to do his job properly in the community and very frequently at the expense of his leisure time. Many colleges are now giving him a careful induction into broader concepts of what is vocationally and personally appropriate for him.

At present, students are divided into four main groups: the technological and technician élites at the top, the craftsmen, and the operatives lower down, with increasing encouragement for students to improve their qualifications and to rise in the technical hierarchy. The purpose of dividing students into four categories is that they represent four main areas of provision with features and opportunities of their own. For example, the technologists are recruited from schools or colleges at which they have taken advanced courses giving them a foundation on which to enter a full-time or a sandwich course leading to a professional qualification. The intellectual needs and the academic potentialities of these students clearly differ considerably from those of technician or craft students. Many of them are capable of embarking on strenuous analysis and study in depth sustained over a long period. They are often at least three years older than craft students on entry into the college. Nevertheless they have points in common with the younger students pursuing less intensive courses. They need the social and educational broadening that comes from contrasting subjects and activities since many of them have pursued a narrow range of courses and interests before coming to the college. When the general studies courses in secondary schools become more widely established, and as the practice grows either of devoting minority time to other subjects, on the lines Crowther recommended, or of increasing the number of main subjects, as others argue, it may be expected that these students will arrive at the technical college better equipped and more generally knowledgeable and versatile than at present. Many colleges are able to give them a substantial amount of general studies. It will soon become exceptional for any of them to receive no general studies whatsoever, and to concentrate the whole of their time on instruction only in the subjects of their examination.

The courses for operatives are still comparatively few. Operatives rarely find their way to technical colleges of their own initiative and many of their employers still see little point in securing further education for workers whose tasks involve little craft practice or theory. Some enlightened employers in both the public and the private sectors encourage their young employees to take day release courses at which a mainly general education is provided. A few have set up their own colleges to do this. Many of the students present difficult problems for the colleges. Those coming from clerical sides of government departments are able to take a wide range of general studies with profit and enjoyment, but their inclinations are frequently towards securing better paper qualifications and they tend to resist general education for its own sake. Operatives from industry are often seriously deficient in the basic skills of reading and writing, and are also disaffected in attitude because of their previous experience of education. To devise courses that will attract and maintain interests all round is no easy task and requires specially good teaching and careful study of the nature and motivation of the students. With craft students the college's main difficulty is to find the time to arrange in addition to the vocational courses a progressive range of general studies relevant to the students' jobs and their personal adjustment to society.

The addition of courses of general studies to the vocational courses is a comparatively recent and spectacular phenomenon. It has produced a controversial but by no means an unpromising situation. General studies are one of the significant aspects of the transformation of technical education, but because of inroads they make into students' time and the critical attitudes they tend to engender, general studies can be a disturbing influence in the life of a college. When well presented, they are not always welcomed; when they are trivial or superficial, they are an affront and they can do more harm than good.

The terms in current use are not the happiest. There is a good deal of confusion between "Liberal" and "General" and terms like "Liberal Studies" can be provocative as well as meaningless. In some quarters, "General" seems to have been a retreat from the consequences of "Liberal". It was a retreat from the frying pan. "Liberal" may be difficult but "General" is too general. "Liberal" may antagonise more than it attracts but "General" could be insidious if all it implies is an extraneous addition to an otherwise unchanged curriculum, narrowly conceived and executed. But whatever labels are affixed to the separate elements in the curriculum, the liberalisation of technical education implying a broader approach to vocational education by means of main, complementary and contrasting studies is essential if technical institutions are to educate as well as train their students. A liberalising process is required which will at least be pervasive, even if stronger in some places in the college than others. It will be exemplified in the variety and quality of the activities pursued inside and outside the lecture rooms and laboratories by the students; it will be revealed in the major aspects of the corporate life of the college; and it will be deficient wherever there are serious deficiencies in the quality of the principal and the staff, and particularly of the staff teaching the main vocational subjects. General studies will only be a part of this liberalising force and, unless they are in good hands, they will make a poor contribution to a liberal element in the college. Imaginatively handled they can exercise an influence second only to a transformation of the teaching of the main subjects. But educational policy must be realistic in terms of the reasonable capacities of teachers and the time available for institutions to put ideas into practice. It should not expect students in one hour a week to transform either their knowledge or their learning attitudes.

Colleges of further education have appointed specialists, mainly with qualifications in literature, history and social studies to teach general studies and in the majority of colleges a department has been established to service other departments. Roughly one in twenty of the teachers of vocational subjects contribute to the general studies programme. In secondary schools, by contrast, there are no specialists in either the teaching or the organisation of general studies and so programmes of general studies usually depend on contributions volunteered by subject specialists in the main disciplines, offering a contrasting experience of study, art or crafts. Some interesting experiments and attractive practices are now in being, which are reflected in the lively quality of the journals produced by the members of the Association for Liberal Education and the General Studies Association, and in the curricula and activities of the schools and colleges.

A number of colleges of further education are undertaking informal educational and social activities indoors and outside. Some of them have accommodation specially built and equipped for youth activities, and about 40 colleges have on their staff a qualified youth worker. This development, though small as yet, has great potentialities. In some rural and semi-rural counties (though not confined to them) interpretations of policy are to be found which may point to one of the main forms of community provision by Local Education Authorities in the future. They posit a clean break with the concept of separate independent units such as youth clubs, village halls and community centres and are based on a complex of buildings. In the simpler form of complex, the village hall, library, clinic etc. are planned as part either of a new or an adapted village school. A more elaborate form integrates youth and adult services in the closest association with a secondary school in a village or community college, a school-based centre of adult and juvenile education under the direction of a warden–headmaster. These concepts seem to spring from three main aims: to put into effect, as community policy, the basic aim of the Act to establish a continuous process through progressive stages of education, to secure the maximum return on existing resources of staff, buildings and the severely restricted allocations of public finance for new buildings, and to provide an attractive social and cultural centre to which people can form the habit of coming and from which extramural services can be organised to supply needs more appropriately met elsewhere.

Behind these projects, as in the outstanding achievements with community centres, have been the resource and conviction of a few individuals who have nursed their schemes through the critical stages. In the field of village and community colleges, it is the Chief Officers of the Local Education Authorities who have given the inspiration and driving force. They have linked their plans and finances in school provision with further education, sometimes in co-operation with other statutory authorities and with voluntary organisations. They have acquired allies wherever they could be found – in minor local authorities, welfare organisations of national boards, trustees of charitable endowments, managers of voluntary schools, student associations and groups and societies of private individuals. In transcending legal difficulties, departmental rigidities and traditional prejudices, they have provided evidence of the potentialities of existing resources and opportunities, especially in combination, which should be more widely known. Only they, with their unrivalled knowledge of the needs and resources of the local situation, could have succeeded in such demanding tasks. Initiative and direction of this kind at the local level is the proper basis for the comprehensive organisation of effective face-to-face relationship of agents and recipients of community effort.

Other examples of imaginative co-ordinated approach are to be found in the large conurbations or in the bigger counties. In some it is now policy to give the Principal of the Institute of Further Education, which is usually based on a variety of school and other buildings, responsibility for general oversight of youth clubs, community centres and of educational work in penal institutions in the catchment area. In others, there is an increasing tendency to link statutory and voluntary provision in community, adult and youth fields to local Councils of Social Service, which cover the whole range of social services.

Recently, new colleges of further education, particularly those built in small towns, have encountered almost from their opening day requests for accommodation and help with adult activities, which they have met as far as they are able. The number of principals of these colleges who look on their buildings and staff as instruments and agents of community service is increasing. Many of them are very ready to stage the local dramatic society's play, to engage professional artists of all kinds and to offer accommodation for amateur enthusiasts of music and drama in the locality, to arrange exhibitions and opportunities for public meetings and debate, to organise classes and practical activities in a wide range of leisure time subjects and occupations, and to bring together

166

young, middle-aged and old in purposeful and friendly association. It would be an overstatement to suggest that these colleges are working as yet to any defined community policy, but they may well acquire one as they adjust themselves to their appropriate role in their areas. Community associations receive advice and aid through the colleges; the colleges act as a focus for the youth service in the area and are a source of pastoral help, training for part-time workers and grant aid to voluntary groups. The colleges' accommodation – library, common rooms, refectory etc. – is made available for adults and some of them have separate youth wings. In few areas, however, will colleges be close enough together to meet the needs of adults and young people without drawing on the resources of other forms of community service. In the existing schemes, therefore, co-operation has been established between the staffs of colleges and of other agencies concerned with community work, especially the voluntary organisations and, in some New Towns, with the Community Development Officers of those towns. The staff of the colleges includes tutor librarians, one or two members responsible for the organisation of evening classes, and a number of tutor-youth officers, at least one of whom is concerned with students' societies; the others function as area youth officers. One result of these combined approaches to community work is to put the adolescent phase more firmly in an uninterrupted process of education. To place youth in an environment where adults may show in practical terms their respect for them as an important part of the community, to give them their own premises and also an opportunity of sharing in decisions that effect the welfare of all, is to provide conditions in which response of youth can be understood and properly assessed.

Youth and delinquency

Most of the youthful participants in these schemes are pupils at schools, or full-time or part-time students in major establishments, but there are many young people who are neither and for them it is the Youth Service which seems to offer the educator one of his few opportunities to play some part, however small, in their development. Accurate information is not available on the backgrounds or proportions of young people in the age groups from 14 to 21 who take part in youth activities over the whole country. It is nevertheless clear that both in the youth club and in the bigger complex including the community centre, the sports and arts centre – more of which are likely to exist in the Seventies than are to be found to-

167

day – there is an opportunity for the educator to help young people enjoy themselves in more acceptable relationships than they have been able to achieve at school or at work.

The Albemarle Report gave the Youth Service a new look and additional resources, just in time. Its consequences in terms of new building, recruitment and training of full-time and part-time workers are impressive. But there are many reservations about its success with the disaffected and the delinquent. Strong support for the youth service, including devoted personal participation, has come in the past from adults anxious to find ways of keeping young people off the streets and out of trouble. Delinquency is uppermost in their minds and of late, thanks to the wide publicity with which the more outrageous forms of crime and behaviour have been treated, juvenile wrong-doing has perhaps become an obsession. The prevailing and possibly conditioning social and economic circumstances are ignored; attention is almost entirely concentrated on the offence and the offender. Obviously society must maintain rules of order and decency and gross expressions of anti-social behaviour must be restrained and, when necessary, punished. Some degree of personal responsibility must be accepted by wrongdoers. Often they seem to slip into crime through misjudgement or temporary instability and some are just the unlucky ones who are detected. The problem of delinquent youth cannot be divorced from the problem of youth generally and the relationships of youth to adults in modern society. They are part of the general problems of the values and quality of the whole community and they concern the rights of young people to be trained more efficiently in the skills of personal expression and to be listened to sympathetically on matters of importance to them. It may be that one factor in the complex problems of juvenile crime, violence and disorder lies in unreflecting and uninformed adult reactions at home, school, work and recreation to what initially are either natural but clumsy expressions of independence in speech and action, or to symptoms of physical and psychological illness.

It is interesting to note that it was the Home Office which in 1918 took the initiative in urging Local Education Authorities to set up "juvenile organisations committees" and that today, when the Department of Education and Science has the statutory responsibility for the Youth Service the question is frequently asked whether youth work is mainly social work and therefore not properly an educational responsibility. The failure of existing concepts and practices in dealing with anti-social elements in youth is the subject of countless enquiries. The situation certainly needs careful re-examination, beginning with the problems of those actually convicted for statutory offences. It would be a safe assumption that social deviance and delinquency will be at least as marked at the beginning of the next decade as they are today. Indeed, many who work with young delinquents will be surprised and gratified if the rate of offending does not rise, with the critical points at the new school leaving age and the late teens. In this situation the partnership between the educator and the organisations charged with the custodial and pre- and post-custodial treatment of offenders is likely to be strengthened at all levels and particularly the local. This partnership is long-standing. It is worth some attention as a significant example of the possibilities of inter-departmental co-operation, in difficult circumstances and often secured between individuals of very contrasting attitudes and experience.

Throughout the last century the grim life of English prisons was softened in places by the ministrations of prison visitors, of men and women who voluntarily brought to the help and instruction of the prisoners their skills and personal interests, and not least of the chaplains who represented a civilising and on some occasions a protesting influence in an environment which remained generally harsh and degrading. Many changes have occurred since the time when Frank Harris recalls Oscar Wilde's complaints to him: "The governor loves to punish, and he punishes by taking my books from me". These words spoken in Reading goal at the end of the last century, mark the end of the predominantly punitive approach to the treatment of wrong-doers in this country. Wilde's incarceration coincided with the beginning of the Ruggles-Brise administration, in which an enlightened man brought new vision to the Prison Commission and the Board of Directors of Convict Prisons. But progress was slow, except in the treatment of young delinquents. The ideas of the educator struggled with a generally restrictive custodial outlook, and educational activity was spasmodic and minimal.

Today, the prime responsibility for the treatment of offenders rests with the Prison Department of the Home Office as a matter of general policy, and with the governors and prison officers in the separate penal establishments for the execution of that policy. It is based on two principles: first, the offender is sent to custody as a punishment, but nor for punishment. (This is an admirable statement of general aim, but in practice the decision to remove an offender from the freedom of outside life is initially punitive, though

169

the treatment inside the establishment may, and usually does, lack punitive intent); second, the treatment is constructive and is designed to fit the offender to return to society, ready of his own volition to lead an honest life. Custody provides the controlling conditions for the offender to be influenced to will his own rehabilitation. Custodial treatment is designed for different types of offenders. It is, like modern education, individual-centred. These principles are proving a satisfactory context in which to make an educational contribution to penal treatment. It still remains, however, even in borstals, ancilliary to the main therapy, and is too often divorced from potentially valuable learning situations in the general life and work of the establishments. It is significant that neither in recent White Papers nor in the Select Committee Report of 1967 is there much reference to education.

Every penal establishment has some educational provision and the responsibility for advising the governor on educational classes and activities rests with the tutor-organiser. The latter is not a permanent member of the staff of the prison service. He is usually on a five-year contract and is generally seconded from a Local Education Authority. Originally these organisers were mainly school teachers, but recent appointments include men experienced in adult education. When an enlightened tutor-organiser deals with an enlightened governor; then education can give to the prisoner something he can understand and value.

There are few situations which test the skill and convictions of the educator more than the penal establishment. Custodial treatment, even when not associated with forbidding buildings and strict régimes, is not an environment in which the educator can employ to best use personal influences and the normal motivations. Its totality and its compulsions place strict limits on the aims of the teacher. He works in an alien and often discouraging situation, and he shares with the governor and the staff of the penal establishment a parmanent dilemma – how to train men for the testing responsibilities of freedom amid the supports and imposed restraints of custody. Nevertheless, over the past twenty years it has been possible to organise in every penal establishment in the country a relationship between educational authorities outside the prison and the training inside which, within its present concepts, is growing in effectiveness and cordiality. In the main this has taken the prescribed and limited form of the provision of fairly orthodox classes in basic education or recreational subjects like art, music etc; it has contributed little directly to the major concepts and practices

170

in custodial treatment, and is often very subordinate to other considerations, e.g. security, on which at present public attitudes are naturally apprehensive, and shortages and changes of disciplinary officers and the unattractiveness and unsuitability of the accommodation.

Borstals and detention centres are the twin pivots on which the main reformative efforts with young people are concentrated and they apply very different principles and contrasting methods of treatment. Detention centres are of two kinds – junior, for offenders between 14 and 17 years, and senior for those between 17 and 21. The duration of treatment is normally three to six months, but opinion is hardening that if the job cannot be done in three months, it cannot be done at all on these lines. It is a severe experience particularly for the young and the weak. The educator is in great difficulty here. The duration of the sentence is too short for much positive education and the circumstances too demanding physically and psychologically for either effective personal contacts or informal education, especially in the evening. Little effective classwork is possible. The purpose and content of education in these circumstances needs a re-appraisal, towards which the Local Education Authorities could offer an appropriate comment.

The detention centre is intended to give a short and salutory reminder to "the silly ass who wants to be pulled up sharp against his foolishness". Most inmates regard it as a severe and punitive experience in which they conform pretty sharply to prescribed rules from first thing in the morning, when they have physical jerks, to lights out. It is left to individual members of staff to recognise the point when the strictness of the régime can be relaxed and when officer-inmate relationships can take on a more informal friendly pattern. The aim is that, after this treatment, the youth will be able to return to society with a more acceptable attitude. Yet reconviction rates remain high. This could be a comment on the effectiveness of the centres; it could also reflect the lack of continued help from the society to which the youth returns.

Borstal training is substantially different in method and duration. The average length of training is 14 months; it is conducted in open and closed institutions, designed to meet varied needs and capacities. Youths are assigned after centralised study and careful allocation; they may find themselves in an ancestral home, a windswept camp or a former prison. Most borstal boys are larcenists and more are convicted for taking and driving away motor vehicles than for violence against a person. A new element is the number of drug takers whom it would be inaccurate to describe as addicts.

Borstal training has been internationally admired. Its attention to the needs and capacity of each individual, its progressive stages of training and its links with the outside community have characterised the best in English penal thinking. It has attracted governors and staff of great devotion and skill. The experience derived from the work of borstals has played and will continue to play a large part in the concepts of custodial treatment for young people in the Seventies. Not that borstals lack critics. One governor in describing the "golden age of borstals" has called them "a sincere attempt to create a series of benign, though feudal manors, each with its governor-squire and enclosed self-sufficient peasant economy". Others note the higher rate of failure, since many offenders who would formerly have gone to borstal are now put on probation and the quality of inmate has declined. The house system and the imitation of public school ideas have also come under fire and in some borstals they are being replaced by schemes of individual attention requiring continuity of relationship between particular staff and inmates throughout.

Nevertheless an enormous amount of imagination, devotion and inventiveness still goes into them. The work attracts men of versatility and character who leave their stamp on the ethos and activities of their institutions. Education matters to them. They go to great pains to build up the right sort of staff attitudes; they explore and make good use of the goodwill and resources of the local community.

More detention centres and borstals are planned or are being built, partly to relieve overcrowding in them in the prisons, but also to prepare for what will probably be an integrated system of borstal and imprisonment in the Seventies. This reform will constitute a major advance. The educational and essentially remedial aspects of Borstal training, the training in vocational skills designed to improve the personal equipment of the youth in order to give him the opportunity of economic independence as soon as possible after his return to the normal community, and the new recreational interests he has acquired, are all aspects of a progressive policy in the treatment of young offenders to which the educator can heartily subscribe. The failure rate in the long run is perhaps less important than the effort made.

For those young people who continue to offend, the framework of penal treatment has every promise of being the most suitable yet devised and one that should win general support, particularly for the proposal to separate young people between 16 and 21 from adults and children. The scrutiny of their offences and their personal records, by special courts constituted from magistrates selected for their understanding of young people, is an assurance that the custodial and non-custodial sentences will be put in a stronger educational setting. They need be no less firm. Sentences will be served in one of a comprehensive system of residential training centres, with a minimum period of nine months and a maximum of two years. The determining factor will be the welfare of the young person and the object will be to make him into a law-abiding and useful citizen. There will be a substantial increase in local responsibility and an encouragement of local voluntary effort in a continuous process of community care.

The Prison Department will in future be able to move with broader terms of reference into a closer association with other statutory agencies. The emphasis in custodial treatment could swing strongly towards education as the main instrument of reformation. The circumstances in the establishments could be suitably adapted – with buildings mainly open; staff acting under whatever title as teachers, trainers, instructors, counsellors and friends; the inmates not cut off in monastic seclusion from the world outside, yet deprived of some of the freedom enjoyed by the non-delinquent. The lines of a further advance in the quality of the education provided could then be, first, a training closely related to the ascertained and expressed wants of the prisoner; in terms of communication skills, his need both to explain himself properly in day to day activity, to write to his family and to deal with personal affairs. Second, the education could be more closely related to the work situation and its problems and particularly to the vocational skills which the prisoner needs. Third, his programme could be built on an anticipation of his economic and social requirements on release. Cultural and recreational interests, hobbies and the like could all be designed to relate to the interests that have been awakened in him. Lastly, there should be waiting for him, ready to run into smooth operation, the essential help and advice necessary to ease the transference from custody to freedom. His release should not be a fresh predicament but a welcome transition from one caring community to another.

In the meantime the educator will continue to offer advice, when asked, at a variety of levels. The most effective situation is obviously in the penal establishment itself. Increasingly governors, and educators are tending to talk the same language. For most

173

custodial situations informal methods are appropriate. In securing the co-operation of the prisoner, the vocational teacher, or the teacher of practical subjects, can often make the most effective beginning; but there is also a need to kindle his interest in music, literature, drama and art, or in the current problems of society, at whichever level is appropriate, and gradually through them to build up his interest and confidence. There will always be a place for straightforward formal teaching in basic educational skills and in the crafts that are necessary for daily life and work; but many prisoners have great personal deficiences and difficulties and they often take these classes successfully without being fundamentally altered. It is in that alteration that the ultimate success of the educational contribution is to be judged. Whoever advises the governor must strive to understand the daily life and work of the establishments. They are all so remarkably different and they change from time to time as different personalities take charge of the custodial situation.

The recent appointment as a Chief Education Officer at the Prison Department of a Senior Officer from the staff of a Local Education Authority should enhance at the centre the relationship between the educators offering advice at all levels. This advice has in the past been concerned mainly with staffing and curricula. It is now extending to the design and furnishing of new buildings. The Penal Institutions Joint Development Group, which is concerned to apply the best techniques available to the design of prisons, is studying a variety of concepts of educational building in the light of the different requirements of each situation. The application of close studies of educational function in relation to buildings, of the kind well-known to education authorities, will enable the Prison Department to meet its obligations, to maintain secure establishments and at the same time to provide a more flexible and attractive housing for educational work on modern lines.

Buildings are one aspect of reform; staff and methods are another. The soundest basis of successful penal treatment could lie in the transformation of the prison officer from a custodian primarily interested in disciplinary routines into an educator with social skills. If disciplinary officers were relieved of their unending chores of custody, by electronic and other technological devices, they could spend more of their time on constructive educational tasks including counselling, discussion group work, and participation in activities. Such professional responsiblities might attract recruits from a much wider field. If suitable encouragement were given, many more youth workers, youth employment officers, social workers, community workers and young teachers might become interested in this work and gain an invaluable first-hand experience. They have some predecessors. At least one governor was one time warden of a community centre.

The penal system of this country is steadily being equipped to tackle, with greater knowledge and resources and an increasing variety of methods and skills, the complex and often baffling problems of juvenile crime. In this task the Prison Department is seeking and receiving the whole-hearted support of other statutory and voluntary bodies. The greatest need is for a more informed public opinion. The educator is well placed to help establish a sounder knowledge of the nature and extent of delinquency. Public interest in the main is in the drama of crime; it is fed by the mass media on heightened fictions. The pathetic inadequacy of the average criminal is not known, nor is the nature and extent of the problems generally realised. In consequence there is a constant danger that isolated incidents may lose public support for reform and retard its pace. If the incidence of delinquency should rise rapidly, the first reaction may be a demand for stern action and sharper custodial treatment, but if this is the only reaction, then a symptom of the disease and not the disease itself will have been tackled. There is no evidence that youth can ever be held for long periods within a merely disciplinary grip and a civilised society has to persevere with an unremitting study of the causes and the appropriate therapy for wrong-doing.

In dealing with youthful behaviour, it is not easy to decide the points at which legitimate self-assertion becomes anti-social conduct, and at which the latter merges into delinquency. It is easier to note when delinquency turns into serious crime. Whilst the extent of youthful disorders is often exaggerated, they endanger the foundations of those values it is the essential task of educational institutions to promote. Therefore the stark offences which cannot pass unnoticed and unpunished in any orderly, healthy community must be separated from the traditional exuberances of youth, which are part of the business of growing-up.

The educator's task is not made easier by the licence permitted to entertainers to undermine by actions as well as words the standards and attitudes encouraged by the good school and home. One may bite a man's ear or punch his jaw, without fear of civil prosecution for assault, provided one is an outstanding footballer and confines one's savageries to the sportsfield. Some would argue that organised team games, especially as played by modern professionals, can bring the worst out of participants and spectators. If games are held to be character-forming it is becoming increasingly necessary to ask – what sort of character? While it is illegal to foment hatred between races, it is perfectly proper to use the pop idols of youth and even the B.B.C. to denigrate the authority of parents and weaken their relationships with their children. The aura of the youthful pop idols is the protective screen behind which indifference, ethical rejection and self-centred intractability are fostered. These examples are infectious. It is surprising in these circumstances that the problems of juvenile behaviour are not larger than at present. On these issues, educators have the duty, not merely of strong protest, but of unremitting counter-attack.

There are simple facts which help to put what appears to be a profound malaise in a better perspective. They need to be studied carefully by educators and to be more widely known. Crime is everywhere a predominantly male activity. Statistics for this country in October 1967 show 34,652 male prisoners including 1,014 young men in prison, 5,897 in borstals and 1,529 in detention centres, compared with only 949 women in custody, of whom 28 were in prison and 176 in borstals. Only one female detention centre was required, housing 26 inmates. Numerically, all the females presenting a really serious problem could easily have been accommodated in a single establishment. In the treatment of criminals, then the educator is concerned predominantly with males. Further, the majority of juvenile offenders do not re-appear in court. The social and educational efforts of society are not failing, despite an increase in criminal violence among older adolescents. In general it is the adult who is addicted to most of the serious and spectacular crimes. A sense of proportion is required in discriminating between undisciplined youths who need a sharp reproof, and those whose conduct requires some form of brief or sustained penal attention.

At the heart of the problem are those young people whose lives and leisure pursuits are trivial, who are often bored with themselves and yet remain indifferent to all educational or social encouragements to participate in creative and satisfying pursuits which will release their potentialities. The opinion is growing among youth leaders and others who work with, and study young people that the more independent youth is encouraged to be the more cooperatively it seems prepared to act; that it is both more charitable, honest and sincere than the adult community; that the majority of adolescents are prepared to conform in behaviour, if not in conviction, if given reasonable areas of freedom of action; in fact, that they believe they could teach adults a lot if they had a mind to learn. Though many young people enjoy a bigger share in the goods and services of the economic system than their elders did, they are not thrilled by their part in making them. Technological society in its present state – for the principles and practices of which adults are responsible – produces consumer satisfactions at a cost in personal frustration which lessens respect for those responsible for its direction. The majority of young people learn well before they come of age that the system fixes them in their place for a long time in circumstances which at worst they detest and at best barely tolerate.

To this predicament of youth the existing Youth Service seems to offer in the main leisure – palliatives which enable young people to extract themselves for part of the time from their predicament, but not to change or influence it. At present the Service is being side – tracked; it seems to be trying to be all things to young people. Despite its fine achievements in the provision of opportunities for association, activity and community service, it tends to emphasise the gulf between the adults in the community and youth.

The Youth Service therefore seems to be at the parting of the ways. It is not making headway with the deviants who refuse to attach themselves to its clubs and activities, however attractively devised to meet contemporary tastes and interests; it is not creating a country-wide network of institutions in which young adults can find a major source of satisfaction either in recreational pursuits or in social and cultural activities. If Newsom's recommendations are implemented, it will lose to the schools the younger teenagers who in many areas constitute the principle membership of the clubs. In trying to do everything for everybody between the age of 14 and 21 it seems often to satisfy nobody. And yet the needs are there and the work must go on.

If the Youth Service is to continue in its present form and to direct its limited resources to the most important aims, it will clearly need to concentrate more effort on people who are reluctant to come within any formal educational or social contact and who must be met in flexible circumstances on their own terms. The main agents of such activities will be face-to-face social workers, not leaders of clubs. If in addition some effort is to be spent on providing older young people with adult opportunities, then both the place of such activity and the participants will need to be set in

177

community enterprises in which it will be difficult and probably undesirable to distinguish at all between youth and adult. Lastly, for either of these tasks new forms of professional training and careers structures will be imperative. At present social workers are trained and recruited separately from youth workers in the education service and community workers in the education service are trained separately from either. Since the material attractions of a career in the youth and educational service are relatively small and the career-structure is narrow, only the dedicated are likely to enter and remain in arduous work on the periphery of the educational service.

It is a most necessary part of the educational and social provision in the community to re-plan training so that all professional workers operating separately may be brought into more effective relation with each other and their transfer to a wider range of educational and social service facilitated. Any training system that assumes that full-time youth or community work in the education service on present lines is a job for life is for the majority of workers probably mistaken. The Albemarle Report said quite distinctly "full-time youth leadership is a life long career for only a few. It would not be fair to attract intelligent men and women into this work unless we made it easy for them to move across to other professional work in education or the social services." This concept is in accord with a growing opinion that careers and functions in education call for the flexibility of outlook and performance which a technological society is demanding in industry and commerce.

The future

This account of the efforts of educators in the Sixties to meet the needs of young people over school age has been mainly concerned with organisation and provision. The establishment of closer relations between secondary and further education institutions dealing with full-time students, the addition of studies to the vocational curriculum of part-time students, the construction of a national pattern of youth clubs and activities designed to attract among others young people averse to formal institutions of further education, and lastly the increasingly significant contribution to the treatment of delinquency in and outside of the custodial setting, are all, in themselves and in their range and extent, an impressive organisational achievement. Much devotion and skill have gone into it, and in places a thin layer of professional skill is spread very widely, or a single educator is on his own.

How far and in what ways the community has been developed it is difficult to say. Does it think more clearly and sensitively? Are most of the professional objectives within sight of realisation? He would be a rash man who would venture any opinion on the degree of success of the Youth Service in reducing delinquency or on how far general studies have prepared technicians and craft apprentices "to find their way successfully about the world both as consumers and citizens" or "to form standards of moral values by which they can live in the new world in which they find themselves", as Crowther hoped. In the theory of community development expressed at the beginning of this paper, one of the principles emphasised was of "active recipients of whatever is publicly provided". How successful has this principle been applied to learning situations in the school or college classrooms, to the pursuits of the Youth Club and to the programmes of the community college or centre? If the test of success in a community centre is whether, after initial help from public funds, the centre becomes a largely self-supporting activator of local community action, few would pass it easily and it would still be necessary to ask – what sort of action? and what has it done for the people concerned? Answers of a kind, based largely on observed behaviour in particular situations, can be given to these questions but most of them will be tentative. The present situation might be generally described as one of experiment and uncertainty. But the scepticism and misgivings reflect an anxiety to improve performance and to make a better use of resources. They are constructive attempts at self-organisation. A major difficulty still in dealing with "unattached" or "unclubbable" young people is to find a geographical point at which to concentrate the youth worker's effort. Failing a requirement of compulsory attendance at a college, the place of work seems to offer the best opportunity for contact. It will be essential in the Seventies to make the most of it. If being a young worker carries with it the inescapable obligation to be trained, and if through the decision of the Training Boards the training includes educational elements, then there will be a point of contact with every young worker and a situation in which the co-operation between educators and trainers can take on new forms. The resistance of employers to concepts of training wider than the straightforward requirements of the trainee's job is not universal. Already one Board is spending money on "character" training. It seems inevitable that the relationships of employers with educators must ultimately involve concern in the agreed

179

objectives about young people as persons as well as workers. Imaginatively handled, it could offer an alternative to the County College which may prove to be the only alternative available in the next decade. Even the keenest protagonists of the original concepts of County Colleges may see a new role for themselves in using the potentialities of the new relationship in which employers accept readily responsibilities as educators as well as organisers of labour forces.

It is often said, with truth, that buildings are less important than people. But buildings are essential and in the present situation many needs for accommodation are not being met; yet existing premises are often under-used. All educational buildings should function as community buildings, and all new building, for whatever phase of education it is intended, should be designed for multiple and not single use. There are already in existence admirable examples of new or adapted primary and secondary schools designed with community additions, some part of which has been paid for directly out of the pockets of the local inhabitants. It will be a great step forward for the image of education if more adults could come to think of educational buildings as really theirs and not just as children's accommodation, of which they have been graciously permitted the occasional use. It is surely obsolete thinking for any one person to regard an educational building as exclusively his sole personal responsibility and sometimes almost his personal possession. The economic arguments as well as the social and educational justification for changes of attitude are strong. The practical difficulties of dual use have been exaggerated. No doubt many adults are loath to enter school premises and many heads are reluctant to share their control with other users. There have been imperfections of behaviour and there is no lack of horrific accounts of maltreatment of school premises out of school hours. It does not always occur at that time. All the faults are not on one side, however, and none are ineradicable. It will be necessary to create a climate of opinion in which the traditional users of educational establishments may accept their position as prime users on a sharing basis – with ready consent and not grudging acquiescence. Problems there will be, since with the prime use goes also prime responsibility. Reasonable attitudes and some restraint will be necessary especially in increasing the wear and tear on playing fields in the English climate. L.E.A.s in most areas have the lion's share of the halls and the public facilities; they also have the most comprehensive view of the situation and the most comprehensive responsibilities to children, adolescents and adults. Many of them are surveying resources and reconsidering the existing ways in which these facilities are utilised and the part they might play in broader communal use in future.

If every area could begin to think of all its educational buildings in full use and with a much bigger contribution from private resources supplementing public finance, it would be possible in the next decade to plan over the whole country colleges and schools as centres of music and arts; as meeting places of broadly constituted youth councils with representation on an occupational basis from the local industries and commerce, as well as from the traditional voluntary organisations and activities; as clubs and institutes of informal adult education, with wide-ranging extra-mural contacts; as information and advice bureaux and as well-organised and well-used centres for sports, outdoor activities and foreign travel. In all these activities young people could be encouraged to take part naturally and as of right. They should be represented in decisions about programmes and the general life of the centres and they and the adult users should pay more than they do now towards the full cost of the facilities. There is some evidence that young people use their present youth premises and facilities for cheap sociability after they have emptied their pockets in commercially provided entertainment. Many further education programmes meet the demands of adults well able to pay the full cost of these pleasures. There is little case for a public subsidy of the further education of either the comparatively affluent or the well-educated. Educators should not be ashamed to make a profit and ways should be devised of leaving it with them to subsidise some of the experimental or inspirational work in the unpromising situations for which public resources are otherwise not likely to be available.

These arrangements will be incomplete unless in every locality there exist complexes of community building in which the former aims of the community centre can be combined with programmes of arts, sports and recreation. Whether these buildings are schools, colleges, or community centres, they will become more easily centres for active recipients of public aid if they are the responsibility of a community association which is properly representative of the community and particularly of the young people. The community association is the most flexible and representative instrument of local self-help yet devised. Its place should be established and its opportunities extended.

The Sixties have been *par excellence* a decade of reports, heart-searching and strenuous analysis, and improvisation. They has produced many resourceful and adaptable educators. The Seventies should see some far-reaching practical consequences. The duty of central government to promote implies forward movement and English education is conceived as a continuous process. For twenty years the children's needs have been paramount. In the Seventies the adults, young and old, should come more into the picture. If the age of majority is reduced to 18 (as recommended by the Latey Committee) then educational and social recognition of 16 as a dividing line between child and man becomes a possibility, the consequences of which could be the beginnings of a much more constructive relationship between young people and adults. If adolescence has been invented by adults it has proved to be one of society's less useful inventions which might in time be discarded. The foundation of economic welfare lies in the orderly disciplined production of goods and services inspired and directed by an elaborate technology. In the complex system of modern industrial society the progress in human relationships must match progress in technology, since any individual or group dissidence can reduce or wreck the effectiveness of the whole. It is in the interest of all parties, young and old, to reach a higher level of accord on objectives and decisions. In the social life of the community too, young people seem now ready to be given a clear recognition of adult status embodied in representative councils and institutions affording them a place in adult decisions and a chance to make some of their own. To refer to these committees problems of disorder and dissidence would be to use only the smaller part of their potentiality. A main activity could be to study, comment on and assist in planning facilities of all kinds to meet the needs of young people in the area. Most English towns and villages are social deserts at night and inadequate for social life at week-end. It could become a matter of pride and competitive interest between neighbourhoods and towns to offer imaginative and acceptable programmes of leisure activities.

Big tasks lie ahead, which may not be within the competence of either the numbers or quality of the educators likely to be available. But whether administering, advising or teaching they can approach the future better equipped to perform their tasks. There is a wealth of practical experience in often adverse conditions. Few fields of educational activity, except possibly in adult education, have not been comprehensively surveyed. The educator has also at hand an expanding – possibly an intimidating – range of educational, sociological and psychological research and guidance, the new concepts and suggestions of the Schools Council and much lively comment in professional journals. The great educational debate grows in interest and relevance, and most of it is based on actual situations and problems. It has to be so, since most educators are concerned to get on with the practicalities of their jobs without undue doubts or distractions, either of methods or purposes.

The educators in the front line could be overwhelmed by too much advice from the rear. Practice could be impaired by excess of theory. The gulf seems to be widening between the practitioners in teaching situations of all kinds and those who administer and advise. It will be a bad day for education if the principle of division of labour is pushed too far. Specialists in administration, research and educational advice need the healthy corrective of regular re-introduction into responsibility for the consequences of advice and policy. Exhorters and advisers need opportunities and persuasion to re-learn on the ground the practical context of their recommendations.

It may also be argued that those who look on these problems from an educator's eye are in danger of building up the educator's professional contribution to the welfare of the community at the expense of other important functions. Indeed, educators in general, in their enthusiasm and conviction, may well tend to exaggerate the contribution which educational policies can make to the happiness, economic wellbeing, and even the readiness to learn of adolescents and adults. In general people know what they want and will not easily accept any view of their needs which is markedly different from their conception of their wants. It is incumbent upon educators to see that needs are met in such a way that the supplier and the recipient find a common satisfaction in the service provided at whatever level and however far removed from the educator's ultimate goal, by ensuring that the manner and matter of their offerings are acceptable to those for whom they are intended. Educators must make their characteristic contribution as adroitly as the situation requires. But they must make it. If that contribution is not forthcoming, an essential ingredient in individual and corporate decisions is missing. The relative scarcity of public resources is unquestionable. This is a further challenge to the educator's imagination. There is scope for exploring ways in which needs can be met from combinations or adaptations of existing resources, or from new private resources. Each year brings evidence of fresh concepts, of a broader basis of financial responsibility, and of originality of achievement on the ground which should be better known. The educational case should never go by default, even if the accountant has the final word.

A realistic view of the Seventies will see it as a period of intensified effort to make education more directly relevant to the needs of young people, which are as yet imperfectly comprehended and inadequately communicated. The next decade should mark an important stage in the development of an efficient society into a community, in which young people are glad to participate. It will not be egalitarian, since no modern society can live completely without its élites, but it will try to be fair. Qualitatively, it promises to be a considerable advance on the present. Points of comparison are interesting and every educator has his own. To the small band still at work, who have personal experience of the dark days of the half-timer and the old elementary school, a little euphoria and optimism may be permitted. In looking to the future, at least one of them would echo the words of Sydney Smith:

> "The good of ancient times let others state
> I think it lucky I was born so late."

YOUTH SERVICE

*

THE REV. ROY HERBERT

It is doubtful whether the most sensitive crystal ball could reflect the future of that branch of educational provision called youth service. The name itself is ambiguous. The word 'youth' is generic and gives no clear picture of the genuine concern for people which once motivated a Baden-Powell or a William Smith, and now inspires a married man with two children to resign from a safe job and undertake instead full-time residential training for youth leadership where there is neither safety nor career structure. The word 'service' has overtones of do-gooding which still attaches to some areas of youth work, but which is healthily and decisively rejected to-day by the young themselves.

Ambiguity of nomenclature, however, is as nothing compared with ambiguity of purpose, aim and definition of role. More than seven years since the publication of the Albemarle Report ("The Youth Service in England and Wales". H.M.S.O.) and its acceptance by the Government of the day (February 3rd, 1960), confusion about aim and role still daunts the Department of Education and Science, the Local Education Authorities and the Voluntary Organisations in their sometimes joint, but all too often separate, search for a viable, rational pattern for the future. Of course it is true that society, and particularly its younger section, is changing and reacts to change all too quickly. Adjustment to such social change is not made easier by the multiple and varied nature of voluntary endeavour nor by the cinderella-like position of youth service within the educational system (itself a super-cinderella). Even the extension of interest and financial support as well as the growth of professionalism and partnership since 1960

185

leaves the service in 1968 going it is not certain where.

There are those, for example, who see in the implementation of Newsom principles (enunciated in "A Report of the Central Advisory Council for Education" – "Half our Future" – H.M.S.O.) a challenge to a new partnership with the schools, while others view this as a threat to traditional method and structure. There are, too, those who see a heightened awareness of social needs as the opportunity for the service to become what it was originally in conception and principle, namely, a welfare and rescue service in the best sense of that term; while others would regard this as an intrusion into their own exclusive provision for leisure, cultural or denominational ends. And there are those who, weary from many years of pioneering and fighting a lonely battle with inadequate means, overwork and understaffing, are content to let controversy pass them by or, with embittered militancy, to oppose change and defend the status quo.

It is not surprising, therefore, that some now pose the question as to whether youth service has a future at all, while others have already begun to leave its ranks. Recent history has not been exactly encouraging. The Albemarle Report marked 1960 as a year of hope which, now deferred and unrealised, has made some of the most ardent hearts grow sick. Before 1960 it was acknowledged that youth service had fallen into disrepute. Lady Albemarle and her Committee gave reasons for this. The Department of Education had shown insufficient initiative; the Local Education Authorities had presented a hotch-potch of haphazard development and the Voluntary Bodies had been unwilling to break new ground. More significantly the partnership between statutory and voluntary bodies, envisaged in 1939 (Ministry of Education circular 1486) as the foundation of the service, was gravely inhibited by partisanship and insistence on areas of influence.

To relieve the gloom and enliven the service the committee proposed and the government accepted a 10 year development plan. A Development Council was set up under the chairmanship of the Minister. A building programme of £3 million and then £4 million per annum of permitted spending was established. The provision of 1,300 full-time leaders was to be speeded through a one-year course at the emergency National College at Leicester and by the Colleges of Education offering a youth service option. Recruitment and training of part-time leaders was to be undertaken jointly instead of in competition. Statutory Youth Committees were to have increased status and Advisory Committees with voluntary representation were to be set up.

There followed in 1962 what is known as the Bessey Report ("The Training of Part-time Youth Leaders and Assistants" – H.M.S.O.) which criticised the method, content and quality of training and recommended the establishment of Joint Training Agencies to meet these criticisms by real partnership and improved standards. By 1964 (December) a Review Committee was set up to assess progress at the half-way mark in the 10 year Albemarle Development Plan. It gave its attention first to the area covered by the Bessey Report two years earlier. By the end of 1965 it reported some progress, but added that the foundation principle of partnership was still misunderstood and misapplied, and that improvement of leadership standards was impeded by the prior need to train the officers responsible for leadership training, and by a continuing confusion about the content of training common to all and about the most effective methods of communicating content. It was a little late to close the stable door, but worse was to come. Full-time leadership was at least as urgent a problem as part-time leadership and this was the next item on the Review Committee's agenda.

Unfortunately it was a ghost item, for after a considerable interval it was announced that the subject could not be dealt with until a more thorough-going review of the whole field of youth service and its priorities had been undertaken. In the meantime the current top of the pops, community service by young people, was to be investigated. The result was a report ("Service by Youth" – H.M.S.O.) which stressed once again the need for greater partnership in meeting real as opposed to manufactured needs and for greater participation in planning and decision-making by the young themselves. It received a cool reception and was killed at birth by fear of co-ordination of effort as a threat to independence and initiative. Joint consultation and experiment and a report on progress, suggested in the Report, have not been forthcoming.[1]

The record of the Review Committee has not been a happy one; its lot neither happy nor enviable. It came up against precisely those fundamental and apparently intractable problems highlighted by Albemarle: a Department of Education bound to take account on the one hand of the legal rights of Local Authorities and, on the other, of the long established tradition of the independence of Voluntary Organisations. Democracy inevitably and rightly involves this restriction upon central initiative. What is not inevitable is a restriction upon insight, vision and forward thinking generally. Perhaps it was an understandable pre-occupation with the technical need to please everybody which confined the Development Council and the Review Committee to the narrow limits of introspective soul-searching within youth service itself. But this was to ignore two important developments.

In the first place the Central Advisory Council for Education was considering the needs of average and below-average 13–16 year olds in school and had in its 1963 Report "Half our Future" (already referred to) spoken of the personal, moral and social needs of young people and the desirability of co-operation between the schools and youth service as well as other community agencies. This emphasis was reinforced by the re-constituted Schools Council in its Working Paper No. 2 ("Raising the School-leaving Age" – H.M.S.O.) in which, after governmental commitment to raise the school-leaving age to 16, school-based provision was seen as a social as well as an academic exercise in which others besides teachers were involved.

In the second place the general trend in society had been shifting significantly. Affluence meant mobility and a lessening of dependence upon purely local provision. Young people had the money and the transport to seek what they wanted where they wanted. They were no longer tied to the home or the local club with its second, third or fourth rate premises and equipment. They could pay for commercial provision of a more sophisticated kind. Educationally more and more were finding the adult atmosphere and social amenities of further education establishments more congenial to academic and technical self-advancement. Horizons had been widened and cultural, artistic, dramatic and sporting activities were available to large numbers as never before. A more sophisticated community was beginning to meet its own needs in these respects. While in others, notably in the matters of drug dependence and an increasing immigrant population, youth service was shown to be but one part of a complex of community services.

In the face of these kinds of developments the Review Committee could no longer look inwards and confine itself simply to matters internal to youth service. It was disbanded and in its place the Development Council appointed three committees which, for the first time in recent history, had terms of reference which directed them to look outwards to immigrants, to the schools and further education, and to the community at large. This most recent (1966/7) change of emphasis represents a silver lining to an otherwise pretty dark cloud of unknowing. Extended discussion of its implications for the future will be given later. For the moment it is perhaps better to retrace our steps and consider the factors which had all along been underlining the need for such a change of emphasis.

The large, though not large enough, army of part-time leaders and assistants has been better trained in recent years. It is, however, pertinent to observe that the real growing points have been those where the service has been influenced from outside its own boundaries. Social or small group work, for example, as a training and communicatory method was imported from America and was in use in other professions before it gained within youth service the important place it now occupies. Supervision and counselling skills, now recognised as essential and only comparatively recently introduced, were earlier developed by the social agencies and by such bodies as the National Marriage Guidance Council. Partnership has been notably strengthened, too, as a result of the involvement of non-youth service personnel from, for example, Departments, Institutes and Colleges of Education. Growing points which have yet to sprout include the recruitment of new and more varied personnel, who are not easily attracted to a service limited in the popular mind to the frightening task of keeping fifty teenagers happy (and quiet?) in an ill-planned, poorly decorated hall; and a universally recognised standard of basic training and more systematic provision for advanced training, so that the image of well-intentioned amateurism may give way to greater parity of esteem and status with other services and professions.

This last point is, of course, even more crucial in the area of full-time leader training. The fact that the overwhelming majority of full-time leaders appointed since 1961 have received only a one year's course at Leicester simply invites the charge of inadequacy and dubious professionalism. Nobody is more aware of this than the Governors and Staff of the National College itself. They have worked miracles in the most difficult conditions. That is not the point. There can be little hope of parity of esteem and status, not to mention interchange of appointments between different professions while, for example, teachers serve a minimum period of three years training with the possibility now of qualifying also for a degree compared with the youth leaders' one-year crash course. The disparity applies to the social services too, but the one growing point is again external to the service. It is found in the

Colleges of Education, a large proportion of which are now offering a youth service option. This could make for parity and
encourage interprofessional understanding, a change for the better which can only improve performance when leader and teacher
later find themselves in the same locality dealing with the same
young people.

Finally, the Albemarle Report exhorted youth service to seek out
and attach, however loosely, those regarded as unattached and outside its ranks. Millions were spent on building youth centres into
which it was hoped youngsters would be attracted. When all
allowance has been made for the "bulge" in the teenage population, the results are not encouraging. At the most 30%, at the least
15%, make use of all youth service facilities, including youth
centres. And already some of these centres are past their peak
membership. Some are in serious financial difficulty, while others
are without leadership and in danger of closing down. Considerable
and entirely genuine as was the effort on the part of many, including the churches, to reach the mass of those outside youth
service, the fact remains that it was an effort tied to the old patterns and traditional structures.

Since 1960 only two pieces of sustained experiment and analysis
outside existing patterns have been undertaken. These were sponsored
by the Young Womens' Christian Association (see "Working with
Unattached Youth" by Goetschius and Tash, Routledge, Kegan and
Paul) and the National Association of Youth Clubs (see "The Unattached" by Mary Morse, Penguin) respectively. Both demonstrated
that real needs go considerably deeper than the provision of a building within which the leader stands beckoning with his finger in the
traditional come-hither stance. The Young Womens' Christian Association Coffee Stall project in particular provided evidence
that a vast number of young people had in fact sampled youth
service provision only to reject it. The overwhelming majority
were unwilling to commit themselves to the four walls of a club
or centre. They were to be found, and contact established, only
outside the four walls; outside in the community where they were
free to choose for themselves where they would go, what they
would do, and to whom they would unburden their desires, their
problems, and their hopes.

Youth service was too slow by half to appreciate the rapid
social changes which had already rendered the new youth centres
out of date. By and large the voluntary bodies had not risen to the
Albemarle challenge to break new ground and the statutory

authorities were in no better case. The Department of Education and Science complained that there was a lack of initiative towards imaginative experimentation while offering only £30,000 per annum as an encouragement to this end. In view of all this, it is deplorable that the Review Committee was not given the teeth (and the money) to launch a full-scale scientific investigation into the effectiveness of the building programme which had already cost the taxpayer and the voluntary contributor something in the region of £15 million without, apparently, any significant increase in provision acceptable to those who in and since 1960 have remained outside the service.

Some such investigation is needed to provide guide-lines for the 1970's, over and above the hard work of the Fairbairn (Schools, Further Education and Youth Service) and the Milson (Youth Service and the Community) Committees. Both committees need to face the facts that at the key-points of full- and part-time leadership, and of reaching out to a new generation less ready and willing for commitment in the traditional sense, youth service has remained largely insular and conservative. Even the national voluntary organisations, who have in recent years engaged in agonising reappraisals (e.g. The Chief Scouts' Advance Party, the Girl Guides' Working Party, The Boys' Brigade Haynes Committee, and the Church Lads' Brigade Exeter Comittee), had as their starting point the need to halt falling membership within the framework of existing structures. This may not be surprising when, for example, one organisation faced the danger of ceasing to be viable on a national scale if within five years a significant increase in membership was not achieved.

Even this, however, is no excuse for failing to recognise the present malaise which perpetuates the concept of membership at a time when it is inevitably at odds with a great many of the personal, social, economic and educational influences which impinge on youth service from outside. Youth service is faced in the 1970's with the necessity of deciding how far it is ready to recognise these influences and to move outside itself and combine in partnership with others to meet needs as and where they arise, rather than to continue to see and deal with needs as and where they fit into existing patterns and structures. A radical change of philosophy and basic conviction is called for. How can such a shift in outlook be expressed?

In three ways, I think. First, whatever may be said about leisure time provision as distinct from academic advancement, the motivation of youth service has been educational. In the broadest sense of the term, youth service personnel are concerned for the development of the whole man. Their function is an enabling one – enabling the young person to achieve for himself that fulfilment which is humanity itself. This is what education is all about. It is *not*, however, what youth service is seen to be all about. Its image is still one of isolated eccentricity, associated with dingy church halls and a 1968 jazzed-up version of the relief work of the 1930's. This only widens the gap which has existed for so long between teachers and youth leaders, for example. Leaders claim for their own informal methods a real understanding of the real youngster, while teachers claim a monopoly of sound method and effective discipline. In fact leaders and teachers are dealing with the same young person and the sooner they come together and accept their common educational motivation the better; for until they do, it is only the young person who suffers by their rivalry.

Second, the context of youth work is social. It cannot be undertaken except within and as part of the community as a whole. That is not, of course, to say that youth service should adjust young people to society, still less society to young people. There remains, however, the vital role of enabling young people to take their place in society and become the makers of history of which society itself is part. Here, too, isolationism has to be cast overboard and closer links established with all other social agencies in the community. There is required a new partnership on the grand scale which goes far beyond the limited pattern envisaged in 1939. Departmental barriers at governmental and local level will have to be demolished if all the services available are to operate in concert rather than in competition to the maximum social benefit of the young.

Third, educationally and socially any service must become and be seen to be professional. The days have gone when to volunteer one's services gave one the right to do the job. This is in no way to eliminate the volunteer, but to insist that he be trained and competent and that his paid full-time colleague should be accepted by other professions on equal terms. This is not the case to-day with youth workers generally and, granted the will to do so, youth service cannot break out of its shell until professional equality has been achieved. We shall return to this theme later, but for the moment there is another aspect of professionalism which calls for comment and it is the ability to be objective. At a time of extremely rapid change there is no room for the self-deception which is content to boost declining numbers or membership. There is time only to assess needs and attempt to meet them, and there is required an objectivity which can vote itself out if that is how real need can truly be met.

Now and into the seventies youth service will, I believe, be challenged to find its rightful place educationally, socially and professionally. It must not only find its place, it must also earn its place. If it does not attempt and succeed, it is doomed to die slowly. What, then, are the areas in which change is required?

Consider first the fact that by 1970[2] all young people will continue to receive full-time education until the age of 16 (and many will choose to stay till 17). The form this education takes is already being re-orientated to meet the needs of people rather than of pupils or examinees. Once the preserve of youth service, person-centred, social-orientated approach and provision are to be found in increasing numbers of schools. The impetus for this comes not only from the Newsom Report, but also from the Schools Council and Goldsmiths' College Laboratory. The movement is seen particularly in the upper forms where learning is linked with experience and becomes a partnership exercise in which the teacher has the role of consultant and growth-evaluator. This process of change in role and emphasis now extends to the Colleges of Education where, as for example at Culham, the trainer/trainee relationship is a foretaste of the new teacher/pupil relationship and where subject barriers are down and team-training is the preparation for team-teaching later.

Informality of provision is the setting for this new approach. In 1966 the Department of Education and Science produced "Additions for the Fifth Form" (H.M.S.O.) in which many examples of informal youth-service-type provision were given. As in the 5th Form Open Unit at Maiden Erleigh School, the work area has the appearance of a super youth centre, is better equipped than most, affords maximum participation and self-programming by pupils and is open (8.30 a.m. to 6.00 p.m.) many more hours per day than most youth centres.

It is at this quite fundamental level of approach and provision that the overlap with the schools up to the age of 16 (and increasingly to 17) calls into question the future of youth service. The point is emphasised further by the increased provision in or by the schools of vocational guidance and school-work courses and by the training (at Keele, Reading and Exeter for example) of counsellors and their appointment to school staffs. Leisure-time activities are also being catered for in an extended school day in places as far apart as Kent, Nortumberland and Cornwall. Dual appointments, such as Youth Tutors and Deputy Heads responsible for informal activities, tend to integrate the academic and the sociocultural under one roof. And this extends beyond the school to Institutes of Further Education where young men and women are attracted by an adult atmosphere in which academic/career achievement and social/leisure activities are both possible.

Much water has clearly flowed under the bridge since the boy quoted in the Newsom Report said of a brand new school: "It's still a bloody school". And to those who think that school is inevitably unattractive to the young, it is worth quoting in contrast the Maiden Erleigh's pupil's remark: "Oh Sir, nobody will want to leave school". The changes in approach and provision in schools are well-advanced and here to stay. It is little use holding up hands in horror at what some regard as poaching on youth service territory. Instead teacher and youth leader, who after all deal with the same young people, could more profitably seek the means of establishing common aims and sharing work-loads. A greater mutual understanding and trust between the professions is an urgent necessity for the seventies and should be pursued through the extension of joint training not only in the Colleges of Education, but also in the Joint Training Agencies responsible for part-time competence. It is a measure of the ground yet to be covered that youth service remains unrepresented on the Schools Council and the same is true of the Local Development Centres springing up all over the country and intended to make plans for 1972 and after.

But essential to any rapprochement is the need for youth service to face honestly two basic questions. First, should it continue to duplicate and to engage in unqualified competition with increasingly sophisticated school-based provision? How far, as informal, personal and social provision spills over more and more into the schools, will separate, additional provision by youth service be required or used by the 100% of young people who stay on in school until at least 16? Second, is it likely that either the state or local government will consider it financially sound to continue a system which encourages separate provision for those labelled "youth service" as well as for those labelled "schools", in respect not only of specialist and highly paid staff but also of separate buildings not receiving maximum use?

The brute economics of the matter do not suggest a rosy future for youth service. In the meantime there is required as between the two professions some careful analysis of what precisely each has to give in common and where each may complement the other. And the criterion to be applied with some discipline to any new assessment of roles and priorities is surely the most productive disposal of all resources for the welfare of young people.

It is precisely the failure to apply such a criterian to relationships between, for example, the schools and the youth service, which gives cause for anxiety. The Schools Council has been at work for a number of years and has spent a million pounds in research and experiment on the curriculum and, on the basis of its second working paper, it is committed to a programme which takes account of the social needs of young people and to the execution of this programme in partnership with others. It is unfortunate, therefore, that, in the documents which have come out since the second working paper, a provision for real social needs appears low in the list of priorities, and partnership is conspicuous by its absence. Membership of the Schools Council itself does not include youth service personnel despite representations having been made on this subject. Meanwhile Local Development Centres are growing rapidly all over the country and these are not only quite without youth service representation, but are also now being called "teachers' centres". It would be tragic if this kind of separation between two professions and agencies, equally concerned with the social well-being of young people, were to continue indefinitely instead of growing as it should into a practical partnership. The difficulties are, of course, great, and include a degree of mutual suspicion and distrust. Difficulties, however, are there to be overcome and, if both professions are unwilling voluntarily to face the difficulties, it may well be that "brute economics" will force them to do so.

Consider next the upper age bracket from 17 years onward. If those below 17 increasingly find the provision they require under school auspices, can youth service turn afresh to those who have left school? Can the service meet the more sophisticated needs of, say, the 17's to 25's, an age range with which to date its success has not been conspicuous? This is an age group which enjoys a large measure of educational, social and economic emancipation and for the most part rejects an old-style youth service. The question has to be asked as to whether existing leadership would or could meet their demands and needs. One suspects that the answer must be a negative one and this is reinforced by the knowledge that the one successful venture among this age group to emerge in recent years, the 18 Plus Federation, has been self-initiated and self-programmed quite outside traditional youth service structures.

To suggest, therefore, that a new Young Adult Service is the answer may be at once over-ambitious and an over-simplification. Are there not, however, new avenues of partnership to be explored? Two suggest themselves. First the area of further education and training which affects very large numbers in this age range. Universities, Colleges of Education and Institutes of Further Education all have within their membership human, personal and social problems and needs of which youth service has experience but a diminishing clientele to benefit from it. Further, the Industrial Training Act empowers Boards to raise and spend money on training, including residential training provided by other agencies. Has the time come for youth service to reassess priorities and redeploy manpower so as to work through these kinds of existing machinery and institutions in partnership rather than, once again, to set up in opposition? Is it not more practical to accept and work upon those areas where the young adult is already on common ground with his contemporaries, and where his personal and social needs occur and are most naturally discussed and may be more spontaneously and appropriately met? This kind of partnership with other sectors of education raises questions of professional competence and parity already mentioned and to which we must return.

There is, however, a second and quite new area where partnership might well be explored. Where specific provision for leisure time is concerned, it seems that nearly all existing youth service provision would be found wanting. By comparison Butlin, Rank, Mecca and others have huge turn-overs among this age group. They do so because the provision – decor, equipment, comfort, refreshment including alcohol, and technical staff – match the requirements of the young adult who is highly selective in his choice of activity and willing to pay for it. Furthermore, commercial enterprises are flexible enough to make frequent changes of provision according to rapidly changing tastes. They have to be because they must show a profit. Here is a more informal area where the young adult is on common ground with his contemporaries. The personal and social needs are just as pressing and many commercial concerns are acutely aware of them while feeling that they really fall outside their own professional boundaries.

Commercial provision is on the increase (one set of figures, for example, include 6 million admissions per year for Ten Pin Bowling and 100 million for dancing) and it seems totally unrealistic for youth service to pretend it can compete on anything like equal terms. Is there not, therefore, a case to be made for a partnership in which commerce provides the capital and profit-making know-how, while youth service provides some of the staff with personal, group and social responsibility? Before such a revolutionary idea is dismissed out of hand, discussions between representatives of commerce and youth service would at least ensure that neither party entered the seventies unaware of the other's existence.

Consider, finally, a third alternative for youth service in the seventies. It is argued by some that youth work is basically a socially-orientated operation and that this should be recognised more widely and acted upon. Its historical roots lie with the under-privileged and the social outcaste or misfit. It began by catering for those who, through poverty, deprived homes, malnutrition and lack of education had no one else to turn to. If now and in the seventies the schools take over until 16 or 17, and other institutions and commercial concerns cater increasingly for the needs of the 18's–25's, what is left for youth service except to become a super rescue service? In support of this it is pointed out that youth work training now contains a large element of social group work, is essentially concerned with relationships, and that this makes obvious the overlap with social workers. Accordingly, youth leaders should become youth workers, receive a 3-year course in social work, and become, as in America, interchangeable professionally with social workers. That is at least a pretty clear-cut scheme of things and would require a revolution in planning and training as well as an emancipation from building-centredness for which youth service shows no readiness.

The very limited extent of experimentation in socially-orientated work outside the 4 walls already referred to and the meagre provision of, for example, counselling services as a social service not tied to membership illustrate the point still further. The fact, too, that grant aid at state and local government level is still tied to numbers, i.e. membership figures, suggests that quantity rather than either quality or, more important, real need is the criterion for financial support. This is short-sighted, if not irresponsible, for the social problems looming large to-day cut right across membership and organisational factors and for the most part render them irrelevant. In particular the new scourge of drug dependence finds youth service largely helpless. The effective preventive and remedial work required is growing only outside its ranks in, for example, the convent at Spelthorne St. Mary, in a counselling and preventive centre in Soho and in the community-involved project at All Saint's Hospital, Birmingham. The structures were not designed for this kind of community enterprise. Perhaps this is why the Hunt Report ("Immigrants and the Youth Service" H.M.S.O.) finds little that is encouraging in youth service provision for immigrants and occupies so much space arguing for a far wider concept of partnership with all other social agencies if, within the next 5-10 years, the immigrant problem is not to become an explosion of great violence.

It may seem that I have cold-bloodedly dissected youth service, left it dismembered and refused to stitch it up again. My reply to such a charge would be that it is the job of all of us to do just this, that nothing like enough of it is done and that, when and if the body is to be made whole again, this too is the task of all of us. Writing personally I cannot be optimistic about youth service in relation to the schools, further education, commerce or society and the community at large unless two things happen.

First, a radical improvement in its professionalism. A service which in peace-time trains the majority of its full-time leaders under an emergency one-year scheme simply cannot expect to be taken seriously by other agencies and professions. There should be a minimum period of 3 years training. It should be training designed to equip a man on a wide educational and social front. It should be possible to extend this training to diploma and degree level so that wide career prospects are possible in allied educational and social professions. Recruitment of students must accordingly be at a higher academic level than the present almost monochrome low level. Changes as drastic as this will not be universally accepted, but little short of these will boost youth service at officer as well as leader level to the point where interprofessional parity of status and esteem, so essential to a new-look outward-facing service, can be achieved.

The need for improvement is equally urgent for part-time leadership. Five years after the publication of the first Bessey Report (referred to earlier) there are, in the nearly 200 local authority areas, only 17 training officers and 49 appointments with special responsibility for training. Numerically youth service would collapse without its army of part-time leaders. Qualitatively it will not in any case survive unless this army is better equipped and this requires more full-time training officers, more effective Joint Training Agencies and a recognised national standard of achievement. Scotland has already established its own "Board for Information and National Tests". England and Wales need a National Institute where research into methods and standards is undertaken and through which a common yard stick can be applied to judge competence and ability.

Second, a radical change in the perspective of partnership. Society is no longer content to be departmentalised, and youth service cannot survive and yet remain in its customary groove. The point is relevant to the voluntary organisations in particular. The voluntary principle has, of course, been applied with honour in this country for a great many years. With it has gone independence, tradition, conditions of membership and the establishment of long-term commitment. All these are now being questioned. Independence, since absolute sovereignty is incompatible with real partnership. Tradition since, for its own sake alone, it is unacceptable and rejected by the young. Conditions of membership, because the young are more ready to make and keep their own conditions. Commitment, since the young with greater honesty are willing to undertake only those short-term commitments which they think they can see through to the end.

Add to this the fact that most voluntary organisations are structured on a member-centred pattern and one is bound to ask whether this can continue if a wider, more flexible partnership is what is required? Have we not rather to work towards a person-orientated pattern which envisages not organisations and the need to perpetuate them by increased membership, but servicing agencies which meet particular needs at particular times for anybody and everybody? Are not small, but often wealthy, organisations bound to see the wisdom of combining resources of man-power, plant, capital and expertise to form more flexible partnership-minded servicing agencies? Many would reply with a resounding negative and complain about loss of identity. But it was not loss of identity, but loss of a valued service to young people which worried some people at the end of 1967 when "Adventure Unlimited" announced its departure from the youth service scene for lack of financial support. It did not conform to the member-centred pattern. It talked about customers and was a servicing agency whose work is now to be taken over by a commercial firm. It is significant, too, that it is the person-orientated servicing agencies, such as Voluntary Service Overseas and Community Service Volunteers, which have a demand which exceeds supply as against falling numbers in the traditional member-centred organisations.

A look at the Seventies involves an inevitable degree of prophecy.

It is a hazardous exercise but, to me, the signs are clearly pointing towards a greater degree of integration of all services which attempt to meet the needs of the young. And, as society itself becomes less departmentalised, the process of integration is likely to extend to all ages, not just the young, so that we begin to think of community rather than age-group provision. It is, I think, still an open question as to whether youth service is or can become equipped to play a part in such an integrated service. It may be that it is being asked or challenged to lose its identity, while retaining what is best and offering it as part of a new pattern much bigger than itself. If the challenge is accepted quickly there will be a new variety of opportunity for all but the most obtuse. If it is not, there may be no youth service worth the name in the Seventies.

NOTES

1 In the event, the Minister has, with an exchequer grant of £100,000, set up a Volunteer Force Foundation to stimulate local action. The manner of its formation appears to have been the reverse of "joint consultation", while "experiment" seems to have given way to yet more organisation.

2 The recent postponement of this until 1972 is unlikely to halt the fundamental changes of provision and approach in schools affecting youth service, while the present period of financial crisis only underlines "the brute economics of the matter".

SPECIAL EDUCATION
FOR THE HANDICAPPED

*

JAMES LUMSDEN

Special education in England in the Sixties is one of the things of which England can be proud. For over 160 years – since the first voluntary schools for the blind and deaf were established – or for over 60 years – since legislative authority was given to the School Boards to provide schools for handicapped children of these and other types – the development of special schools and services has equalled that in any other country, and in very many directions is regarded with envy by students from other lands. Only in a few of the smaller countries of Europe, Denmark and Holland, can one feel that the parents of a handicapped child can expect to get free and appropriate education for him, linked with the other services he needs such as health, welfare, and preparation for work. Visitors from this country to the United States, though they return full of admiration for the best schools they have visited, regretfully have to admit that services are inadequate, costly to the parent and haphazard in their incidence.

Therefore it is not necessary for us to feel that our system of special education needs to be pulled up by the roots and planted afresh in the Seventies, that the best schools need to be disturbed, or in fact, that things have gone wrong and need to be put right. Rather the opportunity should be taken, 25 years after the Education Act of 1944 – which was in fact being framed in 1943 – 25 years ago this year, to point to places where even a good system creaks and needs attention, or, to change the metaphor, to look at places where the shoe pinches and having done so to see how future developments might take place.

Briefly, the responsibility is laid on the Local Education Authority to look for children who are being impeded in their educational progress for physical or mental reasons and to provide forms of education suitable for them. This is education which will circumvent their disabilities if this is possible, or build on what remains to them if irreparable damage has occurred, with a view to developing young citizens who will – like others – make the best use of their own interests and those of the community. If these children are not found, or are found too late to give special education the best chance to influence them, or if the special education is inefficient, they become or remain a burden in their homes, a dead weight on the community, and a misery to themselves.

"A few of them will not be self-supporting when they grow up but their education will make them better members of their family circle, better neighbours, less troublesome patients should they have to live in hospitals or institutions and possibly enable them to contribute something in cash and, more important, in happiness to their household. The vast majority of the handicapped however can with appropriate education become self-supporting. The uneducated and untrained, blind or deaf person is practically unemployable; the educated one can support himself and a family. The uneducated mentally retarded child grows up into an unemployable or unstable casual worker; the educated one into a more dependable and useful citizen. The uneducated cripple is a burden to his family; the educated one may become a useful worker. This applies to every category of the handicapped. It is a matter of common prudence as well as humanity to do everything possible to equip these children to take their place as self-reliant and responsible members of the community".

So stated the Ministry of Education in Pamphlet No 5 brought out in 1945 to suggest to L.E.A.'s how they should go about their duties under the then new Act.

The L.E.A. cannot contract out of its duty of looking for handicapped children, though it cannot carry it out efficiently without the cooperation of family doctors and hospitals as well as its own teachers and school medical officers and the staffs of the medical and welfare services established by other committees of the local authority. It can however pay voluntary bodies to provide forms of special education it does not provide itself, e.g. the older schools for the blind or deaf established by local charitable trusts, or the newer national charities operating services for very rare types of disability like the Spastics Society. Thus the larger and more highly organized authorities tend themselves to provide for almost any type of disability, while the smaller use the resources of other authorities or voluntary bodies to a greater or less extent. It is however noteworthy that even London, with an enviably complete and complex system of special education, finds it desirable to send some deaf-subnormal and some seriously maladjusted children, for example, to schools outside their area, maintained by other bodies. The fact emphasises one of the greatest difficulties of special education, the almost infinite variety of calls upon it to cater for unusual handicaps and combinations of handicap, a variety so great that only by some regional or even national coopera-tion among bodies can all be well served. The variety of special needs calls also for great expertise on the part of those who are to recommend the most suitable kind of special education for each child.

That all the services of special education are free of cost to the parent, as are special transport, and the provision of any special glasses, hearing aids, orthopaedic apparatus, wheelchairs and so on necessary for the child's education seems to us natural and un-worthy of remark. It is far otherwise even in wealthy U.S.A., not to speak of the poorer countries. That the Youth Employment Service set up for all children gives special care to the handicapped we again take for granted, and tend to grumble should it fall down even on the most difficult cases. The L.E.A. does accept an obligation to provide schooling for *all* children however handi-capped if they can by any means benefit from school – a thought which, we may be sure, would have seemed very strange to Plato or Milton. No child should be left out because it is difficult to fit him in: this the good L.E.A. takes as its daily business, not just as a far off impracticable aim. The law as it stands hardly ever pre-vents the L.E.A. from doing what it considers right for a handi-capped child because of administrative difficulties or financial taboos; and we can hardly ask more of the legislators. The De-partment of Education and Science – when will it abandon this meaningless and cumbrous title and revert to former simplicity? – looks with benevolent encouragement upon all efforts by L.E.A.'s and voluntary bodies to pioneer new and more appropriate forms of special education and manages to fit them in to an administra-tive framework designed 25 years ago. At that time schools for autistic children were unheard of, brain damage was not an educational concept, and classes for children with communication difficulties were unknown. Yet all these have now been establish-ed without new regulations having to be brought in. There are no tensions between L.E.A.'s and the D.E.S., and no religious difficulties. In such apparently satisfactory – even paradisal – conditions why should the Seventies not just enjoy the conditions of the Sixties?

Clearly the framework has nothing much wrong with it and the hearts of the educators and the public who support them are in the right place. But there are certain problems, generally those that were not pressing 25 years ago, which now call for more attention and better solutions, medicine has changed the picture of some handicaps, and above all, parents and public ask for more than they did at that time.

I propose first to deal with 4 separate points (among many) where the present system of special education in special schools could well be improved, and second, under a separate head, to look at the approaching need to extend provision of special education to less handicapped children who do not require to be educated in a separate building, and should have their education in the ordinary primary and secondary schools.

Calls for Improvement

1. *Help for the parents.* Not unnaturally the educational system was based on the needs of the child, and apart from a few mentions in the Act, such as his duty to have his child educated and his rights of appeal against this or that, the parent was not considered. This may have been all right in the past, but Plowden has shown what an effect the parents can have on the progress of children in general, and for a long time those dealing with handicapped children have been realising how much better they can do for their children if the parents take an intelligent and active share in their upbringing. More recently the plight of the home with a handicapped child has been more appreciated, but still not nearly enough. The Carnegie Report on Handicapped Children and their Families 1964[1], in the course of investigating the adequacy of services for this group, brought to the surface some of their crying needs for personal help. Many teachers in special schools who manage to establish really close contacts with some of their children's families over a period of years know what a major influence on the family's whole style of life, ambitions, and activities is exerted by their having one handicapped member. Recently one of my students made an investigation in some detail of the families of four children suffering from spina bifida, a distressing

condition involving paralysis from the waist down accompanied by incontinence. These children were only 5 years old, and the mothers could recall vividly what it had meant to them, their husbands and the other children, the neighbours and relations. They worried about genetic factors – the ignorance of even the best educated lay members of the communitity of what is and what is not inherited and what should be done about further births is not surprising in view of the complexity of the factors involved, – but the agonies endured needlessly in these families were not being appreciated by their medical attendants. They had extra costs on laundry – what a boon a spin dryer would have been! – their holidays were restricted, for a boarding house was ruled out because of sensitiveness over the incontinence and smell, – a caravan was the answer – parents could not go out together because they could not trust baby sitters with *their* child, they could not manage the wheelchair because of steps or stairs or narrow and awkward doors. Yet none was in a slum home, and all the fathers had regular reasonable weekly wages: the trouble was the extra needs caused by the child – and that in spite of friendly help from the Welfare Authority which could not do as much for them as it would like to. What comes out is that we really do not know how best to help parents of handicapped children. Medical social workers, health visitors, mental welfare officers, school welfare staff, teachers, and of course medical practitioners, are all in contact with them but investigations like those of the Newsons[2] show how little can result from the efforts of them all. We spend time and money investigating methods of educating children: our next move must be to do likewise with parents. Many questions require answers – who should try to do the job? Is it for the all-purpose social worker or an expert specialist? Where should it be done? Since the school is the major continuing influence which society brings daily to bear on the child, should the work be school-based? Or since the medical expert is found in the hospital – though he is seen only at rare intervals – should it be based there? Or since the home is found in a street somewhere, should it be based on geography? Whatever answers are found one thing stands out clearly – special education must include the family if handicapped children are to grow up as little handicapped as they can. To develop means of doing this is, in my view, the Number One problem for the Seventies.

2. *The dilemma between convenience and expertness.* It is clearly

convenient to have children educated near home, and clearly any solution to the parent problem would be easier if home and school were close. But by inference "special" children are rare – they are not to be found in every street and some types not even in every town, and the special expertness of teachers and doctors is not to be found near all homes. Should the children be collected into centres where there are experts, or should the experts be taken to the children? We are now seeing this – almost for the first time – as a question calling for solution.

The older forms of special education, the residential schools, had no doubt – the children had to be taken to the experts. The Yorkshire School for the Blind was founded in the 19th Century in York where few children lived, rather than in the industrial and highly populated parts of the W. Riding. The East Anglian Schools for Blind and Deaf were founded early in the 20th in Gorleston on the *edge* of the area. There is only one school (opened in the 1940's) offering bright deaf children courses leading to A level, and all have to go to Newbury whether their homes are in Berwick on Tweed or Brighton. The founders of these schools considered that what was required was to get together enough children of a kind to justify having a large staff of expert teachers having among them a variety of gifts appropriate to provide a progressive course of study covering a long period of years in the child's life. They found that the children learned well and made little of their severe handicaps in a boarding school community designed for them. They knew that the local school could offer nothing to the blind or deaf child and that even the generality of deaf schools could not offer curricula and teaching which would bring deaf children to levels of achievement reached by hearing children of similar age. The case for taking the child to the expert was not challenged.

The growth of day special schools by the L.E.A.'s from early this century brought special education nearer home. As Jessie Thomas reminds us in her recent book 'Hope for the Handicapped'[3] the early schools for cripples in London were set up close enough for children to be brought by horse-cab in an hour from their homes. The same time – but by special bus or taxi – still limits the catchment area of day special schools now. But such schools tend, in towns other than the largest, to be all-purpose schools for a very wide range of physical disabilities, or for mentally retarded children. There are no day schools for the blind or epileptic because the one-hour limit does not include enough children anywhere to fill a well organized school, and a class would have so wide an age range as to be unworkable. There are few day schools for the partially sighted, the maladjusted, and the deaf outside the largest cities, because the children are so few. Sixty years have shown up the limitations of the day special school, however admirable they have suited in large urban areas.

But the fairly local boarding school with weekends at home and easy access for parents with medical supervision from the home area, as in the case of the county school for mentally retarded (or educationally subnormal) children, seems to have much to commend it, both for the rural child and for the less common types of handicap in all areas. Yet, except for the E.S.N., these are rare. Instead we have Yorkshire maladjusted children going to schools in Sussex, East Anglian subnormal spastics to Cumberland, partially sighted children from the midlands to Exeter. This is just because highly specialised schools for them exist in very few places. Such journeying does not make sense. Children cannot travel alone, but must be escorted; they cannot come home for weekends; contact between home and school is minimal; the L.E.A. supporting the child cannot keep a personal eye on his progress; and the risk of wrong placement is great. It must be one of the jobs of the Seventies to find some compromise between the claims of highly specialised and very appropriate schooling and geography. Any solution would cause some upset to established ways, and would need detailed planning in a field in which long term planning is notoriously difficult because of changes in the numbers of children needing special education, but if the education of the family along with the child is to take place it is essential that steps be taken to repress the tendency to greater and greater specialisation.

3. *Regional Development.* Some forms of regionalisation seem to offer hope. The Percy Hedley School for Spastics in Newcastle-upon-Tyne, for example, can give to cerebral palsied children of practically every type in the northern counties an appropriate education. It is almost unknown for a child from the wide area it serves to have to go outside that area for education. Services, medical, social, parental and vocational as well as educational are centred on one school with its boarding wings. It is maintained by a local charitable trust, but cooperates in every way with the local authorities. There seems little doubt that such centres could be made to serve other areas of comparable size, not only for spastics, who amount to about a third of the physically handicapped category, but for the whole of that group. Different solutions would have to be found for

207

the very small and decreasing blind group, which is organised already on a regional basis – but with very large regions – e.g. only one secondary school for the whole of the 7 northern counties. If the development of services within the ordinary schools should grow, the residue of blind children who cannot thrive there would be even smaller and call for even longer journeys than at present. Each category presents different problems.

The reason for the long journeys of so many of the maladjusted, almost always from north to south, is the paucity of schools in the north: the L.E.A.'s are reluctant to build, and private schools are found almost exclusively south of a line from the Bristol channel to London. This cannot much longer remain the scandal it is. Possibly the deliberations of the Summerfield committee on the supply and training of school psychologists will lead to the opening of additional sources of supply of these key professional workers and enable the northern L.E.A.'s to provide child guidance services on a larger scale. Any new training schools for these psychologists opened in the Seventies should be situated north of the Trent: southerners do not readily go north, but native Yorkists and Lancastrians, though in demand in the south, do not scorn to live in the north if there are opportunities for employment at home.

The very great variety of problems of children with multiple handicaps – deaf-subnormal, deaf-spastic, deaf-maladjusted, deaf-blind etc. cannot possibly be solved by increasing the number of very specialised schools with national range. We have hardly begun to think of what would be involved in having institutions for a great variety of these, but we should: at least one regional example should be tried out.

The experimental centre in Shrewsbury for very young children of mixed handicaps, where they can be given education suitable to them all before the need arises for more specialised education (by age and ability and aptitude as well as handicap), may have lessons to teach us in the multiple handicap field without causing us to underrate the contributions and knowledge of such highly specialised units as the deaf-blind one (for the whole country) at Condover Hall nearby.

4. *Preparation of Teachers of the Handicapped.* At the present time this is highly unsatisfactory in that, though they must all have an initial qualification as teachers, only those teaching the blind and deaf must have a special qualification. There is no way of getting this special qualification during initial training. While initial

training in the Colleges of Education has been lengthened from 2 years to 3, with fourth years for those working for the B. Ed., no part of this time can be used for specialisation in work for the handicapped. Indeed few colleges even have staff conversant with the problems of identifying handicapping conditions in children within their ordinary school classes let alone of providing for them when they are not removed to special schools. The exceptions are the Colleges which accept experienced qualified teachers who have returned for a specialised course. Its tutors are in a position to influence the students in the initial courses, though not to staff classes for them. One of the major tasks for the Seventies is to increase the proportion of teachers working with handicapped children who have made a satisfactory study of their needs and methods of meeting them. The problems of doing this are many and complex. Only some teachers of the handicapped want to do this for all their teaching life: it is therefore expensive to give others a long training for only a few years work (as it is to train girls whose service before the birth of their first child is only a few years). Teachers are scarce: should they leave their schools to take a long (say 1 or 2 years') special training? What is the "right" length – or rather what can be done in a short, perhaps one-term full time course as in Scotland, and what needs at least a year if not two? What is the place of the part time in-service course as developed successfully in Holland – though without much observation in schools other than the candidate's own? Is there a place – and if so what – for the practice which is fairly widespread in U.S. of specialising – at an elementary level – in the teaching of one kind of handicapped child as part of initial training? Experiment has been slow in England though there have been in-service diplomas for the blind and deaf for over half a century, and one whole-time course in the education of the deaf for almost as long. When, after the war, a committee reported to the National Advisory Council,[4] it pinned its faith to one-year full-time courses and to an eventual compulsory special qualification. This may have been right at the time, and there *has* been a slow growth of these courses which now turn out some 500 teachers a year – a mere drop in the bucket when the needs of the special schools, let alone the ordinary schools, are considered. But a new look is needed at the varieties of training which are possible; and the fatal English habit of suggesting that there is one best answer (if only we can find it) and that no other is any good, must be suppressed. This habit is reinforced by the suggestion, dear to the teachers' associations, that compulsion is desirable, for if something is to be compulsory, then that, and that alone is acceptable. Instead, the maximum of training – of all kinds – should be envisaged and encouraged. Facilities should also be open to those who have taken a course of one kind to take a more advanced one later and to receive academic recognition. This would in time lead to the production of a supply of real specialists in special education, now only sporadic. The non-medical specialists in special education at present working are in the main teachers who came into it without any special training and learned by experience in the job they happened to have and by private reading and study – a means not to be despised if there is need only for occasional specialists but no way to produce a supply. The few present academic qualifications in it are research degrees which do not pretend to be evidence of practical or wide-reaching competencies. The medical professionals are in no better case: their most fortunate members are those medical and surgical specialists and senior school medical officers whose employment has brought them into close touch with special schools: they too have learned by experience. The prodigious growth of university courses in the various fields of special education in the U.S. is bringing into the study of handicapped children in that country a supply of able graduates who are not generally attracted here. This must be said, although we may claim that our one-year courses for already experienced teachers seems to us to be a better preparation for the classroom end of special education than any of those known to us in the U.S.

Special Education in the Ordinary Schools

The earlier attempts to educate the handicapped assumed that they had to be taken out of the ordinary schools if they were to get what they needed. Though there was provision before the war for the Board of Education to certify special classes as well as special schools it is doubtful if any were so certified. None appears in the pre-war Lists, though there were some one-class special schools. It was the 1944 Act and the regulations made under it which envisaged the education of less seriously handicapped children in ordinary schools. For several reasons this has not been seen to any great extent. In the first place those who valued the special school saw this as an attack on the special school rather than as a chance to extend special education to children who would not otherwise get it. Endless discussions took place under the title "Special School or Ordinary School" exacerbating feeling, instead of considering that both were needed and that the question at issue was the best balance and development of better arrangements for distinction. Second, many if not most of the ordinary schools have been in a state of pressure and change since 1944 which distracted their attention from advances that could not take place without increases of staff and buildings. Third, the Ministry of Education, after starting off very well by making a regulation that the names of handicapped children in ordinary schools should be marked for special attention in the registers, withdrew it because of protests that this "labelled" the children undesirably. Classes for retarded children, where set up, were for this reason not recognised in statistical returns because of difficulties in describing what was and what was not such a class and such children without cumbrous examinations. Without official recognition in staffing schedules there was little encouragement, and many reasons for discouragement: misunderstanding by other members of the staff, disbandment of this (small) class in every emergency, technical difficulties over head-teachers' salaries based on number of pupils etc.

A change came with the development of classes for partially hearing children in ordinary schools, beginning in London in the early 'fifties. These were very carefully and critically assessed by the Ministry's medical and inspecting staffs who saw to it that they should be taught only by teachers who had an additional qualification in this field, that classes should be small and children selected by experts, that the rooms should be acoustically treated and equipped with amplifying apparatus. This gave teacher, class and room a distinctive status. The head could not admit or transfer pupils in or out of this class without discussion with someone outside his school: the room could not in emergency be used for a class of 40. Under this régime these classes have flourished and grown mightily in numbers so that the conditions under which at least one kind of special education can be given in ordinary schools can be studied. The lessons drawn from them should be tested out with other types of partial handicaps not at present appropriately dealt with in special schools. "Labelling" has been found to be necessary: without it no one can be sure what is in the bottle, and what to do with it. Recognition by the D.E.S. – at least in formative stages when L.E.A.'s are feeling their way in a new field is desirable. Some permanence is essential for teacher, pupils and school. Advice from outside the school is necessary on admissions, and almost certainly also on work done, for teachers of these classes can get little professional help from their colleagues or the head. Only in the case of fairly common handicaps, like mental retardation, will there be enough classes even in a large school to have a head of department.

The Seventies should see a large development of classes for handicapped children of the less severe types in ordinary schools. The more successful they are, the more serious cases they will become able to take: but where difficulties arise, there is always the special expertness of the staffs of the special school to take over.

This development assumes that the ordinary school will have a special *class* for its handicapped children. But there is another possibility for some children to be accepted and suitably educated as members of an ordinary class under the ordinary non-specialist teacher of that class. So far only sporadic cases have occurred – not enough to make it easy to list the conditions for success. Several examples are known of blind children educated in blind schools till they were expert in braille and typing and then successfully attending grammar schools with small forms. There are also cases of seriously deaf children attending prep schools where classes were small, polio cases who had to be helped upstairs at grammar schools by members of the rugger teams and so on. At the other extreme there are cases of severely physically handicapped children attending nursery schools among normal children and benefiting from it. Should this be encouraged? On the face of it, it appears to be a denial of special education to children whose disability is serious: when more closely examined, it may not be so. The significance of the disability for education depends not only on the child himself but on the school. It is not without relevance that the first group were all bright children, since the schools in question were grammar schools. They were also in relatively small classes having personal attention. They had had time to get used to being handicapped before they went, and their fitness for these particular schools had been carefully weighed up. The schools also had been free to accept or decline them, to say at any time that they were not being successful in meeting the demands of the curriculum. The young children on the other hand were in classes which did not make specific demands on skill, communication, or level of achievement. Under both circumstances the disability proved only a light educational handicap which a bright child might overcome. Under other conditions the results would have been different.

There is no place for a policy of "just leaving him in an ordinary class". If a handicapped child is to be successfully educated in an ordinary class he must be specifically *placed* there, not left there. While there is not much experience to go on it may be suggested that the following conditions make it more likely that there will be success, (and in their absence that failure may be anticipated).

1. That child and family are well balanced emotionally and able to see the handicap as a real one, not to be underestimated.
2. That the child is of good ability.
3. That he is healthy and does not require to be made a frequent absentee to obtain medical treatment.
4. That the school is really prepared to have him, to allow for things he cannot do without making him feel guilty that he cannot do what others do, and to make any effort needed to make him a full member of the school community, not an outsider.
5. That the staff concerned know enough about the handicap neither to under- or over-estimate its significance.
6. That there should be readily accessible outside advice and counsel to family and school. It is not enough merely to have medical advice that the regime is not harming the child's health. He must be a success educationally: it is not enough for him to "manage" to "get by".

A recent investigation[5] by Miss E. M. Johnson of the progress of children with defects of hearing who were – as individuals – in ordinary schools left a great feeling of disquiet that some children in whose care the above conditions were not fulfilled were suffering in ways that would not have occurred had they been in special schools or classes. Before more recommendations are made that handicapped children are placed in ordinary classes in ordinary schools further investigations of similar type should be made. It will surely be found that it is necessary for the L.E.A. to keep a much closer watch on such children, that no objections be raised to "labelling" them for special help, and that the conditions for such placement be carefully worked out – possibly on the lines suggested above.

If more is to be done for handicapped children in ordinary schools, either in classes or as individuals, the Seventies have a task before them. Unless it is carried out, only severe cases of handicap – suited for special schools – will have their needs met. The less severe will still be left without appropriate education.

Other desiderata for special education in the Seventies for which there is no scope in this chapter are

1. consideration of the future of those voluntary schools which no longer have sources of new capital or income. Does there remain a place for day committees to act as agents for L.E.A.'s if they have neither funds nor special expertness?
2. separation of medical assessment of the nature and degree of the child's disability from the educational assessment of his needs for schooling. At present these are often confused and placement in one kind of school or other is done on the advice of medical personnel who are not closely acquainted with the schools in question. This has increased since hospital-based assessment procedures have developed, taking the responsibility from the L.E.A. staff who know the schools.
3. improvement in the integration of services for the handicapped child and his family when he comes to leave school. This is very well done in some areas but neglected in others: the Seventies should see great advances here.
4. the creation or development of research departments in a few special schools in which staff psychologists, experimental educators, and therapists could combine with the regular teaching staff to carry out studies which have not been possible while the experts are not members of staff. Money for these could not come out of the ordinary school budget: it is a research matter. Some of the best U.S. schools point the way here.

NOTES

1 *Handicapped Children and Their Families.* Dunfermline. The Carnegie Trust, 1964.
2 J. & E. Newson: *Infant Care in an Urban Community,* Allen & Unwin, 1963.
3 Thomas J. E. *Hope for the Handicapped.* Bodley Head. London, 1967.
4 National Advisory Council for the Training and Supply of Teachers. *4th Report on the Training and Supply of Teachers of Handicapped Pupils.* Ministry of Education, 1954. H.M.S.O.
5 A report on a Survey of deaf children who have been transferred from special schools or units to ordinary schools. Miss E. M. Johnson. Ministry of Education, 1963. London. H.M.S.O.

GIFTED CHILDREN

*

MARGARET BRANCH

Among all the problems facing us in the Seventies, one of the most challenging, and certainly the most stimulating is that presented by the Gifted Children in our midst. Plato called them the Children of Gold and pointed out that, while in general children tended to be like their parents, sometimes these children were born to parents of iron or brass, the farmers or the craftsmen in the community. It was stressed that when such a child has been recognised that he should be promoted according to his value. That these children have always existed, no one will deny, but their recognition has presented those who try to do so with almost insuperable difficulties, whether the seekers be the Rulers of the Republic or in our own day, teachers, parents, or those of us who are vitally interested in seeing that, through recognition, understanding and the education best suited to that particular gifted child, he is able to reach his true potential.

These aims of course should be our aims for all our children but, without this early recognition, much harm can be done to the gifted and "there's the rub!" How do we know what we are looking for? Many attempts at defining these children have been made. In 1940 Paul A. Witty said that a gifted child was one "whose performance was consistently remarkable in any potentially valuable area". At a conference at Columbia University, held in the same year, it was stated that "the intellectually gifted child is one who excells markedly in ability to think, reason, judge, invent or create". In the Plowden Report, published in the Spring of 1967, the committee did devote a small chapter to the education of gifted children, although they did not undertake or

215

commission any special study of this group; nevertheless their observations are of interest in pointing out the difficulty of definition. They stressed that gifted children did have special needs and the right to have these needs met. Most of the committee felt that these needs could be met in the kind of Primary school envisaged in the Report but admitted that not all schools came up to this very exacting standard.

Having established that gifted children do exist and have special needs, how are they to be selected? Guy Whipple, in 1919, published a monograph called "Classes for Gifted Children", and Dr. Lewis A. Terman used the word in the sub-title of Volume 1. of his Genetic Studies, "Mental and Physical Traits of a Thousand Gifted Children". Since that time, many hundreds of books and articles have been published, mostly by Americans but in this country there have been far fewer. Among the people who have shown sustained interest in the subject are, however, Dr. W. D. Wall of the National Foundation for Research in Education, who published an article in 1960 "Highly Intelligent Children – The Psychology of the Gifted", while in the following year Sir Cyril Burt wrote about gifted children in the British Journal of Statistical Psychology and the whole of the 1962 Yearbook of Education, edited by Professor Joseph Lauwerys and Professor George Z. Bereday, was devoted to the Gifted Child and carried articles and accounts of work being done with these children in many parts of the world. One of the most comprehensive and interesting books on the subject was published in 1966. In her "Introduction to the Gifted", Professor Gertrude T. Hildreth draws on her experiences with gifted children who have come her way in the course of her work and reviews the work that has been done, mostly in the United States, in the last fifty years.

In the mind of many members of the public and even still of some teachers, the word "gifted" is equated only with the kind of intelligence that can be measured by an intelligence test, although it is now realised that a great deal of re-thinking must go on throughout the Seventies as far as these tests are concerned. Standardisation takes time, however good the machinery, and the "guinea pig" children must be matched as far as age, background and culture pattern to ensure the suitability of the test for children to whom it will be administered if the test is to be of any value. Although many criticisms can be levelled at the group tests as they are used in selection procedures, we must not forget the pioneer work of Sir Cyril Burt, both during the nineteen years that he was Psychologist to the L.C.C. and later when he was a Professor in the University of London. He stressed over and over again the importance of the intelligence test being used in the selection of children for Secondary Schools, in addition to the tests in formal arithmetic and English which had been the sole criterea until then. Through the introduction of these tests, thousands of children from poor homes were given the chance they would not have had, owing to low attainment due to their appalling home circumstances. Even to-day, some children fail to do themselves justice because their gifts lie not in the purely academic, but in the technical, creative and social fields and we have not yet worked out valid tests for these qualities.

Perhaps Dr. Liam Hudson's with his open-ended tests, showing two main groups of convergers and divergers may be more helpful in spotting the gifted child than the more conventional type of tests. Certainly his results are interesting, especially his finding that arts orientated boys tended to do better with the open-ended tests and to be divergers, while the boys interested in science and mechanics tended to do less well and to be convergers. Up to now his numbers have been comparatively small but during the Seventies it is to be hoped that he will continue his work, for surely we have need of people like himself who can question popular beliefs before they become myths and stereotypes.

There remain, however, some boys with known original ability, whom the open-ended tests absolutely failed to rouse and Dr. Hudson thought this might be due to the fact that they were uninterested in the test material and so made no effort. This may to some extent be true but just because of this we must go on trying to find out, and during the Seventies, the work of Professor Warburton at Manchester University may well break new ground as far as the vexed question of creativity is concerned.

What are Gifted Children Like?

As far as physical development goes, there seems to be wide deviations. Some of them seem to pass the milestones early, like *Sarah,* whose parents live in a busy Midland town; she was walking steadily at 11 months, talking in sentences by 11 months, started reading from advertisements just before she was 3 years old and was reading by 4. At this point she wanted to write and taught herself to do so in about a month by copying letters. At 4 months she had four teeth, was always an independent child and at 1 year insisted on feeding herself. In her first year at school she seemed to be bored; the teacher told the mother Sarah "has too much imagination". Now at 7 years she is much happier although a rather serious little girl with some difficulty in making friends. The parents always try to answer her questions but were hard put to it when on her second birthday she asked the difference between atomic energy and ordinary energy saying that the latter "was the thing inside us that makes us able to work". Tested on Stanford Binet – her I.Q. was 152.

Duncan shows how a child subjected to many changes of environment can stand up to these if the marital situation is stable and the child is an "allrounder". Duncan's parents were both born in one of the Commonwealth countries and moved to another one for reasons of conscience when he was quite small. The father works for an international concern and Duncan who is just 11 years has had many changes of school. In one year he had five changes. When they arrived in England, he was placed at short notice in a very rigid Prep School and, for the first time, he was really bored and unhappy; at 9 years he had been tested and the psychologist had remarked that "he is an excellent reader with the vocabulary of a 15 year old he handles numbers with great facility, he is a mature, positive and well-adjusted youngster". Now he has been moved to another school and has settled well. He is not interested in organised games but prefers rowing, ju-jitsu, swimming and cycling. He walked actively at 1 year, said 5-6 word sentences at the same time but did not read until nearly 5 years.

Amanda talked early at 6 months – brush, comb and the name of the dog. At 1 year she wanted to know names of letters and learned them quickly, at 2 years 3 months she read the first Ladybird Books. She learned mostly from posters, shop windows and street names. She has always needed a lot of sleep; walked at 21 months; she was not interested in learning to dress herself; much prefers writing stories, reading, astronomy and looking for fossils. She would like to play with older children but is rebuffed by them and minds this.

John, now 8 years 3 months was tested at 7 years 10 months on latest revision of the Stanford Binet, his score was 13 years 10 months. The psychologist noted that he made immediate and friendly contact and quickly settled down. He showed his ability to think clearly by studying the folded paper cutting items before picking up his pencil and then scored at a 13 year old level; he thought for a few minutes about the item covering differences in abstract words and then gave the correct reply in a single sentence. He says he gets sums wrong and can't write very fast. It is interesting that he is left-handed. John was a bad sleeper when younger, now he takes books to bed. He never crawled but pulled himself up and walked at 13 months, and talked in sentences at about the same age. He is an active happy child but needs a great deal of overt affection from his mother.

These four children are four of the lucky ones, in each case the parents recognised that the child was doing some things in advance of others in his age group and they tried to answer questions and to co-operate with the school in meeting the child's educational needs.

Some parents however are completely bewildered by having a gifted child; they simply do not realise that because his intellectual, and usually his physical development are advanced, there may be a greater chance of a dichotomy between these and his emotional development. Like Amanda, a child can read very early and yet be unable to dress herself or tie her own shoe laces. This may be due to a variety of reasons. Sometimes not being able to do things is the only way of getting attention from a busy mother. At others, it is a sign that the child needs the parents to recognise that he is still a child and needs to feel "looked after" and cared for. A third group of children may be concentrating so hard on what they are thinking about at the time that they are oblivious to instructions to do something else which they consider less important. This intense absorption and length of concentration has been noticed by many working with gifted children; it is often seen very early when the ordinary toddler has a very short attention span. It does however require a great deal of patience on the part of the mother and there would seem to be a real need for parents' counselling sessions where information can be exchanged and guidance given, much in the way it is given at present to parents of mentally retarded and handicapped children. The fact that until two years ago there was no organisation in this country to which parents, teachers, psychologists and others interested in gifted children might belong, appears to show that we, as a nation, tend to play down the very able child. Parents say that when they tell their friends that Fred is starting to read at three they are either disbelieved or thought to be boasting and that when this has happened with monotonous regularity they cease to talk of the child's exploits and begin to wish that he "was just like everyone else".

Far from parents of the gifted thinking that their geese are

219

swans, they find him a rather uncomfortable child to have around; all children ask questions but these children ask more and deeper ones, they will not take no for an answer and yet some of them meet with unexpected difficulties. Marjori Fleming wrote in her journal at the age of eight, "I am now going to tell you about the horrible and wretched plaege that my multication gives me you can't conceive it – the most Devilish thing is 8 times 8 and 7 times 7 is what nature itselfe can't endure". Help from her parents and modern mathematics at school might have solved this particular problem. It is the climate created by the parents in the home that enables the gifted to thrive and meet the problems that confront all of them to some extent when they go to school or nursery class and find how few of the group share their interests. Of course not all gifted children have these difficulties but enough of them do, to make the education of gifted children an essential part of every teacher's training course with special emphasis in the courses for teachers at Nursery and Infant schools. Often the parents think that once the children go to school they will get the stimulus and understanding they need but sometimes, even to-day, teachers will insist on a child starting on the first of the Janet and John books disregarding the mother's rather diffident remark that John has in fact been reading for over a year. In Nursery Schools where the emphasis is quite rightly on play, there should be plenty of books, books on all subjects, books with good illustrations and well written texts. The sight of these will reassure both the gifted child and the parent and make it possible for both of them to accept sand and water as part of the growing up process.

There appear to be ages at which gifted children would seem to be at greatest risk, one of these is at five years when so many new experiences are crowding in on them, gifted children are often self-critical and at five their physical co-ordination is not equal to their need to reach a high standard, temper tantrums which they painfully learned to control may overtake them again much more violently and if these are not dealt with in an understanding way, both at home and at school, may persist right through to adolescence.

At seven some gifted children run into trouble, for by now most of the class are reading fluently and the non-readers are at an obvious disadvantage. Word blind gifted children do exist although controversy continues on the causes for this. In addition to their difficulty in reading many of them continue with the mirror writing common in young children and others use scrambled egg writing in which all the right letters appear in a word but in a meaningless order. Much more research needs to be done in this field, in 1968 we only have one clinic dealing with this problem. Psychologists and teachers need to meet regularly with the parents to discuss how best to help the child, the gifted child beset by this problem may be harmed for years by his feelings of failure and inferiority.

As the child progresses through Junior or Prep School it might be hoped that even the gifted would be catered for but in fact the two most vital and dangerous years for these children lie ahead – the years from nine to eleven.

During these two years gifted children may lose heart and become a casualty. It is now that he needs maximum help and encouragement, both at home and at school and if he does not get them, he reacts violently. Some become the clowns of the class and spend much time in the corridor or on treks to the Headmaster's study; others become apathetic and give up. An unwise remark by a busy teacher to the effect that Mark "always knows the answer and must give others a chance" may, if repeated, be the prime factor in a child's withdrawing from the situation and preferring to dream rather than work. A minority show maladjustment "within the meaning of the act" – bedwetting, stealing, as opposed to normal pilfering, truanting and behaviour disorders of all kinds. These symptoms are of course shown by disturbed children with normal or subnormal intelligence but when a gifted child has to be referred to the Clinic because he is suffering from boredom, it is surely time to change the climate in the school. Among the Juvenile Delinquents of this age we shall also find some of the gifted.

Let us see to it that during the Seventies no child prefers winter to summer because he shoves a book under his sweater to read in the corridor when he has been turned out of the class room, or after lengthy and expensive investigations a child has to be sent to a school for "High I.Q. Maladjusted Children" because his Junior school, whether State or Independent was not able to provide the stimulus he needed.

What then are we to do for the Gifted? Their main need seems to be for education in depth at all ages, the recognition of their changing interests and their need for the opportunity to meet each other. Comprehensive schools are setting up remedial classes for slow learners – what about opportunity classes for the gifted? In these they would be with their peer group for a few hours a week and with children of their chronological age group the rest of the time, for they must learn to get along with the rest of us. To a College of Education a group of forty children from four Junior schools in the neighbourhood are brought for one afternoon a week. They can be stretched in their chosen subjects and their Headmasters report that they stimulate project work in their own classes. Students from the College also benefit; while one can acknowledge that a nine year old is more intelligent than oneself, it does not mean that one cannot teach him. One County has conducted a pilot survey into the facilities for the gifted in its Junior and Secondary schools. In the Seventies these surveys must be extended.

Research is badly needed; we do not even know how many gifted children we have. Professor Tempest from the University of Liverpool has set up an experimental class of gifted children within a local Primary school; by the early Seventies some of his results will be available but sociological research is desperately needed into the families of the gifted. This would throw new light onto the theory of Heredity Genius as Galton called it almost one hundred years ago, and maybe give us some clues as to why in this egalitarian age parents feel almost as threatened by having a bright child as a dull one.

Special schools for the gifted certainly do *not* seem to be called for, they have been tried both in America and Russia but the results so far do not look very promising. For two specialist groups, however, schools do seem needed; these are for young musicians especially the string players and for the child who is fitted and eager to take up dancing seriously. However, here it is worth noting that all the children who enter the Royal Ballet School would, as things stand at present, be able to benefit from a Grammar School education and the same would seem to hold true for those at the Yehudi Menuhin School, where the choice sometimes lies between the concert platform and a scholarship to a famous Public School.

The 1944 Act does not need amendment to deal with the gifted. They, like all other children in the country, are entitled to education according to "age, ability and aptitude". Youth Services will give a chance to the socially gifted and, for some of the academically able, Prep Schools are more than willing to offer places. This was stated once again at the I.A.P.S. Conference in 1967 and, while looking to the future, let us remember schools like Winchester, where for five hundred years College Men have lived in an almost closed community although in fact they are taught in mixed ability forms. Perhaps it is the reading, eating and making gallons of coffee together that creates the climate in which future Prime Ministers are bred. We must not dismiss the experience of schools like this when we are planning for the future.

It is the loneliness of the gifted that is sometimes forgotten. In Nursery and Infant school a gifted child would be extremely lucky to find another like himself simply owing to the small number of children involved and the fact that children in these schools are drawn from a small area near to the school in order to avoid traveling for children and parents. This means of course that in the "twilight zones", where Nursery Schools are often non-existent and the Infant schools overcrowded, the gifted child from a poorly housed and possible immigrant family has even more chance of being missed than in more prosperous areas.

Loneliness is only one of the factors in underachievement, the most common "illness" afflicting the gifted like many other conditions, it can flare up into an acute stage or it can have a long insidious onset and affect the whole personality. Lack of effort is often the cause at the beginning of his school life; things came easily, he was not challenged or extended and no pattern of hard work was laid down. Work habits are terribly important for gifted children otherwise when they change schools they are not flexible enough to make the necessary effort, or they do not realise that a different kind of thinking is required, like the child who, because he is bright, passes ten "O" level subjects at 14 years, only to find that he is unable to cope with the change to "A" level work which demands the beginning of a scholarly approach.

One other important factor in under-achievement is the child's wish to "cash in" for acceptance by the group. We all have this need for acceptance and, because in some schools, ability in games has been given more acclamation than achievement in work, the gifted child will play down his abilities to blend with the landscape.

At Junior schools it is not enough to have books in the library; there should also be someone there who can teach the children how to find the facts they require. In fact, learning to "read in" a book is one of the most useful things any child can acquire, but it needs skill on the part of the person who is giving the guidance. As well as books, all modern teaching aids are essential. The fact that science is now starting earlier sets some of these children "alight" – how much better actually to be doing a thing than just reading about it.

Thought must be given the best way of handling the gifted within the school structure, sets would seem to be better than rigid streaming and fluid grouping better than both of them. For these children have need of their peer group both in school and socially to show them that they are not alone. This cross fertilisation is useful too in opening up new interests, for it is of vital importance that these children do not specialise too soon, because at 10 or 11 years a child is interested in star-gazing, it does not mean that he is going to be the next Astronomer Royal. They have need of education in width as well as in depth and most of all, of course, the need for first-class teaching. Surely it is not too much to ask that as in the Colleges of Education, in the Seventies young teachers be trained to recognise the gifted and that this same training be given to graduate teachers at the Institutes of Education.

When talking with experienced teachers, most of them can remember having at least one or two of these children in their classes and what a pleasure and privilege it was to teach them. If we are to avoid exploitation, even unconscious exploitation, by parents and teachers, training must be given at College level and backed up by refresher courses and conferences. Gifted children need exposure to excellence: this holds good with teaching materials but above all to teaching. Of course not many of the teachers of the gifted will themselves be of this calibre but some of them will be and perhaps the Seventies will see further training for some of them.

At present not enough thought is being given to this subject, like other social problems it is going by default. We need to realise that the gifted have problems, that many of them cannot "get by" without our help although they are much better endowed than we are. We do not know enough about them or indeed:

> "...Who fished the murex up
> What porridge had John Keats."

In Russia they are called "Eagles", in France "Bien doué", in Germany William Stern called them "Gutbegabte" and in America Lita Hollingworth "Prodigious Children"; here we call them Gifted, but whatever name they go by let us see to it that in the Seventies this small group of children are given the help and understanding of which they so desperately stand in need so that they can reach their true potential and make their contribution to the future.

EDUCATIONAL BROADCASTING

*

RICHMOND POSTGATE

In his contribution Kenneth Adam outlined the advantages of making educational broadcasting a part of general broadcasting, and of broadcasting being a public service. I would wish to apply these general ideas to the narrower terms of my theme, which is the contribution of educational broadcasting (in a strict sense) to the educational system as others foresee it becoming.

I take it as a datum that educational broadcasting must be a public service provided by a broadcasting organisation. From this it follows that the providing body must follow educational policies in harmony with those of the educational bodies. In this country the B.B.C. obtains this guidance through two Councils – the School Broadcasting Council and the Further Education Advisory Council. The composition, powers and working methods of these bodies have been gradually evolved to attain a somewhat difficult dual objective – that, on the one hand, the control of educational policy rests with the educational world and, on the other, that the B.B.C. staff have the measure of professional freedom and initiative that will result in the broadcasting media being used to their full extent. It would take too much space to describe the minutiae of the arrangements governing these relationships; nor is it yet possible to outline the third relationship now to be settled – that between the B.B.C. and the Authority which will direct the Open University. My point is that a part of our inheritance is the posession of guidance mechanisms that have been tested and elaborated over many years and are effective and flexible. This, in my belief, applies equally to the I.T.A.

The second element of our inheritance is one that produces a

225

high production unit cost per broadcast and an extremely low price per consumer. The average cost per hour of originating educational broadcasting is, for school radio £1,000; and for school television £8,500. This cost relates to new broadcasts as opposed to repeats and covers all overheads except plant depreciation. It provides payment at professional rates for all contributions and the various internal budgets allow a great measure of decentralised discretion and initiative. The total volume of the B.B.C. undertaking – with about 180 professionally qualified staff – is large enough to carry a big specialist element. These factors should – and I hope generally do – ensure a high-quality product, accurately aimed at the right educational targets, and amply backed up by written and other material to make it easy to use well.

In this compact densely populated country very few people are out of the reach of the broadcast services. Educational institutions may need to spend something extra on the publications accompanying broadcasts. But the whole service is extremely cheap. The B.B.C. expenditure upon educational broadcasting annually is something over £3 million, out of a total income of £72 million. The L.E.A.s, out of a total budget on text books, etc., of £50 million, spend about £½ million on educational broadcasting publications. No one could call these allocations excessive relative to the total expenditure on these organisations; the L.E.A. expenditure, even when the cost of receiving equipment is added is a fleabite. If we express the sum of these two figures as a cost per pupil actually using a broadcast, the resulting figures are, for school radio 0.012 pence and, for school television 0.143 pence. The latter figure is likely to drop in a few years when television receivers are in all schools instead of about a half as at present, and when on-site video-recording becomes economical and permissible.

A quality product produced by a large professional team by a guidance system gearing it effectively to educational needs, universally available at a minute cost per user – this is our inheritance. One has to go abroad to appreciate how strong a foundation this provides for the future. In the U.S.A. for instance, the richest country in the world, nearly all educational broadcasting is run on a shoe-string and by general testimony its output is usually mediocre. In many developing countries in which full recognition is given to educational broadcasting as an essential item in the educational system, it is the plaything of politicians and its resources subject to their favour. The instances in which stable and adequate resources can be found alongside professional freedom and effective educational guidance are pretty rare.

Yet this advantage we in this country possess is at present very incompletely exploited. On the broadcasting side the fact that the B.B.C. operates two media should be more fully reflected in integrated co-ordinated planning using each to its best advantage and combining the two when desirable. We have not yet outgrown the separatism between radio and television which accompanied the emancipation of television from radio; though this is coming now that all homes and an increasing number of schools possess both radio and television receivers. At the receiving-end one can only describe as patchy the acceptance of educational broadcasting as an important educational agent among teachers, chief officers, committee members and training institutions. By no means all authorities have adopted supply and maintenance policies for receivers, etc. that would be in force if educational broadcasting were really valued – though the position is improving. By no means all teacher-training institutions acquaint their students adequately with what they will find available or how to use it effectively – though this is perhaps improving. By no means all heads make it easy for their staff to use the service, nor are the Governmental publications or the H.M. Inspectorate's attitude always encouraging or informed.[1] In short, as many from abroad have noted, while the mechanisms of educational guidance work and the actual service is of a generally admired standard, the scale and skill of its use are still disappointing. Utilisation is a major headache.

Turning to the immediate future, educational broadcasting is faced with a series of challenges and opportunities quite unprecedented in its history: for, just as almost every change in thought and social life bears upon general broadcasting, all the growing points described by other contributors to this book influence and may in twin be influenced by educational broadcasting.

First are the commitments arising from Government decision. The raising of the compulsory leaving age in 1970 and its widespread voluntary anticipation require a five-year instead of a four-year course for students who will be young adults at its end. The devising during a period of increasing teacher-shortage, of suitable content, method and approaches is a problem still unsolved, as is the dissemination among the profession of successful solutions. Here is a chance for broadcasting to help at the school and adult level for the students and their teachers. The Industrial Training Act, which requires continuing education and training

227

and re-education and re-training throughout the working life of the entire population raises educational problems of an entirely new scale and order and urgency. The prime impact of this Act is upon two groups – the Further Education system which must be greatly expanded, and the many undertakings inside factories and firms which will have to cater for the training and retraining of their employees. The sums which the Training Boards will handle when they are fully operational are very large. It is speculatively estimated that the twenty Boards already in existence can together command about £500 million a year. The second group is in the greatest difficulty because their immediate problem is the recruitment and training of Training Officers to train the instructors of the students; but both groups suffer from the familiar disabilities of the last-comer in facilities, staff and status (Last come, worst served). That they could use the material that educational broadcasting has learnt to provide is obvious, though the specialised nature of the requirement means that local transmission systems, the sale of film and tape and hire from libraries will be necessary in addition to national transmissions. Thirdly, there is the Open University of which the local main load of the broadcasting component will fall upon the B.B.C. initially. The University is due to start in 1970 and will form the largest single increase yet falling upon educational broadcasting. It will involve the creation of courses composed of reading and private study, correspondence work, local laboratory work and seminars, tied in closely with the broadcasting component. It will also, as mentioned before, involve the creation of a third relationship between the B.B.C. and the body responsible for educational guidance i.e. the University Authority.

All in all, so much new has never yet been asked of educational broadcasting. Its capacity to respond adequately will be the main test of the Seventies.

These developments will take place during a period of continuous and fundamental reconsideration of the objectives, content and methods of learning and teaching now proceeding in many places – such as the Nuffield Foundation, the Schools Council, the centres studying programmed learning and the various research units in Universities. It is important that these enquiries now commonly pass beyond the strictly educational into the sociological field. Educational broadcasting, though it is inevitably analytical and conscious of what it is attempting and why, must increasingly take account of these developments and seek to be organisationally associated with many of them. Reciprocally, these agencies are coming to realise that educational broadcasting, both at school and adult level, is a major agent in reporting and illustrating their conclusions to the educational public. In France research and its popularisation are achieved by the Ministry itself transmitting over the national broadcasting system. In this country the process seems likely to take place through a participant partnership, the B.B.C. being involved in educational study-groups helping to identify the opportunities for broadcasting, which it then develops into broadcasting proposals and eventually transmits. I foresee this pattern of relationships, in which innovation and research are closely linked, becoming increasingly common in the Seventies. I would hope that it will be applied to the Open University project. If this were done we should, as a country, emerge with something genuinely new, that has taken from the start full account of present knowledge of learning processes and self-tuition, and of the personal and social situation of the adult students as well as of the claims of the subject-matter. Radio is as necessary a component as television, indeed probably in bulk more important; so also is the need to exploit the strong points of network broadcasting, namely that talent and material can be drawn from all over the kingdom and, indeed, from all over the world.

Then there are the remarkable advantages and extensions primarily dependent upon improved technology – the establishment of intra-mural and municipal systems of radio and television and their mutual links and connections with the national systems. Briefly, as many will know, the systems are at three levels: University, such as Glasgow, Leeds and Sussex; municipal, such as London; Glasgow and Plymouth; and in colleges of education, at present in about a dozen places but expected to be about 60 in the early Seventies. The rate of proliferation will no doubt be regulated principally by finance; but the educational significance of these developments is surely very great indeed and bound eventually to affect the educational system as a whole and the national broadcasting provision profoundly, For, first, the new installations will carry educational broadcasting to new audiences offering them services which the networks could never provide. The Glasgow City system is using television to introduce a new secondary mathematics syllabus to its schools with a degree of participation by teachers which a national network could not attempt. Secondly, it is possible for small-scale systems to mount research-linked projects calling for matching groups. The organisational problems which would face the networks if they attempted this would be insuperable. One hopes that the small-scale system will exploit this advantage to the full for the benefit of all. Thirdly, a great range of teachers and lecturers will become personally involved in the creation and evaluation of broadcast material. As Socrates suggested, it is by harping that one becomes a harpist. It is also by harping that one becomes aware of what the harp can and cannot do. At the centre of the utilisation problem I mentioned earlier is the fact that too few people really know from personal experience what educational broadcasting, on whatever transmission scale, can and cannot do and how to make the best use of it. An enlarged and informed body of such people is a first requirement in remedying this situation. There are those who believe that small-scale systems will eventually kill the network provision. I differ from this view. I believe that unless we are all extremely foolish, the two will support each other, and that the role of network broadcasting, stemming from what I have called our inheritance, will provide the whole country with high-grade standard-setting material over the whole range of the educational system at a lower cost per user than any other system can provide.

Last among the advances attributable primarily to technological advance is the capacity to record broadcast material in permanent form for re-transmission and distribution by gift, sale and hire. We now have cheap efficient and easy-to-handle audio tape-recorders. We shall soon have similar video-recorders. And we pretty certainly shall have other devices in cassette or other form which will drastically reduce the manufacturing cost of putting educational material into permanent and convenient form that requires no manipulative skill from the user. Allied to these developments are others involving massive storage and retrieval systems based on computers. I confess to being too ignorant to forecast where these developments will take the ordinary schools and institutions of this country, or at what rate. Technology seems to take amazing leaps at times, but there can also be extraordinary delays between the invention and its becoming universally available. Nevertheless, it seems impossible that any form of publication which involves the creation of large numbers of articles whether they be films or tapes, can ever be as cheap a method of disseminating material as broadcasting it. In the educational sphere, it is possible that broadcasting may become the first *mode* of publication, a kind of universal preview, the best of which in its original or adapted form will be converted to other modes

230

of publication.

So far as the B.B.C. is immediately concerned, we are aware of two things. First, that our constitutional task is to broadcast, and that all other activities are subordinate to that. Secondly, that these developments have opened up very considerable opportunities for the extended use of the broadcast material by publication in permanent form. As an institution we have the advantage that we are already operating in all the essential fields – radio, television (which includes film-making); film strip and film loop; letterpress and illustrations; and what might be comprehensively called "kits" and that all of these stem from the broadcasting operation. Moreover, as a consequence of our inheritance, we have a tradition of "high-grade software" and a large home-market to build upon. In 1966-7 B.B.C. educational publications numbered 442 and the distribution topped 14 million. In the same year we disposed of 31,350 film strips and 813 16 m.m. copies of educational programmes. All this was freely bought by people spending at their own choice. None of it was at the expense of the licence income, and all the school publications were on a non-profit-making basis. Unless the overall economic situation worsens significantly I would be disappointed if these figures do not rise steadily in the Seventies.

I hope that from this rapid review of the past and the present may have emerged a general impression of many new necessities to add to the old and many new devices and extensions to the ways of meeting them. As the component elements are likely to develop continuously over the next ten years at differing and unpredictable rates the resultant situation is likely to be one in which appropriate solutions must be expected to change. We should also expect a fair stream of enthusiastic advocacy for particular ideas and schemes on the part of their originators. One may describe this as creative chaos, axe-grinding, or necessary promotion as one's mood is; but it is probably inevitable and in the long run healthy if kept within bounds. Not all the ideas will be good ones. On the other hand they are all being offered to a profession naturally – and rightly – predisposed to preserving what is good in our cultural inheritance and devoted to individual and personal decision-making; and working in a system that favours stability rather than change. Moreover, most of the new solutions are radical in the sense that they cut at the idea of teaching being a face-to-face relationship between a group of 30 or 40 pupils in a sealed box and a single, sovereign adult, and resemble modern manufacture in that they are only fully effective and economically

231

justified if they attain a large following that willingly participates in the roles assigned to the users by the scheme. The need for intelligent, informed and willing co-operation between the users and the providers is paramount, both in local and national schemes. It is easier to achieve in the former.

If this picture is broadly true, it seems to me that a number of conclusions follow. First, we need to explore and display the new ideas through plenty of trials and pilot schemes using the new media, singly or in combination with each other and with the established methods of teaching. The B.B.C. has begun to make a contribution in this field by trial combinations of broadcasting with correspondence work, by using radio with classroom instruction planned on programmed learning lines and so forth. More is to come. Secondly, these experiments should be observed and reported on to a greater extent than at present by professionally competent analysts. Further, it must be accepted that reports in the language acceptable to such analysts is not publication in any real sense. The gist and main conclusions should be made known in language which the ordinary teacher can absorb and utilise. I believe that this long-standing difficulty may be one to which the Foundations might devote attention. Just as the responsibility for organising and financing research is not one which can be reasonably landed upon any single organisation, but must be shared between Government, Universities, L.E.A.s and bodies like the B.B.C., so the translation of academic research into material usable by the general practitioners is something which at present, being nobody's baby, falls between several stools.

Thirdly, we must all, but especially the providers, do as much as our preoccupations permit to become fully aware of the full range of development in thought and technology of the whole educational picture. But keeping abreast in any real sense is now a full-time job; we therefore need help. I imagine the provision of this help will be one of the most important services that the new National Council for Educational Technology, established by Anthony Crosland, when Secretary of State for Education, can provide.

In this essay, I have written principally about likely changes and innovations. But I would not like to leave an over-emphasis upon the avant garde, spear-heading function of educational broadcasting, or suggest that it should cater principally for those of above-average adventurousness or ability. Traditionally the B.B.C. as a public service has aimed at the whole baggage-train and its services have probably been most valuable to those whose professional qualifications and environmental situation is average or below. I am convinced that this should not be lost sight of, and that the balance between giving help to people in the way in which they want it is as important as providing material which will encourage them to move away from what they are doing to something better. In order to illustrate what I mean may I list somewhat baldly what I feel are the six principal priority tasks to which the B.B.C. should pay particular attention over the next few years.

First, as the quickest and cheapest way of assisting the in-service training of teachers in new content, methods and apparatus of subjects undergoing substantial change, it would provide series which outline to teachers the new possibilities, and series for class-use which apply them.

Second, as a proved means of assisting teachers who are under-qualified or in unfavourable environmental surroundings it should provide series for this purpose, very amply supported by support literature and other material.

Thirdly, it should provide material for the solitary student outside the range of institutional education.

Fourthly, it should display advances in technology and modern practice in the broad field of industry and commerce and take particular steps to deepen the impact of these programmes by securing the distribution of the programmes in permanent form.

Fifthly, it should make extra provision for the two groups now coming under the influence of institutional provision i.e. the fifth year at the secondary stage, and those affected by the Industrial Training Act.

Sixthly, it should make a major effort in support of the Open University to make it not only an extension of education for adults, but an influence bearing upon the quality of Higher Education as a whole.

NOTES

1 Between 1959 and 1967, with only one or two exceptions, the D.E.S. publications (Reports on Education, Pamphlets and Trend) have either totally ignored the contribution which school and further education broadcasting are making to education (even when this constitutes a major part of the teaching and gives the strongest lead available in the development

of the subject, as in music), or they make references so marginal, out-of-date, and ill-informed as to give a misleading impression of what is actually happening in the schools.

A recent publication by H.M.S.O., commissioned by the D.E.S., and written by a recently retired H.M.I. (a chief inspector), is not uncharasteristic. "Inside the Primary School" mentions television and radio only once, and then only in connection with programmed learning.

BOOKS & NEWSPAPERS

*

WALTER JAMES

Even in this particular time, change moves rather slower in fact than we often seem to be promised. Nothing cries out more loudly for technological revolution than the newspaper industry, which is slowly suffocating under the weight of outmoded plant and working practices, but the new forms of cheaper production are slow in development, and even slower in gaining acceptance by the printing unions. I view therefore with some scepticism the still more distant promise of the newspaper that arrives electronically by the side of your bed. These wonders are no longer difficult to perform. They merely require a large outlay of capital. The speed of technological development when backed without stint by government can be seen in the American and Russian progress towards putting a man on the moon. If half the money spent on that went to driving information retrieval ahead, we should all doubtless be sitting in our homes by screens linked to the computer in the public library. No longer would we need to thumb through successive volumes to find the facts we were after. Instead we should wire through our query to the machine which in a bare few seconds would flick as it were through the pages of a million volumes, find what we wanted, and produce it on our domestic screen. Some talk already as though in this the doom of encyclopaedias may be read. It is all perfectly feasible; indeed working models exist. The difficulty lies in persuading people to invest enough money to turn remarkable experiments into everyday practice. Old fashioned encyclopaedias would seem to me to be safe for a long time yet.

What is already upon us in educational publication is a grand expansion of the ways of learning which appears to threaten the

235

supremacy of the book. There is of course a vast amount of exaggeration in discussions of what is happening. People speak sometimes as though this were the great age of visual aids to learning. Actually the medieval world relied far more upon the visual than we shall ever do. If we spend hours before television sets for entertainment, they relied largely upon images for an understanding of the deeper purposes of life. The medieval teacher taught medieval man, who in general could not read, from carving, fresco, and stained glass.

All the same, the modern facility of illustration must affect books, especially those supplying factual information, as distinct from imaginative literature. Books by themselves, unsupported, are no longer an adequate presentation of their subject. Let us take for example the biography of a modern statesman. Clearly the reader would like to know more about the human subject than the book by itself can tell. We shall never recapture the tones in which the elder Pitt addressed the House of Commons or catch the flash of that imperious eye. We depend upon verbal descriptions or, where one exists, upon a static sketch. Thus we are gravely limited, for no description of a great orator can tell us anything like as much as the sight and sound of him. There is no longer need for the biography of a modern politician to suffer from these limitations. In fact, if publishers are enterprising, one would expect to see over the next decade a growing practice of supplying with books cassettes of film and accompanying tape. Such records of the subject of a biography supply answers to natural questions which words alone cannot resolve. How did he walk? What was his smile? If a man is said to have had great charm, like Disraeli, or to have had extraordinary love affairs, like Dilke, the reader's instinct is to want to see the man for himself. Now for any great man of our own day this can be arranged. One day a political biography that does not supply a short selection of films of its subject will be considered a pretty lame production.

The call for a full use of modern means of illustration by book publishers is even more obvious in some other directions. There are books, for instance, which describe the movements of the ballet. It is astonishing to think that in these days books can be brought out on such topics without any accompanying illustration, now so easy to provide. Of course, books about the ballet are filled with still photographs, and to those who have watched ballet these doubtless convey something. But the essence of the whole art is movement and when this can be illustrated it is absurd to leave it out.

The accompaniment of books with film fits at present more naturally into school than into the ordinary home. We should expect to see increasing use made of these teaching kits – combination of books, film, recording, etc. – which are already well on their way. Schools possess machines for presenting the illustrative material – film projectors, record pick-ups, and so on.

Homes are not at present all so provided and if books in the future are to be published with cassettes of film for illustration everyone who reads books will need some simple and economical means of reproduction. Standardization and ubiquity of equipment will be important, as with the spread in hotels and private homes of plugs for electric razors.

While accompanying film will greatly enhance the value of some books, it will not be needed for imaginative literature. *War and Peace* or *David Copperfield,* of which films have been made, can stand on their own feet as before. The reader does not ask to hear Barkis's voice or see the light in the eyes of the young Natasha; he makes them up for himself. Though he may go to the cinema and see what someone else's imagination makes of these stories, his own will remain sufficient for him. It is books that touch on reality which demand illustration by modern means.

Perhaps it is worth issuing a caveat for which the wise teacher may already have seen the necessity. A few feet of film will indicate far more of a man's character than the still photograph, but it is still dangerously selective. It may come to dominate one's imaginative picture of the subject more than mere words could cause, and thus gravely mislead. One thinks of an actual statesman whose public appeal, based on a handsome presence, was already great, though what struck those who had to work with him most were the wild and terrifying rages into which he regularly fell. In any cassette of film prepared for such a man, one would find the presence, but not the rages. History itself, however, is filled with their difficulties of selection. They would not seem to justify denying the simple human wishes to hear and see its chief personages as is now possible.

More specifically in school, one of the questions to be determined in the nest few years is how far programmed learning, in book form or on machines, will supplant the present textbooks or even present ways of teaching. A programme is a logically sequenced series of small items of information which, when a machine is used, are set out in frames. The student works his way through the frames, and is required to respond to questions, his answers being confirmed or corrected by the succeeding frame. So, all by himself, he learns.

Up to now in Britain programmed instruction has been used most successfully in the armed services and in industrial training. This is significant, for what is needed in both these instances is a quick and efficient mastery of certain facts and processes. The objectives are entirely simple and clear. But the teachers' aim in a school cannot be as narrowly and precisely defined as an army instructor's in a weapons course. The imparting of factual knowledge is only part of the teacher's aim in school and thus an over reliance on programmed learning would be limiting. The teacher, whatever subject he is taking, is concerned with the whole development of child's mind, and in this the fixed lines of a programmed course are constrictive.

A study of carefully built programmes may well improve the efficiency of text book writers. They should confine their attention to programmes that have been well tested and validated before being put on the market, so that their effectiveness with a known percentage of the students for whom they were designed is assured. But in my view the programme is unlikely to replace in school text books which are themselves improving all the time. The logical completeness of the programme, although an advantage in one line of learning, is a weakness in another. Children in all material presented to them have to learn what to select and what to discard, what to remember and what to forget. It seems to me that even the imperfections of the text book, its occasional diffuseness or excess of information, support the slow learning of this necessary power better than the efficient logic of the programme. In general, it is not factual information that education should purvey so much as the art of finding out. Just because everything in a programme is given, it is not an ideal exercise for the mind.

All the same, it has a place in schools, if a smaller place than its enthusiasts would expect. I always remember my first and only encounter with trigonometry. I never mastered the first steps and the class went ahead, leaving me behind at the starting post. Nowadays I could be put through those first principles on a programme over and over again until I had understood them. It is a good device for making sure that a difficult section of any course has been understood. When pupils are beginning on a new subject, it helps in bringing all of them up to the level of basic knowledge required. It can bring a pupil who joins a class late up to the level reached by his fellows. Programmed learning has a place in remedial work, and in revision courses. It promises to be most useful in the sciences and mathematics, which form the subject matter of nearly two-thirds of all programmes so far published. But I doubt whether its educational limitation will ever let it take the place of the book.

The language laboratory, of course, is going to spread, and is bound to influence publication. At the time of writing there are about 1000–1300 in use in the United Kingdom, and one would like to think that by 1980 there will be at least one in every secondary school. Doubtless this is too sanguine – finance prevents our moving as fast as we should – but the language laboratory should eventually end for ever the feeble performance of our people in speaking foreign languages. It should bring about a more equal balance between the spoken and the written word in language learning. The books that go with the language laboratories are more likely to be guides for the teacher than text books for the pupil. But clearly learning to speak the language still leaves much about it unexplained. There will be as much need for text books as now, though they are going in future to be written with the existence of the language laboratory in mind. Pupils must write the language as well as speak it, they must cover much of the literature. One can be enormously grateful for the support the electronic advance will give to teaching, without rashly supposing that technology will one day oust the book.

I hope readers will forgive if I spend a perhaps disproportionate amount of space in this chapter on educational newspapers and magazines. It is because one of them has been my main business in life. This is the only excuse, for nothing suggests to me that in the next ten years they will greatly change. In that short space of time, any technological advance in production is unlikely to extend beyond the national chains. Even colour will remain too expensive to feature much in educational journals.

Still their own newspapers and magazines are important to teachers. Most of them will teach in a particular corner, but one corner leads into another, and teachers need to see the world of education as a whole and to follow the developing relationships of their own corner to the rest. They want news of what is afoot and comment on the news to provoke discussion and argument. They want summaries of the latest research. Ideally, they will best be served by independent journals, untied to any association or interest. Most teachers belong to professional associations and most associations have a publication which they hope their members will read. Keener teachers in a particular subject will probably belong to an association devoted to its concerns and they too will wish to subscribe to its journal.

But journals run by associations, necessary though they are to the association's life, suffer from the connection. Associations rightly have policies and the editors of their journals must accept these policies ready made. This makes for dullness. The members of an association know its policies and however much they may approve of them their constant reiteration in its journal removes the element of novelty and surprise. Further, the associational tie has a stultifying effect on the journal as a natural organism. We have only to consider how great newspapers and journals of opinion have operated. None of them to my knowledge has been run by an executive committee. All of them have been the creation of good editors, who chose good staffs, and had an understanding of their readership. The policy, the attitude, of a newspaper is best formed by one man. It is however totally wrong to suppose that a newspaper can be successful by one man imposing his prejudices and idiosyncrasies on his staff and his readers. This is to misunderstand the character of the editorial function. An editor and his staff are in one sense the mouthpiece of an undefined community. They are intensely aware of the community of readers, which expresses itself through a stream of communications as well as by rarer but frequent personal contact, and are willingly open to its influence. They are not servile to this influence but respectful of it. At one moment the editor will seek to guide, at another he will follow. Editors and staffs need to be keenly sensitive to opinion and feeling in the sphere in which they publish. They lead opinion, and in turn are led by opinion. There should be a two-way traffic between a journal's staff and its readers. This will be reflected in the journal's leading articles and other statements of editorial opinion; it will also be recognized in the general attitude of the paper, in its selection and presentation of the news. But in these sides of the paper, the prime movers are the editor and his staff, even though they are aware all the time of their readership. This readership, of course, is extremely mixed in its opinions and experience; it will include many who disagree with the paper's line, but find the disagreement stimulating.

Few fields of human activity are more filled with clashes of view and constant controversy than education. It is the duty of all newspapers, but particularly of an educational newspaper, to give a faithful representation of this conflict of ideas. It has complete freedom to express its own views; it should allow its readers no less. Readers grow to trust a newspaper when they see that it will print any argument or compilation of facts, in articles or letters to editor, that is set out intelligently, no matter how hostile the content may be to the newspapers own opinions – or, what is perhaps more to the point, to the fashionable trends of the day.

The source of a newspaper's strength is its readers. Its main duty lies to its ordinary readers, not to government, or to people in high places, or even to those who are chosen by educationists and teachers to lead them in other contexts. People often grow dissatisfied with those set over them, even when they themselves have elected them, and are glad when their newspapers express that dissatisfaction. A newspaper's proper target is power and those who wield it. It seems to me that it is in criticism that a newspaper makes its chief contribution to society.

If there is one danger in Britain to the press today, particularly the quality press, it is an obsession with the power centres in London. There is an enormous fascination with government – understandable enough perhaps in an ever more centralized and planned society. Journalists hang about Ministers for their lightest word and dash back to the office to write it down. Discussion of the various alternatives before public policy is endless in the newspapers. At times it seems that journalism has almost become an appendage of the central machine, its public relations department, if you like, and strangely this can be true of papers that are opposed to the government of the day.

Because its main business is to give the news, a paper must certainly present to the people a complete picture of government policy with the public explanations and defences of it made by Ministers. Someone called newspapers the agenda sheets of democracy, and this is true. One part of the newspaper's role is to inform the public thoroughly of the government's intentions. But this is only one part – the down side of the escalator, as it were. The other side of the newspaper's role is to send up to government the reactions and criticisms of ordinary people and of persons outside the government circles. A newspaper has the role of representing its readership to government. Governments are rarely loved by the governed, and that is why sound newspapers will criticize more than praise the powers that be. Ministers should rarely enjoy a good press and ought not to resent this. They ought to be grateful

241

for a clear picture day by day of where the shoe they are trying to fit pinches. It is no part of the newspapers' job to assist the smooth exercise of government. They belong to the governed, from whom they draw their living. In a dictatorship the newspapers are the propaganda sheets of the men in control. In a democracy, their role is reversed; taken all together, they should tell government what the people think and want.

This may seem to have taken us rather far from educational journals, but all newspapers are of one family and share the same basic function. Education is as much political as any other subject. Just because it is an activity unproductive of taxable wealth and instead is dependent on government finance, those engaged in it may be tempted to be more regardful of authority than others. There is a greater reason then for its journals to be critical.

Journalists serving them have the same need as others to realize the reserve that should be maintained between them and the organs and personalities of government. It never did any journalist good to consort overmuch with Ministers or Civil Servants. If he becomes too close a friend of Ministers he is apt to let their interests bulk larger than his readers'. Some say that it is perfectly easy to dine with politicians one day and tear them to shreds the next. Personally, I believe that friendship tends to blur the eyes of judgment. Further, a friendliness with politicians can lead journalists onto the stage of government or at least into its wings, where they have no right to be. Ministers and journalists serve the same public in quite different ways, and a certain tension between them, a mutual suspicion, indicates that the relationship between them is healthy.

It was the tragedy of that great editor, Geoffrey Dawson, who directed *The Times* in the appeasement years, that his personal friendship with leading politicians played a large part in his espousal of the policy that led to Munich. If he had kept to his office like Barnes, who made *The Times* in the early nineteenth century, he might have retained a clearer judgment. As it was, his delight in public life and his political friendships were his undoing. An editor, in my view, is wise to use his staff as his means of access to Ministers. They too should maintain reserve – not easy, for most of us find it rather elevating to hobnob with the men of power. In public and in private a Minister is concerned to advance his policies; he will extol their merits and cloak their drawbacks. He will drop titbits of information, laced with secret gossip, to build up a little group of journalist friends. They should always remember, whatever their own political sympathies, that they are not working for him, but for the people who put him in power and others who did not want to see him in power at all. I once apologized to a Minister, an old acquaintance, for not having looked him up since he took office. He received it in good part. "You're quite right, of course", he said, "my only object with journalists is to brainwash them." It would be wrong to read something prejudicial to Ministers into his answer. Ministers have a duty to seek to use the Press, and any other means of persuasion, to forward their policies and strengthen the hold of their government.

C. P. Scott, of the *Manchester Guardian,* would never accept a peerage, and it was once a rule of *The Times* that no one while on the staff should accept an honour or award. Such high principled aloofness expressed very well the right attitude to government for the press to take.

Britain is fortunate in her educational press, for the range of its coverage has no counterpart elsewhere. To take only my own paper, *The Times Educational Supplement,* even America has nothing like it. Apart from a few associational journals and reviews, none of which pretend to be an educational newspaper, American teachers are poorly provided. If one asks why Britain is so well off, the answer lies in the practice of British local education authorities in advertising their jobs. The classified advertisement provides the basic livelihood of specialist journals. If it keeps journals alive, it also allows teachers a remarkable freedom. In France, for example, if a teacher in Lille wants to teach in Caen, he writes to the department of Calvados and puts his name on a list. Much later, when his name has worked up the list, he may be offered a job. This is different from the right the teacher has in England to see the whole range of jobs on offer throughout the country and to try for any one of them at any time. If the British teacher lost this right, he would be seriously diminished.

Clearly, the advertisement of school teaching jobs costs public money. But it fits in with the idea of the school as a community, for it allows a head to choose the man or woman who seems to suit his particular school best. As I have said, the system of advertising provides support for educational journals. If local education authorities were to concentrate all their job advertising in one journal, this would rapidly achieve a monopoly by the extinction of all the others. In educational journalism, as in national, several voices are more stimulating than one. This is a question which local education authorities should hold before them in the next decade, for they do in a measure determine the range and quality of educational journalism in Britain.

I should not be doing my duty by educational journalism in the next decade if I did not set down my ideas about recruitment. As I see it, recruitment to educational journalism is recruitment to the profession in general, for a young man or woman who joins an educational paper in his twenties will not want to stay there forever. Journalism is an extremely difficult art and recruiting should aim high. It is difficult through what is required. The public, which is apt to dwell on the mistakes and errors of taste and judgment committed by newspapers, ought to be more sympathetic to the speed with which the work of journalists has to be done. A weekly has no more time than a daily because its staff is far smaller. A journalist has to inform at the moment when his readers are most interested. His subjects are thrust upon him quickly, and the time allowed to gain a relative mastery of them is always short. I remember long ago, before my entry into educational journalism, I was asked to produce a leader on some new theory about the Etruscan language, of which I then knew nothing and of which no one still knows enough, in about two hours flat. The leader I wrote was more than inadequate, as the professor most acquainted with the subject in the local university pointed out to me a day or two later – as I recall, he kindly never wrote a letter to the editor – but no doubt one or two of the totally uninitiated may have had their interest in the Etruscan language stirred by my feeble effort to say something about it. I cite this only as an example of what the news, which no one can predict, constantly forces a journalist to do. He must attempt to master new subjects, new developments, with an almost unnatural rapidity. Society maintains him to have the first word. I have always felt that the tempo of journalistic activity requires the profession to have an early claim on the brightest talents on offer. Clearly the Civil Service should be able to recruit each year a good selection of the highest ability – but a Civil Servant rarely has to decide at the pace of a journalist, with the night trains waiting. Naturally I agree that industry should attract many of our ablest young men, because our standard of living depends upon their enterprise and the happiness of our work people on their humanity – but industry rarely needs to take an all important decision between 11 p.m. and midnight, as newspaper editors constantly have to do.

If the function of newspapers is to be critics of government and administration, then clearly they must recruit to their staffs some men and women as able intellectually as those others who will climb to the top of government or the Civil Service. The only moment to catch such people is as they leave university. We can qualify this by saying that graduate recruitment should not be made an inflexible rule. If the *Manchester Guardian* had made it so, they would have turned away A. P. Wadsworth, who became their editor, as well as Sir Neville Cardus. I usually find that I have on my staff one or two able writers who for some reason or other even in these days never went to university. Talent arrives from the most unexpected directions and it is lamentable, though easy alas, to fail to discern it.

Undergraduate work in the honours schools is similar to that of journalism in many ways. The student taking notes in the lecture room is being trained in precis. In writing his weekly essays he is trained to master a subject quickly and set the main points of it down in order. His final test is to sit an exacting examination in competition with his fellows where success comes to the man who can work against the clock and maintain his efficiency of mind in conditions of strain. A man who had cracked under examination would be a bad bet for the reporters' room. The university is in a true sense a school of journalism and success at the university is as good a prognostic as any of success on a newspaper.

I have not, I must confess, except in my early years on the T.E.S., emulated the zeal of C. P. Scott who would spend weekends in Oxford combing through the ablest undergraduates of their year for the benefit of the *Manchester Guardian*. His eye for good firsts brought Sidebotham, Ensor, Crozier and Ivor Brown on to the paper. The prevailing passion for academic distinction on the old *Manchester Guardian* was delightfully expressed by J. L. Hammond in his biography of Scott when in referring to two of the best journalists the paper ever had he found it necessary to begin "Arnold, like Montague after him, had fallen into the second class in Greats..." Such disasters, he seemed to imply, could be lived down, but it took time. A modern editor who has followed the Scott policy with great effect on the success of his newspaper is Mr. Gordon Newton of the *Financial Times*.

Television now competes with the newspapers for the special type of graduate ability they both need. For all its impact, television can take no political matter as deep as it can be taken by the press. Anyhow, it is easy to pass on to television or radio, if one still wants to, after a few years as a journalist.

Clearly if a weekly educational newspaper aims at recruiting the highest talent, it is always young. The young people come, stay for a year or two, and then go – usually to a national newspaper or to the B.B.C. or independent television. A weekly is too small to retain more than a handful over the years – though the whole policy of relying so largely on youth depends on this handful of stayers whose experience holds the whole paper together. Of course, one suffers sometimes from having so many men and women in their early twenties. A general ability cannot substitute for knowledge. Sometimes I am told we want a few more middle aged long stops. But in my heart of hearts I shall always feel that the paper can draw more from the salad days of brilliance than from prudential middle age. If you want first-rate men over 30 you have to pay them £3000 a year or more. No weekly can stand much of that. So we have to catch them young and lose them early.

Sometimes I am asked how many ex-teachers are employed on *The Times Educational Supplement*. I do not remember that at any stage we have been without ex-teachers on the staff. But this is not the point. An educational newspaper should not be run by a group of experts on education, but by a group of people proficient in newspapers. Its business is to give the news and to maintain the channels of free discussion. It is a task that requires its own professionals.

Education can expect in the 1970s to enjoy more coverage in the national press than it receives even at present – which is vastly more than 10 years ago. But it will still need weekly newspapers of its own. The greater the independence these newspapers preserve from any outside interests, and the abler the staffs they recruit, the better education will be served.

THE MAINTAINED SCHOOLS: RECOVERING THE INITIATIVE

*

T. R. YOUNG

It seems a truism in certain quarters to say that the provisions of the 1944 Act as they concerned Religious Instruction in maintained schools have failed, have fallen far short of the hopes and intentions of their authors. Such a statement seems to assume that we can say definitely what their aims were, and, by implication, what ours should be in the teaching of this most difficult and controversial of subjects.

For what, really, are we after? Do we conceive our task as evangelisation, on a massive scale, of a captive audience? Were we really to try this, we should build up untold resentment: but the teaching profession as a whole has sounder instincts that would allow it to fall into this trap. Is religion then only part of man's history in the world – albeit an important and often thrilling part of that history – but with no relevance to a modern technological society which had largely outgrown what it is pleased to think of as superstition? If so, it hardly deserves to be a subject in its own right. Ultimately it seems we can only justify the inclusion of Divinity in the curriculum if we are convinced that there is a religious dimension to man's life, if we believe that because man can look both backwards and forwards he insists on making some sense of the whole of his experience and imposing a pattern on it. That which forms, as it were, the catalyst between the individual man and the whole of "the other" is what might be called religion, and in this sense it must include humanism, rightly understood, as well as the great ethnic faiths.

But if we look at society to-day, the society into which our adolescents are rapidly passing, the need for such a catalyst, or even for such a dimension, seems to be either denied, or more frequently, ignored. In a real sense, as Chesterton has pointed out, Bradlaugh was a passionately religious man: he believed that Christians had the wrong catalyst, and he wanted to put them right. He was in a very different camp from those who are not concerned whether Christianity is right or wrong because, frankly, it doesn't matter, and they can get on quite well without trying to pose or answer these difficult questions.

For if we were to try and form a stereotype of the typical adolescent of to-day, on the point of leaving school, I suspect his attitude to religion would be that he did not need to prove its falsity, because in any case it has been out-of-date and irrelevant since its dogma was replaced by that of science. His state of confusion would be reinforced by a misunderstanding of what he had heard of the last half-century of theological scholarship and speculation, which he takes to mean that religion has abandoned all claim to objective truth, and by a parallel misunderstanding of the true nature of the debate between religion and science. If he has any clear ideas at all, which one may doubt, he sees this problem in late nineteenth-century terms as a headlong opposition between a mechanistic, Lamarckian, view of man, and a fundamentalist religion which has barely disavowed Archbishop Ussher's chronology. While he has a vague feeling of guilt associated with the abandonment of traditional mores and their replacement by "permissiveness", he is adamant that he is not required to adopt the social patterns laid down by his elders, since he has rejected the father-figure in favour of the peer-group as the instrument of socialisation. And a religious interpretation of life runs completely counter to the hedonism which adult commercial and advertising pressures urge on him as the way to full happiness. The combination of any, or all, of these factors produces a more or less sub-humanist ethos which rejects anything "given", adjudges religion, particularly Christianity, to be essentially "given" and therefore seeks its sanctions in a centripetal view of man as capable of perfection by his own efforts.

Of course very few youngsters would or could be so explicit about what they feel: but if this analysis is right in its bare outline it is clear that what R.I. is about has got squeezed out somehow between vocational interests on the one hand and the activities of the peer-group on the other. Our young people simply fail to see why they should find time for something neither important nor interesting.

The Maintained Schools: Recovering the Initiative

The last generation made only one assumption in the 1944 Act: the assumption that it was evident to everyone and would continue to be evident that there was, in fact, a religious dimension to life which it was important to study. Hindsight tells us that this was the one assumption they could not safely make. But within the limits of the assumption they make sensible provision, according to their lights, for initiating children into that dimension of life. In other words their tactics were sound, if needing revision from time to time. But what is needed now is a broader strategy.

New curricula, better training of teachers, more and sounder visual aids: all these things are needed urgently. But these are tactical considerations. Tactics start only when your strategy has produced a confrontation which you can exploit. Or to change the metaphor, it is useless having the best actors, the most perfect stage-machinery, the slickest production if no-one wants to see the play. Over Divinity we have lost the initiative, our theatre is empty in spirit if not in fact, and we need a grand strategy to recover ourselves. We cannot indefinitely go on teaching well or badly, by traditional or up-to-date methods, with or without visual aids, if the subject-matter of our studies is such that the majority of our students either believe it does not exist at all, or that it does not matter at all to them whether it exists or not. We are not combating other religions; those who hold them are by definition religious; we are not even in conflict with atheism or scientific humanism because these reactions arise in and from the religious dimension of life even when they end by denying it. We are faced with accidia, which is a worse sin than sloth; with the state of mind which cannot be bothered to affirm or deny that there exists anything outside man and his immediate environment, because man can live satisfactorily to himself alone; with the lukewarmness of the Laodiceans magnified to an insane degree and spread by mass-communication so that we end by being interested in everything but denying that anything is to be held as an act of faith because it exists of itself and makes demands on man.

What has been written so far is only an attempt to gloss the simple statement made by many teachers to-day: "our young people are not actively hostile to religion; things would be easier if they were. They are just apathetic." But if it is useful at all to analyse what is meant by that word "apathy" it is because it may help us to create a new strategy, to take the first tentative steps towards regaining the initiative we have lost. This is a daunting task, but one which we must undertake: as a first contribution to it perhaps three points are worth raising, the first of a general or background nature, the second linked closely with the developing powers and needs of the children actually in school, and the last dealing more specifically with the teaching situation in the classroom.

The first may equally well be described as an appreciation of the preparation, of the teacher for his task. If we are to restore the religious dimension to contemporary life it must be done in contemporary terms: so long as we tend to teach Divinity in, as it were, a Victorian matrix of thought we are foredoomed to failure. We must not fall into the trap of trying to meet the humanists on their own ground and rationalising or explaining away the content of the Gospel and the faith based on it on mechanistic or psychological grounds. We must accept with honesty and intellectual rigour our task of mediating the Christian myth. For this faith of ours cannot be contained within man-made symbols: if it were capable of being so expressed we should be talking about a God who was made by man in his own image. It is because the Christian postulates a God who is different from man not only in degree but in the very essence of his being that human language cannot contain him. And if this measure of awe and mystery is absent from our own concept of God we shall always be in danger of judging and teaching any scripture as something comprehensible and to be assessed and criticised in terms of our own limited abilities. Because a myth is not less than the truth, but a way of expressing a truth for which no other vehicle, in human terms, is possible, it must always be written in oblique, in allusive language. So it would appear that our first, and basic task, is to communicate to our pupils something of the difference between symbol and reality. We must not be afraid to let the young adult know, before he leaves school, that in the nature of things religious dogma can only be an approximation to an unrealisable truth, and of course this should be an implicit assumption in the teacher's mind whatever the age of the children in front of him.

For it appears that so long as we try to justify our belief in a religious dimension to man's life in language which the pupil knows to be out-of-date he cannot take us seriously. It is only when we have ourselves accepted gladly that our God is so great that we must believe that the symbols we use are grossly imperfect that we can begin to think our own way through to what Lesslie Newbigin calls a "reasonable faith for secular man". And it is only from this background that we can communicate with young people embedded in a secular society. The first task appears therefore to fall squarely in the laps of the Colleges of Education and post-graduate training agencies. Continued concentration on textual study and church history without a compensating element of twentieth century theology is not going to prepare teachers for their exacting task. For now, as never before, the teacher needs a tough, comprehensive corpus fidei. It is perhaps less important to have a detailed knowledge of the editorial history of the Pentateuch or of Paul's journeys or of the Synoptic problem than it is to have a true twentieth century theology, one which by no means despises these source documents but does not imagine that the truth of God resides solely in them or can be apprehended by their study.

Obviously the Colleges of Education will have to decide for themselves how much time they can devote to the general or basic course and what provision they can make for optional courses. But the nature and content of the basic course is of paramount importance, both because this is all that many teachers will have, and also because it must serve as the focus, the tie-rod, the nodal point, to link and structure all the work done by the Department. Would it be unrealistic to ask that this course should be one in Biblical Theology? It would have to look one way into the texts since they are the basis of the study: but it would not demand textual study to any great degree. It would introduce students to the concepts and the vocabulary used by theologians, and contain thereby its own "demythologizing" element. It should also look the other way to simple casuistry, to the relevance of theological concepts to man's condition in the world. It would above all be a course about ideas, about interpretation of the Scriptures and of life at the same time. It would, without doubt, let students see that teleology and ontology are as respectable modes of thought as is empiricism, which is all that most of them employ. Specialists would also wish to study texts and teaching methods: but after all texts can be studied privately with the aid of a commentary, as simple or profound as the student cares to select. And many would say that there is no special mystique about teaching methods in R.I., and the student will pick up enough from his general psychology and method lectures. What the precious time devoted to R.I. must be used for is to help the student to create his own theological framework. Such a course as suggested would be useful both in terms of the 1944 Act and towards any more "open-ended" approach which may be introduced in the future.

Would it be permissible, if a little facile, to suggest that our first move should be to stop calling the subject R.I. or Divinity or Scripture and simply call it Theology? It is tempting to draw the parallel with Mathematics: we have surely found that in that subject even in primary schools to get behind the process to the philosophy has paid good results. Perhaps this simple change in nomenclature would be the surest way to indicate to teachers and pupils alike the alteration in emphasis which is possible. But to teach theology we need theologians and not those, however honest and sincere, who stop short at critical examination of the imperfect symbol. If we could create this climate of opinion and train teachers who saw their job as mediating to their pupils the Christian myth of which they had a sound and structured knowledge we should be able to tackle our real job with renewed vigour.

For theology is undoubtedly a difficult subject, and we must always keep our eyes fixed on the needs and limitations of our pupils. A "child-centred theology" is an unworthy if not an impossible phrase, but we still have to temper the wind to the shorn lamb and present our material so that it can be comprehended, and does not give rise to misconceptions which it may be impossible to eradicate. In recent years the psychologists have made us all familiar with the stages of development leading up to adult ways of thought. In the first, roughly to be equated with the infant school and the lower juniors, the child is in a pre-causal state of mind, where reality and fantasy are inextricably interwoven. This is followed by a concrete causal phase in which the child clearly sees the relationship between cause and effect, but tends to cast everything into physical, Old Testament imagery. Only when the power of abstraction of principles from experience occurs may the pupil really be said to be adopting adult thought patterns.

It would appear, therefore, that the younger the child the more important is the inculcation of the right attitudes and the less capable he is of arguing out why things should be so. It would seem at least likely that we can stunt the future spiritual growth by telling him stories at that age which he can not understand, and which he has to deform seriously to fit in with the concepts he is capable of forming. So if he is to emerge from this stage with attitudes towards God and man on which we can later build, we must be very careful. Could we apply this test to any story, particularly Biblical stories, which we want to tell him? Is the story one which he can reasonably be expected to understand, and about which we can talk to him, however simply? If not, is it one which he should hear for the sake of its residual effect, because even if we cannot

252

explain it to him, the values which he will extract from it at a subliminal level are good and worthy values? If it qualifies under neither head it almost certainly ought to be out. All teaching at this stage, if directed to the forming of good attitudes and value-judgments, must of necessity contain a high emotional content. And wrong ideas implanted at this stage are almost impossible to correct.

But if the important thing at this stage is to exercise great caution because of the child's very limited powers, how long is this caution to be extended? Clearly in the concrete-causal stage of development the caution takes a different form. This is the time when our pupils are in greatest danger of forming the concept of a monolithic Bible, of a God based on Old Testament imagery, of a religion contained in its symbol and to be accepted or rejected by assessing the symbol as if it had an objective reality. This is the time to introduce a demythologizing element, to let the pupil understand something of the limitations of language (of which he is probably well aware if only inasmuch as he finds difficulty in expressing himself). The historical approach which would have been inappropriate earlier can well come in here and the outline of the Biblical narrative can be traced as a simple piece of history, rather playing down those moral judgments implicit in the Judaic view of history for which he is not yet ready.

But he is rapidly coming to the point at which caution must be abandoned in favour of boldness. Sometime about the third year of his secondary school the pupil is putting away childish things. We may well agree with the Church of Scotland that up to this point many teachers hesitate "not because of doubt or agnosticism, but out of a scrupulous regard for pupils faced with theological concepts beyond their understanding". If this colours our thinking in the earlier stages of education, we are following a very sound instinct. But there comes a point in the secondary school as we well know when, without much prodding from us, the pupil's viewpoint changes: he begins to weigh evidence, he wants to use adult vocabulary, he grows out of the stage of being happy with a rag-bag of generalised information and wants to structure it to make sense. In every other way we welcome this and try to cope with it: does some false piety hold us back in this one subject? How much of the deplorably low standard of discussions on religious topics in the VIth Form – often a mere sharing of ignorance and prejudice – stems from the fact that we have not made our maximum effort at this point in the pupil's development? We all know about the shortage of specialist teachers, and the shortage of time for non-examination

253

subjects, particularly in the grammar school. But if this is the time of greatest need, when the pupil must be eased out of his childish concepts of religious matters into a truly adult viewpoint, and given the necessary vocabulary in which to express himself, it is also the point of maximum opportunity. Salvage operations in the VI Form are not very useful; nor should they be necessary. Whatever skilled teaching force we have, whatever time can be squeezed out of the unforgiving timetable, whatever physical resources the school has for the subjects, should they not be concentrated at this crisis point? If the young adults are to grow up in this sense as in every other, if they are not to abandon all thought about religion because they still think and verbalise their thoughts in terms which no longer satisfy them, it seems at least worth trying to help them over this hurdle.

One hesitates to try and schematise anything so organic as the educational process, but if one regards it as a symbol rather than a diagram, this model may help:

AGE	THE CHILD	THE DANGERS	THE AIMS	THE CONTENT	THE CRISES
16	Stage 3 Abstract thought	Dissatisfaction with childish symbol	Interpretation and relevance	Theology	From childish to adult symbols
15					
14					
13					
12					
11	Stage 2 Concrete Causal Thought	Literalism and Misunderstanding	Factual material and simple interpret-ation	Carefully-graded Biblical material	
10					
9					
8					
7					
6	Stage 1 Pre-Religious	Misunderstanding	Attitudes and Ideals	Stories Heroes and Saints	From natural to revealed religion
5					
4					

Clearly, such a neat picture is not the whole truth. It is obvious that the diagonal lines in each column are vague generalisations: not all children pass from one habit of thought to another at the same age, and none does so clearly overnight. But it is suggested that there is a horizontal link-up and if we start from the nature of the child at a certain stage of development we can find out what his difficulties are likely to be, adjust our aims and methods to help him in those difficulties, and even identify our crisis points.

For the child in stage 1, it is doubtful whether we could make R.I. a separate lesson even if we wanted to: before he sees the religious dimension of life separately, we cannot isolate it for him. In stage 2 he often likes to collect his fund of knowledge under separate heads, and if the teacher has the skill to let him realise that he is learning a "special" sort of history, and if the Biblical material he is asked to study is carefully graded, probably this is the time to master the outline of the Biblical narrative. Goldman's caveat against the premature use of the Bible seems to suggest first that children find the emergence from "natural" to "revealed" religion a difficult one and second, that the implications of containing revealed truth in myth cannot be appreciated in the "concrete-causal" stage of development. It may well be, however, that this reflects not the unsuitability of the material so much as the teacher's allowing the child to look on the Biblical narrative as being on all fours with his history and geography stories. It seems an unfair assumption that the junior child is incapable of the simpler forms of ontological or teleogical thought just because we generally train him to think empirically. It is, of course, not possible to dogmatise, but since we cannot insulate him in school against the Bible (if only as he sees it at the cinema) we must be careful to introduce him to it under guidance. So the first crisis (which indeed goes on for a long time) can only really be solved if we attempt at all times to distinguish the form from the substance, as has been suggested earlier in this essay.

The second crisis has already been discussed at some length. Perhaps one could sum up by saying that we face the first difficulty by introducing him to a non-empirical truth, and the second by telling him how adults interpret it.

And if we can help them in this way, if they come to the final years of their school career with thoughts and words about theology mature enough to vindicate their status as young adults, it is conceivable that something exciting might happen. They could have, on the one hand, a renewed desire to go back to the source books and look at them again: they could equally well see that the "subject" is a purely artificial one and is only part of man's reaction to the world. Minority time studies in the VI Form are becoming more respectable; a number of schools are experimenting with integrated courses in the humanities for the younger school leaver. Both these possibilities should be seized by the theology specialist. If he can show his colleagues that it is impossible to study man in the round in any context without remembering that he is homo adorans he will help to restore the religious dimension and show that the Christian God is not a mere "god of the gaps".

At the beginning of this paper new curricula and better training of teachers were dismissed in a rather cavalier fashion as tactical rather than strategical developments. The rest of the paper has been devoted largely to talk about these two things. But perhaps the inconsistency is more evident than real: these things are only important inasmuch as they contribute to the strategical plan. There is a lot more work to be done; it is inconceivable that any one person can come up with the complete solution. But there may be some measure of agreement on priorities: first we must think out a twentieth century theological corpus for ourselves in adult terms; then and only then can we, as teachers, begin to use our professional skill to mediate it to our pupils, bearing always in mind the developing powers and needs of the children on the one hand, and the learning situation on the other. It is a pity that strategy, dealing as it does with generalities and broad concepts, can only really be written in platitudes.

As a corrective to these generalisations it might be useful to indicate in the barest outline how a teacher might make an appreciation of the problem and work out his approach for one class only in one term. The details are, of course, less important than the application of the principle. As Head of Department he has decided to take the third-year class for the reasons earlier suggested. The class is a good average ability, say the third stream of a 7-form entry comprehensive school, and has previously given no trouble in R.I. lessons, but has not been particularly interested. The Agreed Syllabus suggests that a final revision be made of the Gospel story in the Synoptics, with particular reference to the post-Crucifixion appearances and the Resurrection. So it will be reasonable to assume that the pupils know the stories and will need no further recapitulation.

When the teacher looks at this he is tempted at first to introduce his pupils to Christology and the Atonement. There is plenty of material here: a lot of specialised vocabulary, many fascinating heresies to amuse and interest, and a good chance of drawing ideas from the class, imparting some real theological interpretation of a familiar story, and generally re-stating Christ's earthly ministry in more adult symbols. On reflection, however, he decides that this is going too fast. What his class needs before they are ready for this is a chance to sort out their reactions to the miraculous element in the New Testament, and this seems on psychological and educational grounds the right time to do it.

The teacher must then decide just how much it is worth trying to do, and what should be his approach. One can almost see the first rough jottings going down on his pad:

1. How many pupils have had experiences they could not communicate? Ask how many really think they "come through" in a letter? an essay? an account of an experiment? a written attempt to argue or persuade? is there a scale of success?

2. Might the evangelists have had the same trouble (read from C. S. Lewis's trilogy where Ransom has trouble in focussing a nonterrestrial landscape).

3. How do you think God "speaks" to men in the Bible? (Try and define simply what Ian Ramsay means by a "cosmic disclosure").

4. Sometimes the writer knew he was writing nonsense – they wist not what to say – sometimes (Pentecost) he borrowed symbols from rhetoric.

5. How to show class that although experience did not necessarily happen as written it was much more than subjective?

6. Try and discount "empty-tomb" theology: stress importance to disciples of identifying post-Resurrection appearance (whatever it was) with Jesus they had known. (Remember D.L. Sayers on ressurection body – Morrison – 1 Cor. 15).

7. Insist disciples knew Christ had not "ascended" into orbit – see if Irenaeus on "our Father in heaven" is possible for them.

May we leave the teacher with his jottings? If he can carry this through with any measure of success what is bound to arise as a term's work will be stimulating, new, demanding a response. No more sketches of Jewish houses, no more text-chopping, not even Streeter's four-document hypothesis: but the "lively oracles of God"; ὁ τοῦ θεοῦ λόγος; the meaning, not the words; the interpretation, not the recapitulation; the striving to reach, not the "it" but the "Thou"; and – dare we say it? – perhaps the Spirit which gives life and not the letter (even the scriptural letter) which can kill all faith, hope, and charity if it is presented as an end in itself and not seen as the vehicle of a God beyond man's understanding.

THE CATHOLIC VOLUNTARY SCHOOLS

*

THE MOST REV. G. A. BECK,
ARCHBISHOP OF LIVERPOOL

Since the passing of the Butler Act in 1944, the voluntary schools have consolidated their position in what is known as the "dual system" of public education in this country. In this system two types of school are maintained by the local education authorities. On the one hand the county schools are provided by the L.E.A.s from public funds and are maintained by them. In these schools the Cowper-Temple provisions of the Education Act of 1870 remain in force. So far as religious teaching is concerned no "catechism or religious formulary distinctive of any particular denomination" may be used. Religious teaching is in accordance with an agreed syllabus, drawn up by the local education authority in consultation with other religious and educational interests. On the other hand are the voluntary schools which are provided in the main by the Church of England and the Roman Catholic community, but are maintained (apart from external repairs) by the local education authority.

I

Since the end of World War II Catholic voluntary schools have continued to grow in numbers and in size. In 1947 there were 350,494 pupils in 1,826 Catholic voluntary schools. The corresponding numbers for 1966 were 655,799 and 2,324 – an increase of 305,305 pupils and 498 schools in 20 years.

What will happen to these schools and the pupils attending them during the next decade? It requires courage to look into the future of our educational system; and even more courage to assess the future of the voluntary schools. There is no doubt, I think, that they will continue to grow in numbers. At present about 67% of Catholic children attend Catholic schools. In some areas the proportion of Catholic children in the total school population is as high as 45%. In rural areas it is usually extremely low.

The policy of the Catholic body, constantly reiterated since the days of Manning, is the traditional one of seeking to provide places in Catholic schools for as many as possible of the Catholic children in the country. The formula that a Catholic child from a Catholic home should be taught by Catholic teachers in a Catholic school undoubtedly strikes a somewhat unecumenical note at the present time, though if the word "believing" is substituted for the word "Catholic" the formula seems less exclusive. It is a formula which can be defended on good educational theory. Everybody agrees that, in the education of a child, home and school should work together in the closest co-operation. Parents are constantly being encouraged to take a more personal interest in what goes on in their children's schools. Teachers are urged to make closer contacts with parents. This trend will be increasingly emphasised in the Seventies. Co-operation of home and school will be seen more and more clearly as the basic condition for the successful education and harmonious development of the whole child. Nowhere is this co-operation more important than in the field of religious instruction and moral training. When parents have clear-cut and definite ideas about the religious and moral upbringing of their sons and daughters, they should have some assurance that their views and wishes in this delicate, personal and intimate matter are reflected by the schools to which they entrust these children. Tensions and divided loyalties at this stage of education can do permanent harm to a child. This is the basic argument for the "dual system" and the establishment of voluntary schools. It is sometimes held that these schools introduce a divisive element in society and that both greater openness and greater uniformity are highly desirable. There seems little evidence that this is the case – perhaps because no adequate social studies on the point are available in this country. If anything, the divisive element, even within a single religious community, seems to arise mainly from the influence of selective secondary schools.[1] Indeed the expression "divisive" is something of a catchword. It is used often enough without serious consideration of the factors which make for unity and those which make for division in modern society. If, as the

Crowther Report suggests, one of the functions of education is to reflect the "broad directives" given by society, then some form of pluralism in our school system is not only justified but highly desirable. In a recent book on the history of education in New Zealand, Dr. John Mackey analyses the current of thought which led to the establishment there of a single national system, secular and free, on the American model, and the rejection of a dual system which had been successfully tried in some of the provinces. This decision embodied in the Act of 1877 is characterized by Dr. Mackey as a defeat for a national system which would "reflect the diversity that belongs to religiously heterogeneous communities", and the triumph of a "unitary state system that would foster an ideal of homogeneity that philosophically does not exist".[2]

Within the Catholic community proposals have been made that strictly denominational schools should not extend beyond the primary stage, and that Catholic children would benefit at the secondary level from closer contacts with other Christian pupils and teachers and with non-Christians. This question, related as it is to the financial commitments of the Catholic Church in this country, will continue to be debated in the Seventies. A decision for the modification of the traditional Catholic policy is unlikely to come easily, especially without more careful consideration of the pattern of religious growth in children from infancy to adolescence. There is a growing awareness among teachers and other experts that, for many pupils, personal religious commitment belongs to the secondary rather than the primary age-group.

Financial conditions have made the continued building of Catholic schools a more practical proposal than it seemed when the Butler Act was passed in 1944. This Act provided Ministry grant at the rate of 50% on the capital expenditure undertaken by the voluntary bodies to replace existing school accommodation. The Butler Act did not envisage or provide funds for an extension of the dual system. No grant was available for new schools. Since 1944 however the financial burden on the voluntary bodies has progressively eased. After an increase in the rate of grant to 75% in 1959, Mr. Crosland's Act of 1967 extended Treasury grant to all capital expenditure on voluntary schools, including new schools, and raised the rate of grant to 80%. This is where it is likely to remain for the foreseeable future. Although the Roman Catholic community in England and Wales is carrying a heavy financial burden in order to meet the costs and loan charges for a school building programme which has reached a gross total of more than £ 100 m. in

20 years, it seems likely that, at the new rate of grant, we may well be able to meet the lower share of future building programmes. It has been calculated that new costs and the servicing of existing loans may require an annual contribution from the Catholic community of about £4,000,000. For a regular Mass going population of approximately 3,000,000 this does not seem an unattainable sum.

In the Seventies the reorganisation of secondary education on comprehensive lines will continue to be worked out for the Catholic voluntary schools in accordance with the general pattern of secondary education in the whole public sector. It is increasingly obvious, however, that the process will be slower than many originally anticipated. Much will depend on the form which reorganisation eventually takes in a given area. If selective secondary education is to be abolished completely, and if grammar schools are to be absorbed into the comprehensive system, the Catholic community may have greater difficulties of adjustment than other bodies. All over the country working parties have been set up in conjunction with the local education authorities to examine in what ways the Catholic aided secondary schools could be reorganised.

Our attitude in this matter has been governed by two considerations. In the first place the organisation of Catholic secondary education in a given area should broadly conform with that of the county schools. It would be highly undesirable to have two systems of secondary education, one selective, the other non-selective, side by side. The co-existence in the same area of rival systems of secondary schools would produce intolerable tensions. This does not mean that the reorganisation of voluntary secondary schools should follow in detail the corresponding county pattern. Very much will depend on the size and position of secondary school buildings. It is these factors above all which will dictate, at least during the Seventies, the type of non-selective secondary reorganisation which will be possible – and not be "botched-up" – in any given area.

The important second consideration concerns freedom of parental choice on religious grounds. In most areas of urban population there are enough Catholic voluntary schools and enough pupils to make a comprehensive system eventually possible and workable. In rural areas, however, and in some urban areas, the present size of the Catholic secondary school population raises doubts as to whether a secondary comprehensive school of the minimum size laid down in the famous Circular 10/65 could be established. What will happen in such cases? Will the voluntary school be doomed to closure because it is not of sufficient size? Will it be expected by the authorities to find a place in a two-tier system, part county and part voluntary? Will the Secretary of State maintain his promise that reorganisation would not deprive parents of freedom of choice on religious grounds? It was made clear in Circular 10/65 that he hoped that all concerned would "be able to negotiate solutions which ensure that, while selection is eliminated, parents are not deprived of places which meet their religious wishes, and on which they have hitherto been able to rely". These are serious problems which will await solution in the seventies.

There are other practical problems needing a solution during the course of the Seventies. There is for example, the question of the Catholic direct grant schools. Of the 179 direct grant schools in the country, 56 are Catholic schools with over 36,000 pupils. Of these schools, 27 are situated within the county boundaries of Lancashire. They cater for about 19,000 pupils and are an integral part of the Catholic secondary school provision in this area. Quite clearly, any reorganisation of secondary education must take into account the places which these schools provide.

In general, moreover, the Catholic move towards comprehensive education is bound to be slow and perhaps considerably slower than will be the case with county schools. In some areas – Lancashire may again be quoted as an example – the vast majority of Catholic secondary schools are housed in comparatively new buildings, which are at such distances from each other that integration or co-ordination in an effective comprehensive unit does not seem to be a practical possibility. New schools during the seventies will be built as comprehensive schools, but unless capital expenditure is sanctioned for a programme of reorganisation it will be impossible to achieve the ideal of a series of straight-through comprehensive schools. It seems inevitable that in most parts of the country a two-tier system will be imposed by the existing buildings. Detailed suggestions on these lines are now being worked out.

II

A note of reservation on religious education signed by Professor A. J. Ayer and five of his colleagues is appended to the Plowden Report. The authors of the note are opposed to any form of religious instruction for pupils in county primary schools. The reasons they offer in support of this attitude need not be discussed here; but there is certainly considerable substance in the criticism that a great part of religious instruction in county primary schools fails to achieve its purpose.

In recent years the researches of Doctor Ronald Goldman and his colleagues into the development of religious ideas in children have underlined some of the reasons for this failure. Dr. Goldman explains his purpose at the beginning of his first book *Religious Thinking from Childhood to Adolescence*.[3]

"In many areas of knowledge such as Mathematics, History, Geography and English Comprehension, a great deal of work has been done in the last thirty years on children's thinking. Led by that prolific writer and investigator Professor J. Piaget, large numbers of researchers in many countries have helped us to understand the growth of thinking, the structure and sequences of thought and the limits of understanding demonstrated by pupils at varying ages. Experiments tend to show how valuable children's misunderstandings can be in indicating the problems of thinking they face, and the kind of curriculum content in a subject that can and cannot be coped with. Some of these investigations will be outlined and discussed later. I mention them now because when I first encountered them it occurred to me how valuable it would be to apply similar research to the religious thinking of children and adolescents."

It is true that Dr. Goldman's researches have deliberately excluded Catholic schools and have been concerned with county schools and with agreed syllabus teaching. Much of what he says, however could be applied, so far as one can judge on the available evidence, to the voluntary schools and the denominational syllabus. He speaks of the concern which we have to build a sound spiritual foundation for our children's lives, and yet, through failure to appreciate the degree of their "readiness for religion", we may have been undermining the very basis of their religious education. We have been "over anxious to provide a ready-made religion, a complete system of beliefs and ideas which we impose on them." Although this may be done from the best motives, it may in fact hinder the child's spiritual growth for "passively acquired information is more easily forgotten and ready-made religion is more easily jettisoned than where truth and belief have been the result of personal growth.[4]

Dr. Goldman is concerned with the religious syllabus based on bible teaching and comes to the conclusion that, in the Infant and

Junior school, it is possible for such teaching to do positive harm to a child's spiritual growth. "There are two dangers apparent in familiarising without understanding, in teaching these Bible stories. The first is the accretion in the child's mind of misconceptions, verbalisms and focus upon trivialities in the story, so that there may be in relation to the story a period of 'arrested development' in which the child is satisfied by his too simple explanation, his thinking is crystallised too soon and he sees no need to think further in relation to the story. 'Too much, too soon' is now regarded as a danger to a child's developing concepts of number, where similarly he can acquire a number vocabulary, counting skill and even computing facility without the necessary insights or growth of concepts to support them. This may not only waste a great deal of valuable educational time but may prolong childish thinking in relation to number. The parallel with religious education is obvious. There must be many for whom the freshness, pungency and simplicity of Christ's parables are lost for ever because they were taught them far too soon, and they crystallised misconceptions of their meaning, never penetrating to further insights... To say that the child will 'grow out of his misunderstandings' is not an accurate statement, since all the evidence points to the fact that most children carry their misunderstandings through with them into early adolescence. They then find the crude ideas untenable, because the alternative is not put before them or left until it is too late, they may then reject religion as intellectually untenable."[5]

Dr. Goldman also emphasises a second danger which is not intellectual, but emotional, and arises from a too early familiarity with the bible story.

"Stories are essentially dramatic presentations of truth. But when a story becomes familiar, by constant retelling, the drama ceases to be dramatic. It no longer has the freshness, the element of surprise and the enjoyment it once had, and the child eventually becomes bored with it. This will directly affect the thinking power brought to bear upon it, for if the pupil is bored by a biblical story, he is not highly motivated in relation to it."[6]

The work of Dr. Goldman and his colleagues, however, has been far from merely negative. They have taken advantage of the current progress in child psychology to assess the development of religious thinking in children from infancy to adolescence, and, as in other subjects, have assessed their developmental limits. Modern educational methods are strongly child-centred in subjects such as number, language and science. It may be a matter for surprise that we have had to wait so long to see developmental assessments applied to religious teaching, yet what are now called the pre-religious, sub-religious and the personal religious stages in the development of a child are, in most cases, clearly discernible and each stage calls for its characteristic teaching. This may be summed up by saying that the teaching must correspond to the growing experience of the child and that enrichment of this experience even at the natural level is an important aspect of religious education.

Thirty years ago religious education in Catholic schools tended to be measured by the amount of information a pupil was able to absorb. With the catechetical renewal the emphasis moved from "information" to "formation". The persistent campaign of Canon Drinkwater through *The Sower* scheme and later through the Birmingham syllabus of religious instruction began eventually to have an effect.[7]

For a long time, however, *The Sower* was almost a lone voice, until it dawned on English Catholics that changes in religious instruction and catechetics were already far advanced on the Continent. Perhaps the most important landmark was the publication in this country in 1958 of an English translation of the German Catechism which was the result of prolonged effort on the part of enthusiasts in Germany for the growing catechetical movement.[8] In this country emphasis was laid above all on new methods of presentation and less on the contents of the syllabus. The visits of Father J. Hofinger, S.J., and the remarkable attendance of hundreds of teachers at his summer schools brought inspiration and a sense of enthusiasm to the movement. A National Catechetical Centre, originally founded as a branch of the Catholic Education Council, was inaugurated by Cardinal Heenan as an independent body and Corpus Christi College, the first catechetical college in this country, was set up in London in October 1965.

At that time the flow of books and materials came mainly from abroad and naturally enough the authors envisaged conditions which did not necessarily apply to this country. Only within the last year or two has a supply of books, discussion notes, and classroom material begun to be available from English sources.[9] Information is increasingly available not only about presenting the "History of Salvation" and the four ways of delivering the Christian message – the Bible, Liturgy, Doctrine and Witness – but also about the whole "kerygmatic" approach to religious education.

266

What is now needed and will undoubtedly come before the next decade is over can best be described as a threefold co-ordination.

In the first place the results of the researches carried out by Dr. Goldman and his colleagues must be adapted to the different conditions prevailing in Catholic schools, and applied specifically to a situation in which home, school and parish community are working for the same end.

Dr. Goldman's work has been welcomed among Catholic teachers, but is not accepted unquestioningly. The comment has already been made, for instance, that Goldman's theme of readiness for religion lays too much emphasis on intellectual formulations. His conclusion that there is a "pre-religious" stage in the development of young children does not seem fully justified. While accepting his findings in a limited field, Catholic teachers and Cathechists – and probably most of all Catholic parents – would hold that even the youngest child is capable of making a genuinely religious response at his own simple level not merely to the awareness of natural mysteries, but also to the experience of God's word, and thus to a genuine religious insight into the meaning of the events in his own life. The stimulus may come from a parent or member of family, from a teacher, or perhaps through the bible or the liturgy. It will be important during the Seventies that further research on the lines laid down by Dr. Goldman should take place in the whole field or denominational religious education.[10]

Secondly, in the light of this knowledge, the syllabus of religious instruction in Catholic schools will probably undergo constant revision. Important work in this field has already been done by Anthony Bullen, David Konstant, Derek Lance, and the staff of Digby-Stuart Training College.[11]

Thirdly, teachers will need a deeper understanding of the nature of God's revelation to man. The purpose of Christian education is not to present a series of propositions to the mind of a child as a preliminary to inspiring him to Christian action, nor is it, as Dr. Goldman seems to suggest, limited to the worship of a God who reveals himself mainly in nature. The teaching of God's revelation history is a long story of the gradual unfolding of his purpose; but it must, of course, begin with the student's own history and growing experience. It must develop in the growing awareness of inter-personal communion between himself and God. The record of revelation in the Bible may be of importance; but it is of far more importance for the teacher to realise "that God enters the history of each man and that each man must find God in his present personal history if he is ever to find God". It is in Christ, true God and true man, that the fullness of God's word is revealed and the fullness of man's reception and response is made. The publication of two books by an American author, Gabriel Moran, *The Theology of Revelation* and *God Still Speaks*, is bound to set off a further stream of thinking about the way in which Christian education is to be shaped and inspired. The aim must be personal and mature commitment to Christ, and communion with him. "The student has to meet Christ, really meet him. There are many places to do that: in one's neighbour, in one's enemy, in a thousand ways in daily life. But of all these opportunities only the encounter in the Eucharist is the *summit* compared to which all other meetings are lower stages on the slope".[12]

In this way, Moran's idea of a renewed theology of revelation embraces both Goldman's developmental idea and the kerygmatic element of scripture and liturgy. It will be for the teacher to seek to awaken in the child an awareness of God's revelation to him in ways both "natural" and directly "religious" at a level appropriate to his stage of intellectual and personal development. This will require the twofold adaptation of both curriculum and method.

There still remains the problem which is implied in all that has gone before – the fashioning of a religious education for adolescents which will take into account their relatively sudden individual development both intellectual and emotional, and also the immense influence on them of a complex pluralistic contemporary society without apparently a very stable core of values. This must be the main purpose of Catholic educational thinking and effort during the seventies.

We are told that at the moment we are at a crossroads in catechetics. The training colleges and our young teachers will be the chief factors in determining during the seventies along which road we shall go. The promise for the future is rich. There could be here a great breakthrough – a genuine revivifying of Christian education. In the final analysis it will depend on the quality of Christian living in our homes and on the informed enthusiasm of our teachers. This is perhaps a measure of the opportunities which are offered to those who undertake this arduous but deeply rewarding work – the staffs and students in our colleges of education.

The Catholic Voluntary Schools

NOTES

1 See the conclusions reached by Dr. Joan Brothers in her study *Church and School* (Liverpool University Press, 1964) and compare the conclusions reached in an earlier study, *Priests and People* (Liverpool University Press, 1961) by Dr. Connor Ward.

An American study on this point does not support the contention that denominational schools, still less a "dual system", are a socially divisive factor of any importance in the community (See Greeley and Rossi, *The Education of Catholic Americans,* Aldine Publishing Co., Chicago, 1966).

2 See *The Making of a State Education System,* (Geoffrey Chapman, 1967).

3 Routledge & Kegan Paul, second ed. 1965.

4 *Readiness for Religion,* Routledge & Kegan Paul, 1965, pp. 11–12.

5 *Religious Thinking from Childhood to Adolescence,* pp. 222–23.

6 Ibid., pp. 223–24.

7 For a brief tribute to the work and influence of Canon Drinkwater on catechetical development in England, see Jungmann *Handing on the Faith* (Burns, Oates, 1959) pp. 55–64, together with appendix IV "Catechesis in England".

8 *A Catholic Catechism* (Herder and Herder, 1958).

9 See, for example, Derek Lance, *Till Christ Be Formed* (Darton, Longman & Todd, 1964); Sister Romain, *Tell My People* (Geoffrey Chapman, 1965); The American *On Our Way* series adapted for this country (Dublin, C. J. Fallon, Ltd.). Suggestions for a basic Catechetical Library are given in the September 1967 issue of *Duckett's Register,* pp. 16 & 17.

10 An important work on this subject is Eve Lewis, *Children and their Religion* (Sheed & Ward, 1962).

11 See A. Bullen, *First Steps to the Father, Growing in Christ, Living for God* (Geoffrey Chapman); D. Konstant, *A Syllabus of Religious Instruction for Catholic Primary Schools* (Burns, Oates) D. Lance, *11 to 16* (Darton, Longman & Todd); *Over to You* (Surdaw Publications, Leicester).

12 See *God Still Speaks,* p. 105.

THE CHURCH OF ENGLAND SCHOOLS I
„TO MATURE MANHOOD"
(Ephesians IV. 13)

*

THE RT. REV. A. J. TRILLO
BISHOP OF HERTFORD

The Christian must be the first to rejoice in the immense revolution which is going on in the world of education. We are all familiar with the far-reaching plans of educationists which are intended to widen the scope of and improve the quality of education in every field, from the nursery school to the university. The thinking and the planning go on and great sums of money will be needed to implement new policies.

In all this the Church is privileged to work in partnership with the State. The significance of the part we have to play is not based on the contribution we have made in this field in the past, great as it was. Nor is it based on our vested interests in existing schools and colleges, nor in the desire to capture the young by indoctrination. We are in, and will remain in, education because that is where we belong. The pursuit of truth and the imparting of it is very much our business, as are the healthy enlargement of men's minds and personalities, the creation of truly human relationships and communities and the establishment of creative standards of living.

It is sometimes argued whether Britain remains, or ever was, a Christian country. Whether this is so or not there is no doubt that we inherit a culture which is still deeply permeated by Christian values and insights, many of which are accepted by humanists and others as part of our common heritage. We willingly work side by side with any and all who accept these values but we are bound to stand firm in the faith and confidence that they rest ultimately in the nature and will of God, as revealed to us supremely in Jesus Christ.

As we look into the future and to the growth which we can expect in the seventies it is with the hope and confidence that the Church will play an increasingly significant part in education in the land. It should be remembered that the Church is represented in every one of its members who undertake religious education or any other subject. It is a cause for great encouragement that there are increasing numbers of graduates and other teachers qualified in divinity. Many of them have been trained in Church Colleges of Education. We may take courage too from recent evidence as to the quality of this teaching. There are awful stories of the ignorance of young people of the fundamentals of the Christian faith and Sir Richard Acland and others have made this point. But the recent researches, for example of Mr. Colin Alves in County Schools all over the country give ample evidence of good teaching well absorbed. A comparative study of the teaching of history and of divinity in a recent survey showed in this case the latter to be more effectively taught. No doubt the teaching of agreed syllabuses has varied widely in its effect but insufficient credit is given to those who have faithfully and effectively taught the subject over the years. The 1944 Education Act provided a unique opportunity for the Church and the architect of the Act, Lord Butler, deserves all credit. He recently expressed his disappointment at the manner in which the Churches have not rallied to religious education in schools. Doubtless we have been at fault but Lord Butler should not underestimate the enormous benefits conferred on children as the result of his Act.

There can be little doubt but that the quality of religious teaching will still further improve. The writings of Piaget have had great influence, as have those of Dr. Ronald Goldman, Mr. Harold Loukes and others. Discussion goes on but already there is a revolution happening in the teaching of divinity, similar to that in the teaching of arithmetic.

All this is taking place against the background of theological ferment which we all in some degree find unsettling but which has brought theology alive and kicking into the market place where it has not been for centuries. The efforts of theologians to restate the basis truths of the Christian faith in contemporary terms will go on, and many teachers of divinity are encouraged and strengthened by it as they in turn struggle to state the same faith in terms suitable to their charges. It may well be that in the seventies some of the uncertainties of the current theological discussion will clear and something like a synthesis will appear, but our understanding of the faith must grow and develop – or die. Meanwhile

272

teachers are relieved as they call to their assistance the work, for example, of Dr. Ian Ramsey, Bishop of Durham, in linguistic philosophy, or that of Dr. F.W. Dillistone in the theology of symbols.

We need not fear that none will hear. There is ample evidence that many people are disenchanted with the brash commercial values which characterise so much of our life. This is seen particularly in young people as in various ways they make their revolt; some in social protest, some in the flouting of convention, some in turning with the Beatles to transcendental meditation and some in giving themselves to service of the community, either overseas or, in very great numbers, at home. Professor E. Wedell wrote recently of the courses which he had organised in adult religious education at Manchester University and which, contrary to expectation, were heavily over-subscribed.

Alongside this is the demand by an overwhelming majority of parents for religious education for their children. It is interesting to speculate on the reason for this demand but it remains a fact which must give pause to those who wish to remove the religious provisions of the Butler Act.

In all this we have been glancing at the general scene and we have paid tribute to all those who have undertaken religious education in county school over the years. Here is the Church working through its members. This work is of infinitely more value than the utterances of bishops or other Church leaders. The teachers are on the frontier and in the end all depend on their dialogue with their pupils.

But we are convinced that there remains a place for the Church schools and here again the demand of parents for places in such schools and for the erection of new church schools is immense and, unfortunately, likely to outstrip our resources.

It is in the church school that we enjoy a unique opportunity to educate for wholeness. We do not wish to indoctrinate children, for this is too freeze and arrest their proper development as persons. Nor do we wish to "sell" the faith and still less the Church but our hope is "to initiate attitudes of mind and will which may enable children to mature as spiritual beings."[1] We accept that education must be "child-centred" but we believe that in the end all will be lost if it is not also God-centred. It is in a Church school, in a community of believers that a truly integrated course can be mounted; where everything from arithmetic to domestic science is seen and taught *sub specie aeternitatis,* as part of a whole which

273

belongs to God. Furthermore the growth of true humanity is possible only in the ambit of worship and the good Church school is by definition a worshipping community with its own life and with links going out to the community around it. I have seen something of this quality of life in county schools but the conditions for it are found very much more easily in Church schools. The end is wholeness. For St. Paul it was the teachers among others in the Church who were given gifts so that we "shall all at last attain to the unity inherent in our faith and our knowledge of the Son of God – to mature manhood, measured by nothing less than the full stature of Christ". (Ephesians IV.13.N.E.B.)

There is a great deal of criticism of the Church, much of it well-founded. But whatever the faults of the institution, and we are working hard to remedy them, the Church remains the Body of Christ, increasingly aware of its unity in Him across the barriers of denomination, and acutely conscious of Christ's command, "Feed my lambs." Herein lies our mandate and our glad responsibility, and the implications carry us into every field of education. It is in this spirit that we look to the Seventies believing that the contribution we are called on to make will grow as the scope of education grows in general. But basically our aim and inspiration will remain the same. As to the rest we have much to learn and we shall remain open to the leading of the Holy Spirit however and through whoever He speaks to us. It is in this confidence that we shall face the cost, in money and other ways, which is bound to be demanded of us. This cost we dare not and do not wish to refuse for it is but a part of the cost of discipleship.

NOTES

1 *Revolution in Religious Education* by H. F. Mathews.

THE CHURCH OF ENGLAND SCHOOLS II

*

KATHLEEN BLISS

By the end of the 1970's it will be nearly fourteen centuries since Augustine and his monks arrived at Canterbury and more than that since Irish monks brought the flowering of Irish culture to the North when they came to preach the gospel there. During those years the Church has believed – and still does – that the promotion of learning and the dispelling of ignorance are part of a Christian witness to the God of truth. Divided at the Reformation the broken parts of the Church continued in the same tradition. Scattered over the earth as settlers and missionaries, Christians of all denominations have founded and maintained schools, colleges and universities. Thus the Churches became the first bearers of the Western tradition of education – including science and medicine as well as the humanities to many parts of Asia, Africa, the Americas and the Pacific and were the educators in many countries of the first generations of national leadership and the creators of many embryonic educational systems. They have pioneered also in teaching and training the handicapped and disadvantaged and in informal education their activities have ranged from literary campaigns to publications from radio stations to family education. Like all pioneers they have had peaks of achievement and arid flats created by spreading inadequate resources too thinly or randomly.

Why range so far afield? First, because all churches (including one with a national name like "the Church of England") have not only a historical but a world-wide geographical dimension to them. Missionary societies (which play something of the role occupied by religions orders in the Roman Catholic Church) have not only been agents of the Church of England in education overseas: they have educated a Church public at home to think of its wider commitments. The ecumenical movement, the Lambeth Conference, the world Anglican Congresses, the religious presses have helped to do the same. Secondly, because the forces at work affecting the place of the Church in education are Universal. Beneath the choppy waters of our national educational problems runs a great tide of world change. Societies are becoming pluralistic in race and faith, urbanized industrialized and re-industrialized: their citizens must have an education that will make them flexible as to employment, adaptable to new communities, ready for change and for constant new learning. If villages are not to suffer decay as the young and enterprising find in education an escape route away from them, they too must undergo change. The new elites who create and are created by the explosion of knowledge are mobile and international.

The vast cost of education and the need to extend its every aspect brings the State to the forefront everywhere as the financial provider and directing force in an education which is itself both effecting and undergoing change. All sorts of new questions emerge. What happens to the family, the small community, the voluntary and informal group on which the development of stable and mature personalities so much depends: can they be convinced that they have a continuing vital role to be helped to perform it? Are there dangers in a state monopoly of education that can be mitigated without the creation of new types of educational privilege? Where are the moral and spiritual energies to be found that will carry nations forward to grapple with the problems that lie not so much within as between sovereign states such as world poverty, racial tension and war?

The Church therefore as itself a more than national institution has to relate to these wider issues, and perhaps voice them, as it looks towards the 1970's and at its own participation in education. The base from which it operates can be quickly described. Voluntary schools (3,080 aided and 4,220 controlled) and 27 church colleges of education form part of the statutory system and contain 12% of the children of school age in England and 20% of all teachers in training. Church Youth centres, clubs and groups in thousands of parishes together make up the largest voluntary component in the Youth Service. The Church of England is, in accordance with the fifth schedule of the 1944 Education Act, a party to every agreed syllabus of religious instruction used in the maintained day schools.

In the independent sector of education, 80% of those independent schools which are called "public schools" are Church of England schools by their trust deeds or by long usage.

The Church is conspicuously absent, in an institutional sense, both from the universities (except for the colleges of religious foundation in Oxford, Cambridge and Durham and at King's College London) and from the field of technical and technological education (except for a very small number of technical secondary schools). The religious provision of the 1944 Act do not apply to these areas of education.

The limitations of this base are obvious: it is heavily slanted, institutionally speaking, towards the primary end of the educational scale. Nor are the Church's schools scattered evenly about the country: there are fantastic differences of incidence from one diocese to another, due to the accidents of history.

Grounds for Hope

First I would put the fact that in relation to its schools the Church has got out of an untenable position into one that can be supported with conviction or opposed with respect. In 1944 nearly half the nations' school buildings were owned by the Church: many were old and ill-provided. With no source of income comparable with the rates from which to improve them, the Church appeared to the public to be *against* educational advance and to be asserting the rights of property over the need for reform. The provisions of the 1944 Act were understood by the Church of England as a straight choice – contribute half the cost of bringing your schools up to standard, make them part of integrated plans of reform and at this price retain a high degree of control over them – or let them go to the Local Authority as controlled schools and lose both your financial burden and all but residual control. Once convinced that there was no other way the Church's spokesmen accepted what was offered. Believing that the Government and local authorities would produce new plans and new money faster than in fact they did most dioceses made their decisions rapidly and some let more schools go controlled than they might have done with longer thought. The Church found money quickly: the diocese became the unit of relationship with local authority and government: the Church was well served by its administrators and legal advisers and the quality of effectiveness of what was left to the Church after a very radical pruning began to improve.

The fruits of this, twenty five years later, are seen in better relationships between, Church, local authorities and government.

The dual system, preserved as a compromise has become much more like a partnership. Successive minor education acts have helped the Church financially, cleared some anomalies and given the Church the chance to build new schools and thus to improve its position in secondary education. Morale has improved too, and though there is much to be done, new buildings and improvements to old ones, new relationships and a clarification of aims have helped the Church to look ahead with more confidence. 32 of its 43 dioceses include school building as part of their regular budgets and 4 others make provision in other ways. This money comes from the parishes and totals over £1 million a year. The number of children in church schools has begun to rise for the first time this century. The strength of the church school lies in its local connections. Tradition is still strong in education, especially local tradition. Whatever they do themselves parents want what are basically Christian standards for their children and expect more continuity of such standards in an overtly Christian school though few would go beyond their own locality of make enquiry at County Hall to find it.

If the Government of the 1970's has the urge and the money to implement the recommendations of the Public Schools Commission, the Church of England may well have a new task. To open up public school boarding education to a far wider public than the financial limitations in its availability at present allow and to open it up to those who most need it (whether for the whole or part of their secondary education) means bringing children from maintained primary schools into what are at present independent schools. A bridge will be needed to carry children to the schools best suited to their individual needs and much closer association will have to be made between schools at present wholly unrelated to one another.

The Church offers no disapproval of private education as a parental choice and responsibility, but it puts its own money into voluntary aided schools, not into the private sector (except for special schools for the handicapped and various other categories of need). The Church might well find opportunities of relating church schools in the maintained sector with schools sharing a common religious outlook in the present independent sector.

The second ground for hope lies in the colleges of education. Their condition in 1944 was little if any better than that of the schools. Support from the Church's Central Board of Finance and a strong

278

champion in the person of Canon (later Bishop) F. A. Cockin as Moderator of the Colleges brought them out of their neglected condition. The cost to the Church Assembly (i.e. again to the parishes) of finding the Church's share of the cost of expansion has been well over £4 million and this debt will be carried throughout the 1970's. It is understandable but regrettable that the Church says "no more money for the colleges". More serious is its uncertainty about its commitment to them. The mood of the colleges is otherwise. They have had for many years independence under their own governing bodies and they have learned to think and act as a group, taking an occasional stand on educational issues and working out many forms of joint action.

Within educational circles their reputation is high. They are well placed to contribute to certain urgent problems; the reconciling of vocational training with the aims of a liberal education, the clarification of the role of the teacher in the community in the midst of social change; the working out of the new professionalism in the consciousness of teachers, carrying into it the best of what is understood by the word "Vocation".

The third ground for hope lies in the new relationship between the Chruches conflicts about educational issues in the past enabling them to bury old strifes (still regretting the harm they did) and work together. On issues of policy they discuss and often act together. One hopes that this will continue and develop and that they will explore together the re-interpretation of the aims deriving from their common origins and their earliest tradition in relation to education. Inside formal education common curricula and examinations, increasing dependence in state finance and conformity to educational planning tend to put into a separate compartment the specifically religious teaching and observance. Relating this to what else is taught will need increasing attention.

Many Church institutions the world over have quietly and unconsciously slipped away from their mooring in circumstances such as our own. It may therefore be both a good thing in itself and good for formal schooling if the churches – none of whom believe that "education" is exhaustibly defined as "what happens in colleges and schools" – gave increasing reflective joint attention to out-of-school education where so much waits to be done for all ages. In the training of adults and the bridging of the gaps between generations, classes and races within our society, in educating parents in the preparation of young people for Christian work (to name only a few) there are new experiments to be made, and many actually being made to-day which could be tested and developed. The Churches need to develop joint study and research co-operating with universities and colleges. The 1970's will bring conflict about the place of religion and of the Churches in education. That the Churches will face it together is certain; but equally urgent is it that they try to take the heat out of political controversy, to show themselves unconcerned with status quo or property or privilege and open to informal criticism in order that right decisions may be reached. If they can by their example gain their critics' commitment to putting the welfare of children first, the vigorous debate and changes ensuing on it will be in the right direction.

THE FUTURE OF JEWISH SCHOOLS

*

EDWARD S. CONWAY

Historical background

The religious education of Jews in England to-day is basically similar to that which Jews the world over have received during the past two millenia. It includes the study of the bible, its commentaries, codes of religious laws which affect the daily lives of people, the history of the people and – insofar as the capacity of teacher and student will permit – the study of texts in the original Hebrew and Aramaic.

Education is an essential ingredient of the Jewish religion and it is incumbent upon every parent to provide the maximum religious education for their children as soon as they are able to receive it.[1] The rabbis always insisted that an ignorant Jew could never be a truly pious one. Illiteracy was not only a social defect but a sin, and the community bestows its highest honours on the man of learning, however humble his birth or impoverished his home.

Throughout the centuries of their dispersion, Jews made their own arrangements for the education of their children because they feared that even if they had been permitted to send their children to schools which were part of the national system of education, they would be subjecting them to the pressures of conversion, since, until comparatively recently, schools throughout Europe had a primary function to ensure that all their pupils grew up as conforming Christians.

Up to the twentieth century, the vast majority of Jews in England were poor because religious tests, official or otherwise, prevented them from participating fully in the social and economic life of the nation. In the eighteenth century many poor Jews were driven to crime as the only means of livelihood which appeared open to them. This was the situation when the blunt warning of Patrick Colquhoun, a London magistrate, goaded Jewish philanthropists into providing a broader education to enable Jewish children to fit into the social life of the wider community. In 1795 he wrote that of the 20,000 Jews in London, some 2,000 were engaged in nefarious practices because they were not trained for useful employment.[2]

So, under the guidance of Dr. Joshua Van Oven, the Honorary Medical Officer to the Poor of the Great Synagogue in London, two major educational institutions were founded: in 1806, the Jews' Hospital "for the reception and support of the aged poor and for the education and industrial employment of the youth of both sexes"; and, in 1817, the Jews' Free School, which, in 1821, transferred to Bell Lane, where it catered for 600 boys and 300 girls.

In 1830, the House Committee of Jews' Hospital reported: "At the time when this Hospital was originally founded, there were no public schools among the Jews and the ignorant state of the lower class of children among them was most deplorable and such as to render it absolutely necessary that it should be formed on its present principles, and that elementary education should form part of the system – although the desideration of the founders of this Institution was to qualify the male branch of its youthful inmates as mechanics and enable them to gain livelihood by following a respectable trade.

"But it must be manifest to all that the first twenty years have made a material alteration in the character and condition of the Anglo-Jewish poor; from a state almost bordering on barbarism, which troubles, poverty and neglect have engendered, they have been raised by the laudable and well-directed efforts of Jewish philanthropy... by the institution of various schools among them, but more particularly by the Free School, which has hitherto been most successful and fairly promises to continue so... comparatively to a state of respectability, comfort and importance."[3]

Following fresh waves of poor Jewish immigrants from eastern Europe, the Jews' Free School expanded and, at the turn of the nineteenth century, it had 4,500 pupils on roll. Other schools opened in different parts of London as well as in many provincial towns. It has been estimated that, at the beginning of the twentieth century, a quarter of the Jewish children in England were being educated in Jewish schools which had become incorporated into the educational system of local authorities.

Each of these schools, however, had an independent body of managers, for they had come into existence to meet the needs of local Jewish children. There was no communal organization responsible either for their establishment or for their administration. Rabbis were invited ot inspect and report upon the standard of religious education, but the schools were controlled by the laity.

In the course of time, whilst religious education occupied an important part of the curriculum, the fundamental aim of the schools was directed to integrating the children into the life of the wider community so that they could play their full part as British citizens. For a variety of reasons, however, the schools began to lose their appeal during the first half of the twentieth century and, when World War II broke out, there was every indication that their days were numbered.

Reasons for the decline in popularity and influence of Jewish schools Locale. The Jewish schools had been erected in densely populated slum areas. Eventually Jews shared in the increased national prosperity and moved into the more pleasant residential districts dispersed over wide areas of the towns. The two world wars accelerated the process of dispersion. Consequently, the schools no longer served neighbourhoods in which the Jewish population was large enough to justify their existence. Some closed down; others admitted increasing numbers of non-Jewish children.

Development of Secondary Schools after Act of 1902
When the Jewish schools had been founded, secondary education was confined to the privileged minority. With the extension of opportunities provided by the Education Act of 1902, there was pressure on all elementary schools to secure the maximum number of free places and scholarships to the grammar schools. There were no Jewish grammar schools, but the vast majority of Jewish parents shared the common view that admission to secondary schools was a hallmark of educational achievement. It was not a far step for these parents to regard Jewish primary schools as inferior to preparatory and independent schools, even to those which had evangelical Christian foundations, because many of them carried the prestige associated with the assurance of admission to the better known grammar and public schools.

Effect of Social Emancipation

The spread of tolerance opened up opportunities for social integration. Many Jews were convinced that, if they discarded outward characteristics of foreign associations, they would become accepted more easily within the social, professional and commercial circles within which they wished to move. So they changed their names and sought to acquire the outward manifestations of British culture. Even the Jewish schools gave priority to the task of assimilating pupils. Israel Zangwill, the famous Jewish novelist, was obliged to leave his teaching post at the Jews' Free School because his headmaster, Moses Angel, disapproved of some of his writings in which Jews were recorded as speaking a corrupt form of English which, Angel claimed, projected a bad image of the Jew. Yiddish was frowned upon. English was introduced in religious services and new religious sects were founded as breakaways from the orthodox tradition, partly in order to substitute English for Hebrew as the medium for prayer and worship.

The consequences of shedding characteristics which identified Jews as a separate group were the weakening of religion, an increase in inter-marriage with non-Jews and inevitably the decay of denominational education.

Development of part-time education

Even before the majority of parents sent their children to non-Jewish schools, provision existed for part-time religious education on week-nights and during week-ends at religious schools known as Talmud Torahs or as Synagogue Classes. This was because many parents were dissatisfied with the quantity and quality of the education given at the day schools. They wanted a more intensive education than the schools were able or willing to provide. Many pupils who attended the day schools and came from very religious homes also attended these evening and week-end schools.

Eventually, many parents who otherwise might have sent their children to Jewish day schools, preferred to send them to the part-time schools because these were under the direct control of religious authorities. This helped to establish a rivalry between the part-time and the day schools whose influence was thus still further undermined.

Although the more committed Jews sent their children regularly to the Talmud Torahs where they studied for a minimum of two hours each night, the majority sent their children less frequently and less regularly. As day schools made greater demands on

284

homework, and as leisure pursuits in a more permissive and sophisticated environment became more attractive, both the attendance and, eventually the interest in Synagogue Classes declined almost to vanishing point.

The Education Act of 1944 gave religious organizations the opportunity to provide denominational education in County schools for a very limited period during normal school hours. The Jewish community took advantage of this facility, but one of the results was that an increasing number of parents came to regard this minimal instruction as adequate and did not feel obliged to send their children either to Jewish Day Schools or to Synagogue Classes.

Thus the expedients adopted to make good the loss of influence of the Jewish Day Schools not only failed to arrest the decline in the standards of religious education, but actually helped to precipitate or aggravate it. Dr. Nathan Morris, the first Director of Education of the Central Council of Jewish Religious Education summarised the position in 1945 as follows: "At any time there are more children outside the Hebrew Classes than in them... Compared with the position at the end of the last war, the standard has dropped calamitously. It is doubtful whether the majority of the present generation of children will even learn sufficient Hebrew to be able to follow a synagogue service."[4]

Talmudical Colleges (Yeshivot)
Talmudical Colleges or Yeshivot are the traditional institutions of higher education and they originated in the pre-Christian era. Students normally join in their early teens. They study intensively the rabbinic commentaries on the bible and the various religious codes of law.

Until the rise of Hitler, the major colleges were on the continent of Europe. Then those that survived transferred to Israel.

Many Yeshivot were established in England, both in London and in the provinces. But, as Jews became assimilated, the colleges lost support. Only the one at Gateshead has acquired an international reputation. Apart from some small Yeshivot which cater for exclusive sects within Jewry, the others developed into part-time institutions catering for orthodox Jews who wanted their children to be acquainted with talmudic culture but who also wanted them to benefit from the advantages of the secondary education in local authority schools.

For generations after the return to England, the Jews were obliged to seek their religious leaders from abroad. But when the community became anglicized, there was a reaction. So Jews' College was established in 1855 to train clergymen who would be no less familiar with English as with Jewish culture. It forged closer links with the University of London than with the Yeshivot. Gradually it grew in stature and produced scholars who acquired international reputations and, included among them, were several who became Chief Rabbis of Great Britain. But the minor ecclesiastical officiants and religious teachers, insofar as they were educated in this country, continued to be recruited from the Yeshivot. When these ceased to attract students, the reservoir of teachers almost dried up.

Changes after World War II

When World War II ended, the day schools seemed doomed. Attendance was perfunctory at the part-time classes, which were diminishing in size and influence. The theological seminaries failed to attract students. On the other hand the growth of tolerance, permissiveness and agnosticism within the general community had made it easy for Jews to be accepted socially without the slightest danger of conversion to an alien religion. Inter-marriage between Jew and non-Jew was increasing at a rate which alarmed the Jewish community. The prospect of the very survival of the Anglo-Jewish community seemed to be in jeopardy when, as so often in dark periods in Jewish history, there emerged an unpredictable reversal of trends. This resulted in a renewed interest in Jewish education which can be illustrated from the following table of the growth in the number of pupils who attended Jewish Day Schools:

Number of pupils (from statistics collected by Dr. J. Braude)

	London	Provinces	Primary Schools	Secondary Schools	Total
Feb. 1954	2706	1694	3607	793	4400
Jan. 1958	3890	2133	4611	1412	6023
May 1959	4400	2654	5069	1985	7054
Apr. 1961	4770	3052	5404	2418	7822
Apr. 1963	5325	3571	6315	2581	8896
May 1965	5840	4142	7324	2658	9982
May 1967	6280	4431	7888	2823	10711

This Jewish renaissance can be attributed to the combination of the following remarkable coincidences of major historical events.

In the first instance there was the massacre of the Jews by the

286

Nazis. This shattered the sense of complacency and security which Jews the world over felt before the Thirties and seemed to lead them inexorably towards complete assimilation, so that, once again in their chequered history, they became inward looking. But, on the other hand, their gigantic and horrific tragedy had assured for them boundless sympathy and a degree of immunity from differential treatment which, hitherto, they assumed could be obtained only through the process of assimilation. So, almost for the first time in their tortured history, they felt able to acclaim their religious separatism and yet be assured of parity of esteem and treatment.

Then, the emergence of the State of Israel gave a fillip to the renaissance in Hebraic culture which strengthened the bond between Jews the world over and provided an intellectual basis for their renewed self-confidence.

The sympathetic acceptance of Jews by gentiles coincided also with the decline of evangelical Christiantiy and with the current growth of humanism. These trends alarmed the leaders of Anglo-Jewry because the impact of humanistic tolerance produced a more corroding effect on the corporate Jewish body than the attempts at conversion or the anti-semitic prejudices of the nineteenth century. The increasing growth in the rate of inter-marriage is regarded as alarming, and, if allowed to continue unchecked, estimates as high as twenty percent are forecast for the current decade. A recent survey by the Jewish Board of Deputies has shown that the rate of synagogue marriages fell from 7.3 per 1,000 of the population in 1941-50 to 4.0 per 1,000 in 1961-65.

It became obvious, even to the most enthusiastic supporters of the system of synagogue classes and Talmud Torahs that these institutions have been unable to arrest the breakaway from Judaism. The casual nature of the attendance of pupils persisted despite the renaissance. The following figures for the last decade contrast their decline with the growth in popularity of the day schools.

Roll at Synagogue Classes and Talmud Torahs in the Greater London Area.[5]

	Total	Boys over 13 years	Girls over 13 years	Withdrawal Classes in County Schools
Nov. 1956	11823	593	233	2698
„ 1958	11618	516	211	2639
„ 1963	9477	451	215	2252
„ 1966	8717	365	163	1743

The attendance record at such classes reveals even more clearly the inadequacy of the system of voluntary part-time education.

Average Percentage Attendance[5]

	Sundays	Weekdays
Nov. 1956	75	44
„ 1958	72	38
„ 1963	73	36
„ 1966	78	32

But, the Education Act of 1944 gave religious organizations a unique opportunity to build the schools which to the religious and lay leaders alike alone seemed adequate to meet the new needs of the Jewish community. The old schools had been "all age" schools but the Act made it obligatory to provide primary and secondary education in separate schools. So, for the first time in England, and, as an indirect result of the revolution in English secondary education, Jewish secondary schools were built as part of the building programmes of local authorities. First in Liverpool, then in London and Manchester, they emerged conforming to the high standards in design and amenities required by the Ministry of Education and they were erected within easy access of the new centres of Jewish population.

The figures already quoted of the annually increasing rolls reflect the growth in popularity of the schools, and plans are in an advanced stage for the enlargement of existing schools as well as for the construction of additional ones. It seems reasonable to predict that, especially in view of the more liberal financial support which the Government is now prepared to give to denominational bodies, Jewish schools will increase sufficiently in number during the seventies to cater for the majority of Jewish children.

Training of Teachers
It would be a poor reflection of the ethos of these schools if their teachers were not themselves examples of the best products they hope to produce.

But, at present – and this will apply for some years to come – the majority of the teachers especially in the secondary schools are not Jewish. Indeed, primary as well as secondary schools, independent as well as aided, have the greatest difficulty in securing an adequate number of orthodox Jewish teachers qualified to teach even religious subjects!

There are many contributory causes of this dearth of qualified religious teachers.

In the first place, because of the absence of Jewish secondary schools before the war, almost all contemporary teachers received their education in non-Jewish schools and had to depend upon the inadequate facilities of Synagogue Classes for their religious education. In the nineteenth century, the Jews' Free School had acted as a training centre for teachers and was recognized as such by the Board of Education. The Headmaster conducted classes for student teachers who were ex-pupils and were imbued with the tradition of the school. Their standard of religious knowledge was elementary but it was sound and adequate for the needs of elementary schools.

There were, however, always the few orthodox and knowledgeable teachers who had received an intensive religious education at Talmud Torahs and Yeshivot whilst they studied at secondary schools and universities. They chose the vocation of teaching because this was one of the few professions which enabled them, with the minimum of difficulty, to remain true to their faith in practice as well as in belief.

But the number of qualified orthodox teachers has always been small because there has never been a denominational college. Now, however, with the increase in the need for teachers because of the growth in number and size of their schools, the Jewish community will be facing a crisis if there is no satisfactory means of ensuring an adequate supply of suitable teachers. In 1965 there were more than 400 full-time and 150 part-time teachers in Jewish Schools. In 1966 the numbers were 526 full-time and 216 part-time teachers. In the Seventies the need will be for at least twice this number.

Whereas in the nineteenth and early twentieth centuries many of the religious teachers were brought to England from the learned centres in Europe, nowadays, the teaching force is supplemented by teachers from Israel who, however, are concerned, in the main, with teaching the Hebrew language.

The staffing position is no less acute in the synagogue classes and Talmud Torahs. Indeed, in some respects, the position there can be regarded as more critical. In the day schools religious lessons can be staggered throughout the time-table, so that it is possible to provide basic religious education for the 10,000 pupils with forty teachers. The other subjects could be taught equally efficiently by non-Jewish teachers. But 400 qualified teachers are required to teach an equal number of pupils in the part-time religious classes and there is not available anything like that number of qualified orthodox teachers. The result is that children are being taught by unqualified teachers, a large number of whom are themselves pupils in the fifth and sixth forms of secondary schools. Although they are sincere young people, they are, not surprisingly, inadequate for the task, and help to lower the prestige of religious education both in the eyes of parents and pupils.

If religious education is to be regarded as something more important than a study of bible stories and a description of the main rituals, then the Jewish community will have to regard the provision of suitably qualified teachers as a major responsibility.

The Impact of Israel

There is no doubt but that the establishment of the State of Israel has been a major cause of the renaissance. The Bible has become a reality and a source book of the most exciting developments in the modern history of the Jewish people. The original language of the Bible is now the spoken language of this re-born State in the Middle East and has been adopted by thousands of Jews in every country in which they live.

Inevitably, Modern Hebrew has become the second language in Jewish Schools although it is not spoken in the home. But it has been introduced into youth organizations and there is a considerable growth of Modern Hebrew Classes in evening institutes and in seminaries for adults.

There is a vigorous religious movement in Israel which is responsible for training teachers for schools there. The progressive pedagogic techniques which they are introducing will eventually influence teaching in Jewish schools the world over. Jews of all shades of religious attachments in the United States have come under the influence of the new educational trends in Israel and they are utilizing their resources to providing new educational material which is already finding its way into the class-rooms in England.

Thousands of young Jews from every part of the world meet annually in Israel where they exchange experiences and return inspired with the modern message of Judaism.

The first quarter of this century witnessed a decline in interest in religion – an almost ostentatious protestation of identification with English culture – a stressing of the tenuous associations of Jews with their past and with their co-religionists abroad – and an emphasis on an exclusive identification with the country of their birth. The next quarter of a century will undoubtedly witness the growth of religiously educated Jews who will regard themselves as closely identified with Jews throughout the world through a common interest in the destiny of the State of Israel as an instrument for the fulfillment of the messianic mission of the Hebrews.

This will present a startling and serious challenge to Jewish educationists. They will have to educate children to accept the responsibilities involved in their identification with a religion which has suddenly taken on a new pragmatic significance. Jewish education will have to teach youth how to translate the Jewish ethical teachings of their prophets into daily practice. It will have to demonstrate the reality of the Jewish teachings of the brotherhood and unity of man. Unless Jewish education succeeds in impressing upon their youth the need to be living witnesses of God's message – wherever they are – this newly found Jewish unity may turn into yet another chauvinistic force.

It has been shown that, once again, in Jewish history, parents are eager to entrust the education of their children to Jewish schools, but the ability of these schools to meet the new challenge will depend upon the availability of suitably qualified and dedicated teachers. The ultimate responsibility falls upon the lay leaders of the community who will have to overcome sectional rivalries and display the necessary foresight as well as administrative ability in order to provide appropriate facilities for higher education which will attract the requisite number of teachers and clergymen.

The Chief Rabbi, Dr. Immanuel Jacobovitz, has pledged himself to regard the provision of education as his principle pre-occupation and many communal leaders are pressing for an effective co-ordination of religious educational institutions.

But it would be wrong to under-estimate the difficulties. At present, there is no common approach to religious education among the many primary schools. There is no co-ordination of schemes of work in the primary and secondary schools. There is no link between the aims of the schools and the Yeshivot. There is a clash of interest between those who wish to concentrate on Classical Hebraic culture and those who would concentrate on Modern Hebraic culture.

The syllabuses of the London Board of Jewish Religious Education and of Jews' College have been related more to the needs of the part-time classes than to those of the day schools, only one of which, the J.F.S. Comprehensive School, incorporates them in

291

their schemes of work. Rival religious educational institutions have different syllabuses, although their ultimate objectives are the same.

The only unifying syllabus in all secondary schools during the last two decades has been that of the General Certificate of Education. This carries a common prestige for all school subjects and the impact of the new interest in Hebrew can be seen in the following figures for candidates taking "O" Level in Classical Hebrew for the University of London:

June 1950: 6,   June 1955: 15,   July 1959: 49,   July 1962: 83,
July 1966: 112

There has been a similar increase in the number taking Advanced Level Examinations and Modern Hebrew at Ordinary Level. There has been strong pressure to introduce an Advanced Level paper in Modern Hebrew because of the increasing interest in the culture of modern Israel.

There are a larger number of undergraduates studying Hebrew, and new University Departments have been opened in London and elsewhere for the study of the language, history and general culture of the Jewish people. This will ensure a supply of teachers of Hebrew but will not, of course, solve the problem of supplying a sufficient number of religious teachers qualified to teach other subjects, too.

It is unlikely that for the next few decades the demands of Jewish schools will justify the establishment of a denominational College of Education. But there is a large number of Jews entering the teaching profession who would welcome a qualification which would make them equally acceptable to non-Jewish as well as Jewish schools. An attainable and attractive solution to the problem of teacher-supply, would be an arrangement with one or more Colleges of Education and Institutes of Education which would be prepared to collaborate with Jewish religious educational authorities to establish departments of Hebrew Religious Studies and to grant Jewish students facilities to practice their religion in the same way as Clifton College has made provision for a Jewish House. In this way, the Jewish community and the educational service of the country as a whole could be served.

Conclusion

If the Jewish schools which are now emerging were to function as separatist schools, that is, as schools no different from others except that they catered exclusively for the education of Jewish children, then they would be a blot on the educational landscape. They would be a self-imposed, yet government supported system of educational apartheid.

But, if they impregnate Jewish children with the ideals and culture of their religion, in order that they can be better fitted, not only to live freely and uninhibitedly as equal citizens with their fellow non-Jews, but also to make a specific and unique contribution to the mosaic of civilization, then they have a valuable function. The inter-mingling of pupils from Jewish schools with those from other schools through normal inter-school activities and the presence of hundreds of non-Jewish teachers in these schools who will be able to recount their experiences, should do much to improve understanding between Jew and non-Jew.

During the Seventies, England should witness the first results of a fascinating new experience in denominational education, because for the first time in Anglo-Jewish history, hundreds of Jewish young men and women will have left the Universities and entered the professions and commerce, after having received an intensive Jewish religious education from the age of five to eighteen years of age in a Jewish school environment.

Will a new type of Anglo-Jewish culture emerge? Will this novel Jewish intelligentsia have any influence on the general cultural, social and religious life of the country? Or will the pervasive growth in influence of humanism, materialism and permissiveness in human relationships succeed in nullifying the effects of this Hebraic renaissance, in the same way as it appears to be weakening the influence of Christianity?

NOTES

1 Printed in 1771, one of the first Jewish publications in England on the education of children stated. "As the child reaches an age which enables it to learn, and this differs according to the intelligence of the child, the parents must be concerned to find a good teacher... One should strive to choose from the outset the best teachers and not believe that at the beginning any teacher is good enough, the opposite to which is really the case..."
Remember the Days p. 149. publ. The Jewish Historical Society of Eng-England, 1966.

2 Treatise on the Police of the Metropolis – P. Colquhoun. Publ. Fry, 1795.

3 The Institutional Care of Children. Ph. D. Thesis. E. S. Conway.
4 *Jewish Education in Time of Total War*. Nr. N. Morris, p. 99. pub. by London Board for Jewish Religious Education, 1945.
5 Figures taken from the Annual Reports of the London Board of Religious Education.

REFLECTIONS & PROJECTIONS
ON MUSIC & YOUTH

*

SIR ROBERT MAYER

Seventy years ago

As a beginning, I feel I should declare my interests. Contrary to most contributors to this symposium, I am neither a professional muscan, nor an educationist, but merely one of a dying species; a patron of music who has given his life to what may be considered contructive pioneer work. During nearly half a century I have gained practical experience in both the educational and musical fields. As a result I am firmly convinced that the English are at least as musical as other nations, that in fact, they have the potential for becoming the leaders in the world of music. This may seem to some readers an extravagant statement; I am encouraged to make it because of the remarkable changes which I have witnessed since I first came to England in 1896, changes probably set in motion through the efforts of the late Sir Henry Wood in his institution of the Promenade Concerts. It was he who first acquainted a popular audience with the world's musical literature, and the result of this tradition can be seen today in the magnificent work done by the B.B.C. under the guidance of William Glock.

This is not all. In the period I speak of orchestral playing was at a very low level. There were different orchestras, it is true, but they were largely composed of the same players, and the deputy system, by which any player could send a deputy to an already rehearsed concert if he should have found a more lucrative engagement, could not ensure a first class performance to say the least of it. The operatic world too left even more to be desired: a short star season at Covent Garden, and an occasional visit from the two travelling companies, was all that London enjoyed. And the provinces were even worse off. The only field in which the British could then be said to compete with the European standards was that of oratorio, but even there the repertoire was limited to the old tried favourites, and a composer such as Edward Elgar was indebted to Germany for the first performances of some of his major works.

After the First World War
It was because of this state of affairs that in 1923 my wife and I were convinced that some way must be found to help those few people who were trying to create both a better musical climate and new audiences. To do this, education must be called to music's aid and we instituted the orchestral concerts for school children which bear my name. We were perhaps not alone in our wish to raise the standard, but we were probably more fundamental in our approach, and we were fortunate to have the enthusiastic support of educationists of all kinds, from teachers in primary schools to His Majesty's Inspectors, of whom three singularly gifted men were oustanding, Cyril Winn and Geoffrey Shaw, succeeded by Bernard Shore.

But the going to concerts and the joy of listening to music was not enough; it had to be continued in the making of music by the young who are always more interested in what they can do themselves than in what can be done for them. After persistent effort some authorities consented to supply instruments to those schools who would introduce orchestral playing to their pupils; and from a small beginning has grown the whole complex of music making in the form of youth orchestras – national, county, municipal and school – which is the envy of other European nations.

During the course of this article other factors will emerge which can rightly fill us with pride and optimism; however, the purpose of my observations is not to indulge in complacency, but to tell the truth and to propose what could and should be done if in the Seventies we are to reach full musical development.

Education
How? there is no short cut; the best and surest method at hand is obviously education. In using that word I do not mean work done in the formal school curriculum, but rather the formation of the tastes and habits of young people outside the curriculum, and often outside the school itself. Such education in essence draws out all that is latent in an individual. It will be generally conceded that musical education can be justified on the same basic grounds as any other kind of non-vocational education. It is just as natural to teach

children good music as, say, good literature. They may not understand it all. That is irrelevant. They do not fully understand all they
read. The main aim is that they must be made aware of music's
existence and be given the chance to make the choice for themselves, if only to counteract the pressure of less valuable counter-
attractions in the world in which they will emerge.

Primary schools
It is true that a certain amount of music has always been a part of
primary schools' activity; but formerly it was mostly confined to the
singing of hymns or to inferior music written for school use which
could only be replaced gradually by works written by George Dyson,
Armstrong Gibbs and others who realised that there was a field
where they could operate for their own and the children's benefit.
Simultaneously the non-competitive movement brought some incen-
tive to both teachers and children. But primary schools were still
deprived of good teachers, decent pianos and other requirements and
broadly the child left primary school without even the ability to
read music at sight. A revolution has occurred in primary schools in
the last ten years, thanks to Maxwell Davies, George Self and other
pioneers as well as the B.B.C. whose contribution is described
later in this article. Also, children's concerts in and out of school,
as well as the activities of enlightened teachers, and music advisers,
resulting in school orchestras, have created a new climate.

Secondary schools
Common sense demands that these achievements should be followed
up in the secondary school; unfortunately this is not the case. The
impetus generated in primary schools is kept up only in respect to
orchestral playing. No statistics are available about the large numbers
of good orchestras which have been organised since the war. The
London School Symphony Orchestra, the Leicestershire School
Orchestra – the result of Mr. Stewart Mason's vision – and a few
others, pay regular visits abroad where they are much acclaimed.
But probably even in the Seventies we will not reach the ideal
whereby every secondary school possesses its own orchestra; and
apart from this happy development, musical secondary education is
falling far behind education in primary schools. The G.C.E. is, it
seems, the enemy of music and so is paternalism, as I can illustrate
by one concrete example. Recently I established direct contact
with a few senior boys from a school. They got together
a large group of boys who had previously not been interested in

music, and have now secured for themselves the benefits deriving from my movement, Youth and Music. Thereupon I asked the head-masters of 38 other schools of a similar type to give me the same chance with their pupils. Not one of them replied. Result: the pupils, without their knowledge, were deprived of the benefits which thousands of others enjoy, and of the chance of organising matters internally, without troubling their teachers.

The plea that the money and care spent on junior pupils has been wasted unless education of the seniors is continued falls on deaf ears; it is often met by the assertion that the musical do play, and that the others are not musical and therefore, do not count. This specious argument is often an excuse for apathy and aversion to action and in any case it overlooks the fact that the large majority of people who are not sufficiently gifted to make music should be given the chance, through education, to become music-lovers.

Leisure

This point should appeal especially to those who want to prepare for the Seventies when the problem of more leisure hours will be facing us. Music is probably one of the best and easiest methods at hand which can fill these hours, especially for the young who can find in it an outlet for their emotions. Modern life without music is, or should be considered unthinkable; and secondary education should be organised accordingly.

Opera

The task of widening and improving musical education will be greatly helped by the advent of a new factor: opera. Practical experience in school and college has proved that young people are greatly drawn to opera. This is the era of visual attraction and this discovery should therefore not be surprising; moreover, it furnishes proof that, given the opportunity, the English are opera minded. The absence of opera in Britain, due to the effects of puritanism and subsequently industrialism has left a wide gap in our musical life which has only now begun to be filled by our two permanent opera houses of which we can be rightly proud. Lilian Baylis's dream has come more than true at Sadlers Wells; and thanks to Sir David Webster, George Solti and others, Covent Garden ranks among the world's leading opera houses. Whether it be the schools who perform opera on their own ground, or the large majority who do not do so, all should be given the opportunity of hearing operas in which the greatest composers have found outlet for their genius. Opera is confined at present mainly to London, though travelling companies and budding art centres reach out to other parts of the country. Youth & Music aims at letting youth benefit from and at the same time help in this expansion. Central and other authorities supporting operatic performances obviously also require public support and especially new audiences which can be made up most easily and effectively by our youth. Fifty years ago concerts given outside schools were a novelty. This is no longer the case, although for lack of concert halls and finance most concerts are still given in school; but concerts outside are naturally more exciting and stimulating, and it is hoped that educators will give a further lead by encouraging attendance in opera houses. In doing so they will have the satisfaction of also supporting the growth of opera in Britain. In the twenties Sir Thomas Beecham launched an operatic campaign, but, though a genius, used the wrong methods. People cannot be bludgeoned into going to opera. Leadership must coincide with public demand. Let youth be articulate. The need for more opera cannot be overstressed, for the growth of opera will bring to the fore much musical and artistic talent which is only latent at present.

Specially gifted children
This is not the only waste of talent. We also deprive children who are exceptionally endowed as instrumentalists of the chance to develop their gifts early enough. Heads of our conservatoires and others have stated repeatedly that such children should receive special instruction in which conventional education need not be disregarded. Menuhin and the Central Tutorial School have begun to tackle the problem of the specially talented children, but action is required on a far larger scale if we wish to advance the cause of music, not only quantitatively but also qualitatively. Where none can excel, nothing excellent can result, be the musician professional or amateur. In fact, the two are closely linked.

Teachers
The production of the right kind of teachers is obviously of paramount importance and deserves more profound discussion than is possible within the framework of this short article. The dismal conditions prevailing in the twenties have been replaced by more enlightened methods of training in music colleges, colleges of education and universities. Professor Mellers at the University of York, Professor Dart at the University of London and others hold original

ideas and pursue progressive policies. The Gulbenkian Report exposed the difficulties under which our music colleges are operating owing to quite insufficient support by the Treasury. The position in the much newer colleges of education appears to have engendered less interest. It may not be unfair to say that, of course with exceptions, people often enter the music teaching profession who may be adequate musicians, but inadequate teachers, or vice versa; and there are also those lacking the experience in handling young people who, especially when adolescent, should add music proper to their interest in commercially advertised pop music. For the task of teaching in primary and secondary schools we require far more teachers who possess, and who can stimulate creative imagination; who spurn uniformity; who use the examination system to a minimum extent; who do not command, but who attempt to inspire their pupils; and above all, who educate through enjoyment, the love and joy of making and listening to music. Foreigners are amazed at the independent authority which our central and local governments delegate to headmasters who, in turn, pass it on to heads of departments. Long may this continue, provided that in the Seventies qualified teachers will definitely secure for music especially in secondary schools, its proper status.

Radio and Television
Fortunately influences coming from outside school have already helped to raise the status of music and to improve the musical climate in schools. Foremost have been broadcasting and Youth & Music. For understandable reasons I will not elaborate on the latter. As to the former, I must go back to 1924 when the late Mary Somerville heard, when she was by chance in a village schoolroom, a broadcast talk on music by Walford Davies. The talk was not intended for a classroom audience, but hearing it in this situation made Miss Somerville see the potential value of broadcasting in school education. At first there was some opposition from the teaching profession who saw the use of radio in the classroom as unfair competition, but in 1929 the Central Council for School Broadcasting was founded, and ever since the B.B.C. has worked hand in hand with the teaching profession.

Music has always been at the heart of school broadcasts – for instance, about twelve thousand schools take the series "Singing Together". Broadcasts have been particularly valuable in schools where there are no teachers confident enough to take music unaided. But because broadcasts are planned to keep abreast of the latest developments in music teaching, and can tap unrivalled musical resources, even gifted music teachers may find them stimulating to use. The emphasis nowadays is on active and creative participation by the classroom audience, with children playing many of the instruments that were popularised by Carl Orff. In 1963 Television joined radio in presenting a regular series of programmes to both Primary and Secondary schools; and in the hands of John Hosier, who moved over from radio to start the new programmes, there has been an emphasis on commissioning new works from leading composers to start a repertoire for Primary schools of good music that children can perform, both vocally and instrumentally, entirely on their own. At a time when Britain denigrates its achievements, it is pleasant to know that B.B.C. Television is unique in the world in presenting a regular and committed series of music programmes to schools.

Resident Quartets
There are other new ideas, conceived outside school, which can help education. One is the scheme to attach resident quartets to universities and towns. So far the scheme has been ratified in Edinburgh, Dartington, Keele and Harlow: a tiny beginning compared with over two hundred resident quartets in American colleges. This innovation can be of real constructive value if the ensemble performs not only for a college or other body, but for the community at large, academic or not; and if, in addition, the players also teach, and lead non-professional orchestras in and outside school or college. The scarcity of public concert halls has already resulted in the use of school halls for public concerts, for the enjoyment of the community. Members of the resident quartet, by participating in the lives of school and community, can help remove barriers between them and thereby engender a much needed common interest and civic pride.

Patronage
In the early twenties when the (then) London County Council refused to support concerts and opera in London, the Government gave a grant of £25,000 to Covent Garden which was abandoned owing to the pettiness of other musical interests. The present policy adopted by the Government has opened a new chapter in our musical history, and, largely thanks to the leadership of Miss Jennie Lee and Lord Goodman, the grants made through the Arts Council are constantly rising. Local authorities, especially the Greater London Council, are also extending their patronage, and so are Foundations

– Gulbenkian, Peter Stuyvesant, Leverhulme, Munster, Vaughan Williams and others. Unfortunately industry as a whole has not yet realized the role which it should play in participating in the country's musical development; social reasons alone point to the wisdom of action in the Seventies. When considering the future the I.L.E.A. would be well advised to change its policy of providing outside operatic or concert performances free to young people because they are given in school. This ruling is based on a hundred year old law made when social conditions were entirely different. Young people today have the money to pay for what they want, and they will value far more an event which they have chosen and paid for. Further, if they are simply sent to a concert or an opera by the school, the majority will simply relate this in their mind with lessons, from which they will be relieved when they go out into the world. The exact opposite is desirable – they should regard the arts as something which will add to enjoyment in their entire life.

Barbican Scheme

The City Authorities have also evinced a new attitude to the arts by sanctioning the Barbican Scheme whereby the Guildhall of Music and the new Concert Hall will be built next to each other, with the London Symphony Orchestra serving as resident orchestra. Its members will also teach in the school. Performing and instructing will thus be in the new pattern, as in the case of resident quartets. I cannot refrain here from commenting on the dual value of this scheme: it can be a focal point for the members of Youth & Music who work in the City of London; and they in turn can help to provide the audiences necessary for the scheme's success.

Conclusions

To conclude. I have endeavoured to present some facets of a very complex situation, and to depict the real progress which has been made in various directions and which justified the optimism expressed at the beginning of this article. The task confronting us in the years ahead requires above all a new spirit; a burning faith in music and the creation of a point of vantage overlooking the entire position. At present we are still bedevilled by a separatism shown in the barriers which exist between the various types of schools and colleges and also between both of them and the rest of society. People may be doing excellent work in their special spheres; but this is by definition very limited. Education and music are divided traditionally by a gap which must be filled by co-ordination, so that each component part knows and profits from what the others are doing. The present situation is not unlike an old-fashioned office, composed of numerous little rooms, each being used by separate interests. Let us scrap it and replace it by one spacious floor, light, free of partitions, the requisite for enthusiastic collaboration. Consolidation is the watch-word in business and could well be copied in the field of music, provided it can be organised within the framework of individualism and enterprise, a pre-requisite of an era of unprecedented revolutionary changes in society. Democracies are generally suspicious of anyone functioning outside the common herd of mankind and therefore lean heavily on conformity; let us beware of this enemy of the arts.

The musical development in Britain and U.S.A. during the last 40 years has been phenomenal, yet we have in Britain large regions which are underdeveloped, or even undeveloped. Reformers therefore have a tremendous task ahead of them before they can claim that we are a musical nation, meaning that the ordinary man feels that music is part of his life. As I have endeavoured to show in this article, this goal can be reached most quickly and effectively by inspiring the youth of the country.

ART EDUCATION

*

SIR HERBERT READ

In the present year (1967) art education in Great Britain is in a state of great confusion. Completely different ideals and methods of teaching prevail at the primary, secondary, technical and university levels. No one in political or professional authority seems to know how much importance should be attached to the subject – indeed, no one seems to know how to give the subject a precise definition that would show its relation to other subjects in the curriculum and permit its integration within the educational system as a whole.

The confusion is endemic to an industrial society and arises from the fact that machine production by its very nature implies a distinction between art and design that has never been resolved either in the philosophy of art or in the practice of education. Before the Industrial Revolution the artist, whether he was a painter, a sculptor, a carpenter or a silversmith, was responsible for the design and workmanship of the object he was making. He may have learned his craft from a master, or attended classes in Fine Art in an academy, but what he was taught was an *ideal* of design. It might be based on the observation of nature or on the imitation of the work of old masters, but the qualities to be embodied were universal and traditional – qualities such as harmony, nobility, serenity, elegance and (in the best of academic art) vitality. These qualities were perhaps only fully appreciated by an educated minority, but this minority gave its "taste" to the whole community. Each period had its style and the style prevailed, in more or less diffuse forms, from the palace to the cottage. Even in periods when the style became luxuriant or decadent among the rich merchant classes, a simplicity of taste, what William Morris called "a love for sweet and lofty things", persisted among the people at large.

When the Industrial Revolution came to England it was at first thought that the qualities that had distinguished the fine arts of the past could be imitated by the machine; that those who owned or operated the machines could be taught "the principles of design" – that is to say, of ideal design as it had been taught in the academies of the past. In 1835 Parliament, which by then represented the manufacturing interests, became acutely aware of the importance of the problem (even from an economic point of view) and appointed a Select Committee on Arts and Manufactures "to enquire into the best means of extending knowledge of the arts and principles of design among the people (especially the manufacturing population) of the country; also to enquire into the constitution of the Royal Academy and the effect of institutions connected with the Arts". The subsequent history of the subject must be read at length in Professor Quentin Bell's excellent book on *The Schools of Design*,[1] but briefly it may be said that the debate that then began is with us still. In spite of several special committees and select committees that have from time to time been appointed to deal with the subject (the latest being the National Council for Diplomas in Art and Design, established in 1961 under the chairmanship of Sir John Summerson confusion) still prevails.

It should perhaps be admitted that at the source of the educational stream the waters now run clearly enough. It has been generally agreed throughout the world, that the child is naturally endowed with aesthetic sensibility, and that given the right environmental influences will spontaneously express this sensibility in formal images (aural as well as visual but I confine myself to the visual). These formal images, already at this spontaneous stage, have great psychological significance in the development of the child's personality, and under sympathetic teachers child-art has become a recognized category of art, distinct from adult art but the basic material for any further instruction in art.

Unfortunately the basic nature of this material is not recognized in the present educational system. It remains an activity peculiar to the infant or primary school and no method of effecting a transition from child art to adult art is recognized *or even known*.

This is the first problem to be solved in the art education of the Seventies – the maintenance of an effective continuity in art education. At present what happens is that art as a subject has to fight for recognition in the secondary stages of education. The official policy seems to be based on the supposition that a certain number of pupils (a very small minority) will have the desire and the necessary talent to become professional artists in the academic sense – that is to say, artists who make a living by painting pictures, carving stone, casting bronze, or teaching these techniques to other aspirants. Otherwise, it is generally assumed, art (as distinct from design) has no place in general education.

It has to be admitted that a considerable number of those who are taught "fine art" either fall by the way (i.e., are failures) or transfer their energies to other professions (including motherhood). This fall-out is likely to increase as the public demand for paintings and sculpture continues to decline – fine art, we may safely prophesy, will become obsolete in the 'seventies, except for purposes of public entertainment (in art galleries, theatres, etc., and in the decoration of public buildings). It may survive as a private 'hobby'.

With some presentiment of this decline and fall of professional fine art the tendency, fostered by the Ministry of Education, has been to emphasize the concept of *design* and even to substitute the word "design" for the word "art". The recognized qualification in the art schools is now the Dip. A.D. – a diploma in art and design. Admittedly the word art still survives in the designation, but the whole pressure (seen in the tendency to integrate schools of art with polytechnics and colleges of technology) is to concentrate on design, as being more relevant to a technological civilization. Even schools of art in which painting and sculpture are still given predominance in the curriculum will now devote a preliminary year to "basic design", one of its purposes being to dissuade the student from any romantic interest in the fine arts.

In this development everything will depend on what is meant by the word design. The art schools that were established on the recommendation of the Select Committee of 1835 were called Schools of Design, but it has been said that this term was used because its originator did not know the English for the French word *dessin*. "École de dessin", which means a drawing school, became a school of design. The original Italian word "desegno" always meant the art of drawing – the ability to draw an outline of a mental image (phenomenal or phantastic). That is not the sense of design in Dip. A.D. Design in this context means "to reduce chaos to order", "to explore the constructive possibilities of a material such as wood, iron, leather, etc. – in general, to solve functional problems,

307

to invent better tools, better machines, better media of mass-communication.

The whole power of the State is brought to bear on this new concept of design — it has practical value, social value, commercial value. But nevertheless it is the wrong concept, for art education, simply because it denies (or betrays) the imagination.

Perhaps I should say it *tends* to deny the imagination; that I fear that in another ten years it will have betrayed the imagination. To express the same thought in other words: it deprives the work of art of its symbolic value, its original function of creating forms expressive of human feeling.

I believe (with Susanne Langer and other contemporary philosophers of art) that to deprive art of this function would be to deprive humanity of one of its basic modes of biological development. Mind cannot function vitally without concrete images to represent its emotional and intellectual tensions, the images we need to articulate feeling. Living form, not functional form, is what matters in art, and living forms we already find in the spontaneous art of children as well as in those works of art that have survived from prehistoric times. Art is not art, in any meaningful historical sense, unless it constantly reflects organic modes of feeling. It was for this reason that Walter Gropius, in the Bauhaus (now, alas, in retrospect the source of so much misunderstanding of art education) balanced his teaching of functional design with the teaching of artists such as Klee and Kandinsky — teachers of magic rather than of logic.

Either we come to this realization in the next few years or we abandon forever (in the educational sphere) the concepts of beauty and vitality. Imagination, not mechanization, should take command in our art schools. By this I do not mean a return to academic art education, to the life-class" and the dead fish and faded flowers of the "nature morte". Nor do I mean the divorce of art from industry. The general purpose of art education for the 'seventies can be expressed in one phrase: to discover how form arises in nature and then use that knowledge to construct forms that are equally vital or organic. In this way, in the education of the future, science would serve art, art science. But it is essential to begin this process at the beginning, in the infant school, and maintain this mutual relationship throughout *all* stages of education, including the final stage, the university.

I believe that the most inspiring book an art teacher can read today is D'Arcy Thompson's *On Growth and Form;* and that the most inspiring book a science teacher can read is Paul Klee's *The Thinking Eye*.[2] Meditation on these two works, each a classic in its own field, would lead the teacher of the Seventies to a true conception of his task.

NOTES

1 *The Schools of Design* is published by Routledge & Kegan Paul, London 1963.
2 *On Growth and Form* is published by the Cambridge University Press; *The Thinking Eye* by Lund Humphries (London).

THE SHAPE OF ENGLISH TEACHING

*

T. R. HENN

I

Crystal-gazing has its compensations; one can afford to be personal, even dogmatic. Perhaps there is some excuse, after forty years of the teaching of literature, and of war. But I have altered the title the Editors gave me. "English, our heritage" sounds to my ear a little pompous, a little popular. I would rather write of English as a university subject, as it is now and as it might be then: if only we could resist the distorting pressures upon it.

I say distorting, deliberately. For I believe that of all subjects taught at the universities English is, as a discipline, the worst: except for the "good" students. And by "good" I do not mean any quality evidenced, or measurable, by the final class-lists of an honours school: in my meaning there may be "bad" students even in the upper seconds, and an occasional "good" one in the thirds. Let us speak more narrowly; and, humbly but inevitably, out of my own experience.

When the English Tripos was set up at Cambridge in 1917, it was mainly the work of H.F. Stewart and "Q". The teachers in its first phase (perhaps until the Tripos was split into two parts in 1930) were all "ex" other disciplines; classics (Tillyard, Aubrey Attwater, S.C. Roberts, F.L. Lucas), history and moral sciences (Mansfield Forbes and I.A. Richards), modern languages (B.W. Downs). H.S. Bennett and C.G. Coulton were professional medievalists. Most of the men and women who were my contemporaries had also been brought up in some other discipline: classics, modern languages, mathematics. The total number of undergraduates,

311

and of their teachers, was small; I think there were only nine published lecturers in the list for 1921. One result, of which Tillyard has written[1], was that our teachers themselves were exploring as they taught, and communicated something of their own excitement in that exploration. The professional text books were few; I remember with gratitude reading W.P. Ker, A.C. Bradley, George Wyndham, R.C. Moulton, Walter Raleigh. There was a good deal of fairly rigorous Shakespeare textual criticism, and the Charles Oldham Shakespeare Scholarship attracted a large entry. But above all I suspect that our teachers provided us, probably unconsciously, with their own reference points in their previous disciplines, without a thought that they were, in a sense, teaching "comparative" literature or even "humane studies". As a matter of experience, the boy who has been taught classics intelligently – but he is a vanishing asset – is still the best potential student of English at the university level.

II

During the early 1930's the Higher Certificate in English gradually hardened towards its present form as the G.C.E. "A". I remember that when the Cambridge Locals first set up a "Comment and Appreciation" paper as an option there was a storm of discontent from the schools, countless letters from schoolmasters saying that they didn't know how to teach for it, and asking for text-books to which they could go.[2] Six candidates out of some five hundred offered it that first year or two. But the examination in other subjects was still small enough for one examiner to mark all the candidates for a single paper. For his judgements he was responsible to the Syndics only, not to an intervening committee. He was free to compensate as he saw fit for short work (always the bane of any rigid system) of outstanding quality, or to reward work which might, if referred to a strict marking instruction, be considered oblique or even irrelevant. (In all English marking this is apt to be a crucial and highly subjective judgement; and, sometimes, the higher the intelligence of the candidate the greater the wrong that may be done.)

But once the numbers get really large a new state of things obtains. A single paper may have to be shared by a dozen different markers, under a chairman or coordinator. The character of the paper set begins to change. One of its chief qualities must be its potentiality for being analyzed by a not-too-complex marking "scheme", and therefore to some extent fragmented into "markable" aspects. And with the present economic situation (this in itself has many and complex repercussions) it is unlikely that many of the younger university lecturers will take time off from their own work (on which their promotion now depends) to do this "drudgery". Therefore the examiners, men and women, will often be engaged as casuals: retired, perhaps, or having taken their own degrees a considerable time ago. It is even possible that they may be ignorant, shall we say, of recent developments in criticism, such as an intelligent and independent sixth-form boy might produce. I have known perfectly reasonable views penalized merely because the examiner had not read a book published three or four years before.

I see no remedy whatever for this situation. The numbers entering for G.C.E. "A" level in English are bound to rise. The same system of setting papers and of examining is bound to continue. Both will reflect, at every turn, on the teaching in the schools. One notorious difficulty is that of finding set books for any "O" or "A" syllabus that will fulfill the conditions of being worth while, unstaled by examination, and unlikely to give offence to this somewhat sensitive mixed market. Indeed, one suspects at times (particularly in the Entrance Scholarship Examinations) that one is examining the teacher rather than the pupil. In many subjects it is possible for a highly efficient teacher to put a veneer on moderately intelligent candidates which does not really stand up to the stresses and frictions of the first year's work at a university.[3] For some reason which I do not understand, the mathematicians are peculiarly susceptible to this: as if (to change the image) their bearings had been burnt out by too heavy and too early a load.

I believe that we can do no more than recognize that the G.C.E. "A" in English is a general guarantee of literacy, of the power to master fairly ordinary details of a few rather limited texts, and the capacity to write four or eight standardized essays on the same number of writers or subjects. It is possible to predict within narrow limits what the examiners can or will set. A competent teacher can exercise pupils in a relatively small number of preparatory essays, and be virtually certain of getting the necessary quota from them: for there are not many wholly different questions that *can* be asked on Chaucer or Milton, Wordsworth or Keats, Shaw or T.S. Eliot. Nor is there much that is new in the sense of being potentially fresh to any sixth form student that can be said about them. This is the central dilemma of English studies both at this level, and for the university undergraduate. There are too many excellent books available on every aspect of every significant literary figure; too many, indeed, for the good of literary studies.[4] A really able pupil can make his own synthesis or extraction for a 1,000-1,500 word essay with ease and efficiency. A moderately intelligent lecturer can do the same. If a don gives one of the survey courses which are so popular, and necessary, on both sides of the Atlantic, the pattern of what he is transmitting will never be original except as a personal synthesis.

III

It is for this reason, among others, that the potentially amorphous quality of English must be buttressed by some linguistic discipline. It may be that by 1970 all entrants to an honours school will be qualified in two languages; one, certainly. The controversy over Middle English and Anglo-Saxon still rages, a little uneasily. I cannot find better words than those of Sir Stanley Leathes in 1913.

"We may have to give the student something he does not exactly ask for; we may have to give him training in language. But we must open to him, at least, those languages which give him the richest return in history, literature, and modern knowledge. If the choice, to be made on these lines lay between Middle English and Anglo-Saxon, and, say, modern German, can there be any doubt how the choice would go? I trust I am not hostile to any form of learning, but I cannot bring myself to regard Middle English and Anglo-Saxon as in any way necessary to an educational course in English literature. I reckon such studies as post-graduate rather than pre-graduate."[5]

And he goes on to argue that one or more of Latin, French, German, Italian, Spanish should be included among the languages. If by 1970 we can demand a reasonably high standard, or entrance, in at least one of these, we shall have the groundwork for one of the most rewarding and testing of all studies, some portions of comparative literature.

IV

English seems to me depressingly unique in this aspect of its unsuitability to provide a range of testing questions. Perhaps History is almost as bad. In the sciences, mathematics, modern languages, the range of "new" material is unlimited.

These deficiencies are, I believe, apparent whenever one examines at a university. They are, perhaps, more blatant in the U.S. and Canadian universities (when the normal essay-type examination is used) than here. But the discrepancy between what an average paper in English literature seems to invite, and what actually appears in the students' scripts will often be depressing in the extreme.

The common horizontal unit for literary study, of 150-200 years, will generally provide, with alternatives, between twenty and thirty questions. Students will, of necessity, have been taught to concentrate on five or six subjects. The less able and the less energetic will be able to make a show of answering their three or four questions with relatively standardized essays; that is, they will embody the same basic facts, the same lecturers' views, often the same basic quotations. They know that the margin left to the examiners for framing wholly fresh questions is a very narrow one; they know also that the matter of the relevance of an answer may be a matter of subjective judgement, and that, if there is doubt, they may well be given the benefit of it. We have therefore the type of "scatter-gun" answer; the candidate plasters the target with generalizations, and hopes that a sufficient number will be near enough to gain a pass. It is also true that the same candidates, when confronted with passages for comment which aren't in the book, may be notably incapable of demonstrating commonsense, knowledge of the historical and social background, and of attempting independent critical judgements. It may well happen that somebody is capable of writing a perfectly sound essay on Chaucer – on orthodox lines, but anyway who can say anything new? – while showing in the same paper that he is incapable of construing accurately a dozen lines of Middle English. This inflexibility is a measure of the failure of the whole method of approach.

With the Shakespearean work, a staple examinable subject of both the G.C.E. and of the university curriculum, the situation is even worse. There is much evidence to suggest that for many people Shakespeare is spoilt beyond redemption by being taught for examinations at school; and the situation grows far worse

315

when the same plays are harrowed again during the first and second years at a university. Shakespeare is, indeed, the test case. Every conceivable aspect has been written over so many times, and there is little new that can be said until knowledge becomes wider, and sensibility is sharpened, the post-graduate area of studies. At the same time a student may easily be misled "where fashion or mere fantasy decrees". The teacher is faced with the most difficult balance of all: between the necessity of seeing that his pupils know what can be known without full understanding, and that understanding through experiences for which they can, as yet, have no reference points in their own adolescent lives.

V

For this is the pride, and importance, and perennial weakness of all teaching of English. As a discipline it demands a framework, and a core of fact; in political and social history, in comparisons with other literatures, and particularly with the roots of the mountains, its own multiplex sources. Yet all the while its study involves the communication, and the assessment, of statements of the most vital importance. They may conveniently be grouped under Dante's three divisions of love, war, and death. Statements about these are constantly being confronted by all students of literature. They must be mediated, interpreted, valued by their teachers. Without this mediation literature, and poetry in particular, will become dead (as irrelevant or meaningless), or even an object of contempt.

For this purpose the teacher of English is in the most vital, responsible and dangerous position. There is no aspect of his subject that does not teach, in some degree, the ultimate values, "the art of living". He cannot handle, shall we say, seventeenth-century poetry without a knowledge of the religious and moral preoccupations that underly this poetry, and he must be able to trace their origins in the past, and even suggest their implications for the present. He must be aware of the power of all great literature to irradiate the present with significance: and to do this requires an intense effort of the creative imagination allied to a high degree of sensibility.

He will, or should be, teaching largely by osmosis, obliquely, at the most important levels. Consciously or unconsciously he will be transmitting his own values to his pupils. It is probable that the most important thing about those values is, not that they should be in any way orthodox or unorthodox, but that they should be held with complete integrity. The young are immensely quick to discover the bogus, the insincere, in their teachers. Because of the double nature of the statements made by literature, and the subtlety of those statements, he may do great harm as well as great good. Is it too much to demand that his pupils should be able to be certain of his own integrity, his wholeness, his right to assess these experiences which he mediates? Beyond all, there must be power to kindle the fires. We may quote C.S.Lewis: "For every one pupil who needs to be guarded from a weak excess of sensibility there are three who need to be awakened from the slumber of cold vulgarity. The task of the modern educator is not to cut down jungles but to irrigate deserts. The right defence against false sentiments is to inculcate just sentiments. By starving the sensibility of our pupils we only make them easier prey to the propagandist when he comes."[6]

This may sound pompous, even fantastical: but I believe that the ideal is not an illusion. I know, through handling their pupils at the university – for the most important of the work is done, for good or ill, at school – that there are teachers of genius scattered, though not thickly, throughout the country. From such men and schools come a succession of pupils who are remarkable, not necessarily for their outstanding intelligence, but for their energy and curiosity as regards their work; and for their urge to integrate themselves and their work into something like a coherent whole.

I have come to believe that these qualities, the assessment of energy, curiosity, and the capacity to engage themselves wholly in the subject, are of central importance in the selection of students. To these qualities the G.C.E., whether at "A" or "S" level, is no more than a general pointer: not merely because of the fallibility of examinations, but because of the complex personalities of the students, and their potentialities for the future. English, and perhaps to a lesser extent history, is a subject into which far too many people drift: either because they take it to be a soft option, or cannot keep to a more demanding subject, or because adolescence has revealed, and a school magazine has apparently justified, some urge to write. If this drift towards English is reinforced by a drift to the university (for I believe that an appreciable number of present day students do not want to go up, but accept the transition dully, as part of a necessary education pattern) we have one explanation for the deadness of much university English. Still worse, the state of things is self-propagating: an appreciable proportion of these people will go on to become teachers themselves, with perfectly respectable second-class degrees but without any sense of vision of what might be done.

VI

"What then?" sang Plato's ghost, "What then?"

With the licence that I have assumed, I would cut the numbers reading for Honours English by a very large factor, perhaps 40%; and this not because they are Thirds or – perhaps worse – "standardized" lower seconds, but because they are basically unfit to benefit from the subjects at all. Methods of selection, both at entry and whenever there is some qualifying hurdle for the second or third year, would be overhauled and stiffened: with more attention to qualities of intelligence, personality and potential for development than to the marks gained. It is worth noting that throughout the system the dice are heavily loaded against the late developer, who is often the most rewarding person.

I would have smaller lecture classes; and of the open and survey or "core" lectures the student would attend not more than five a week.[7] Each lecture would have issued with it a précis, and perhaps a bibliography. Each lecture would be succeeded by seminars, on the same day: groups of 12-15 students at which the lecture would be discussed, extended, developed, with at least one other lecturer present. This would serve, among other purposes, to make large faculties more homogeneous; too often its members are unfamiliar with what the others are doing, apart from the nominal subject covered, and sometimes it is considered not quite delicate to inquire about, still less to attend, a colleague's lecture.

Every student would be taken twice weekly in supervisions/tutorials, in groups of two. But these groups should be adjusted, both by initial selection, and by regrouping after a few weeks, so that the personalities complement each other: or, better, clash to provide some mutual stimulus. Of the two weekly periods, one might be given up to an essay requiring some original thinking, the other to some exercise of the practical criticism type. Each group of two should change supervision at intervals, but not too frequently, for otherwise it is difficult to form a fair picture of a student's total potentiality and personality.

Examinations would be worked on a system of compound evidence, and the committee or body responsible would themeselves exercise a high degree of intelligence and care. At a guess, "Finals" might consist of the following:

40%; three or four written papers, constantly varying in form so as to avoid presenting the stereotypes so often available in old books of papers.

20% on a single essay, done at leisure, some 5-8,000 words in length. The subject for this would have to be approved by some responsible body, but considerable latitude would be given for excursions into related disciplines.

40% of the assessment would be on *written* reports on each student: by at least *two* tutors or supervisors.

All borderline cases would be determined by a searching *viva,* which would be adjusted to compensate, as regards the written papers, for "nerves", accidents family troubles and so forth. This in itself would present a major problem; we may suspect that the time allowed between the writing of the examination, and the rigid requirements of a university calendar as regards marking, is often far too short. Class lists (with all their disadvantages) would have to be retained in their present form: they are too firmly tied into innumerable systems such as prizes, post-graduate work and studentships, and (I think lamentably) into the promotion of teachers. But they should invariably have a divided second-class. There is an enormous gap between the good two-one who has shown alpha quality during the previous year, or the laborious two-one who makes it on sheer hard work and knowledge, and the lucky or slick or even laboriously dim student who just clears the thirds. The two-one class becomes the more important because of the reluctance of all universities to give firsts in English. The reasons are not wholly clear; perhaps in a subject whose judgements are largely subjective examiners tend to have a Platonic idea of what a first-class should be, and indeed the best work is fantastically good. Yet when, as at Cambridge, the raw material includes a very large number of entrance scholars and exhibitioners, who have been elected after the most rigorous type of selection, there seems to be too little co-relation between these and the classes which are in theory appropriate to their rank in a college.

VII

But above all I would try to reverse the current trend, the dichotomy between the "teacher" and the "researcher" in university work. Thirty years ago professorships and readerships were so rare as to be almost wholly outside the expectation of the younger don. With the university explosion there are many within his reach. But now his road to promotion is clear and well-trodden: post-graduate work, a Ph. D., publication, an assistant lecturership, more publication, attendances at conferences; the whole complex operation of "getting known". If he has followed the current fashion in marrying early he may well be living at a considerable distance from his pupils; and, in any event, to borrow Bacon's stately phrase, "charity will hardly suffice to water the ground when it must first fill a well". Charity then should be, in the oldest and broadest sense, between teacher and taught; in the shape of friendship, patient availability, at all hours; a knowledge of cities and men, of business and affairs. But such an ideal state demands a high price today: the devoted teacher may be little regarded in comparison with the writer, the researcher, and, occasionally, the broadcaster. It is even possible – I have heard this argued – that a younger teacher may rationalize the situation by assuring himself that his first duty is to his family, their security and his promotion. At the same time he is, or should be, steadily building up a sort of family of ex-pupils and friends: who will turn to him constantly throughout their subsequent careers for advice, criticism of their own creative work, testimonials for their own promotion. It is part of his task to devise some method of keeping records of all those he has taught, and this in itself is a large and considerable burden.

As to publication, I receive every year perhaps a score of papers, many of them from across the Atlantic, on many subjects. Few of them are worth more than a cursory glance. The writers, if pressed, will admit that these are for show. I know of one university where the professors are required to submit yearly, as evidence for their possible promotion, every scrap of paper they have published, down to the smallest poem. Such things are rewarded. It is not uncommon for a professor to stipulate, on a new contract, that he will only teach post-graduate work. If there is excessive wastage – and many universities reject 40% after the first year[8] – the junior years may well be taught by young and relatively inexperienced instructors. This is a reversal of an ancient and, I think, valuable tradition; that only the most eminent teachers are good enough to teach the first year.

We may look into the crystal, or the ink-pool, again. Perhaps we might recognize one day that English, as an honours subject at a university, should only be for carefully selected students; that the delicacy and complexity of the response of the individual, and the crucial importance of the values transmitted, makes any system of mass-instruction actively pernicious. That our students should be taught to master a small number of weighty and significant texts before they adventure on even the most enlightened criticism; and that they should be taught to weigh that criticism before they accept it. That they should be encouraged towards understanding of aesthetic form by reading aloud, learning to interpret latent subtleties and music by the voice. That they should memorize great tracts of poetry, and perhaps some prose (in the old tradition), because it is only by living with it in this way that they can know it in the marrow-bone. That we should provide them with teachers who acknowledge no other claims than the rigorous ones of their vocation, and who know that a scholar who produces in a life-time two books that will be read fifty years after his death deserves the best from his university.

Under these conditions we might find that the study of English *might* become vital, of incalculable importance, in that assertion and transmission of values of which it is capable.

NOTES

1 E.M.W. Tillyard, *The Muse Unchained*.
2 There are now far too many books that purport to offer such guidance, particularly in the U.S. See, *passim,* C. S. Lewis's lecture *The Abolition of Man.*
3 This is clearly one reason for withdrawals and breakdowns.
4 Witness the common diversion from originals into every kind of selection or anthology; and F. L. Lucas's remark "The imagination has been laid in a great tomb of criticism."
5 *The Teaching of English at the Universities,* English Association Pamphlet No. 26, October 1913.
6 C.S. Lewis, *The Abolition of Man.*
7 A certain civic university demands an average of nineteen lectures a week during the first year.
8 It has been suggested in a recent article that certain universities plan for built-in wastage: partly to facilitate admissions, partly to proclaim their own high standards.

BIOGRAPHIES

KENNETH ADAM, C.B.E., F.R.S.A., M.A., is Director of B.B.C. Television. He was educated at Nottingham High School, and at St. Johns College Cambridge where he was senior scholar and prizeman. He was a member of the editorial staff of the Manchester Guardian from 1930 until 1934 when he became Home News Editor for the B.B.C. for two years. In 1936 he became a special correspondent of the Star and in 1940 Press Officer for B.O.A.C. In 1941 he was appointed Director of B.B.C. Publicity and in 1950 Controller of the B.B.C. Light Programme. In 1955 he became joint General Manager of the Hulton Press for two years and in 1957 was appointed Controller of B.B.C. Television Programmes. In 1961 he became Director. He is a Governor of the Charing Cross Hospital and the British Film Institute.

The Most Rev. G. A. BECK, A.A., ARCHBISHOP OF LIVERPOOL was educated at Clapham College and St. Michael's College, Hitchin. He became a priest in 1927, and in 1934 received a B.A. (Hons) from London University. He was on the staff of St. Michael's College Hitchin until 1941 when he became its Headmaster. In 1944 he became Headmaster of The Becket School, Nottingham where he remained until 1948 when he was consecrated Titular Bishop of Tigia and Co-adjutor Bishop of Brentwood by Cardinal Griffin. He was Bishop of Brentwood from 1951 until 1955 when he became Bishop of Salford. In 1964 he became Archbishop. He has been Chairman of the Catholic Education Council since 1949.

Dr. Beck's publications include *Assumptionist Spirituality* (1936), *The Family and the Future* (1948), (editor with A. C. F. Beales)

323

English translation of Gonella's *The Papacy and World Peace* (1944) and edited *The English Catholics 1850–1950* (1950).

JOHN BLACKIE, C.B., is now a part time lecturer at Homerton College, Cambridge Institute of Education and a writer, having retired as a Chief Inspector of the Department of Education and Science in 1966. He was educated at Bradfield College, and at Magdalene College Cambridge. He was an assistant master at Lawrenceville School, New Jersey, U.S.A. from 1926 to 1927 and at Bradfield from 1928 until 1933. He was Assistant Director of the Public Schools Empire Tour to New Zealand from 1932 to 1933 when he was appointed one of Her Majesty's Inspectors of Schools. He was District Inspector for Manchester from 1936 until 1947 when he became Divisional Inspector for the Eastern Division. He was appointed Chief Inspector in 1951. He belonged to the 47th County of Lancashire Home Guard from 1940 until 1944. He is a Fellow of the Royal Entomological Society of London.

His publications include *Family Holidays Abroad* (with Pamela Blackie) (1961), *Good Enough for the Children?* (1963, and *Inside Primary Schools* (1967).

KATHLEEN BLISS, M.A., is a Lecturer at the University of Sussex. She was educated at Girton College, Cambridge. From 1932 until 1939 she did educational work in India. After the War she was Editor of the *Christian Newsletter* from 1945 until 1949, and from 1951 until 1955 she was Research Assistant (Talks) at the B.B.C. In the following year she became Research Assistant to the Y.M.C.A dealing with education in industry which position she held until 1957. In 1958 she became General Secretary to the Church of England Board of Education which position she held until 1967. She is a member of the Central and Executive Committees of the World Council of Churches and is a member of the Council of the University of Essex. She received an Honorary Doctorate of Divinity from the University of Aberdeen in 1949.

Her publications include *The Service and Status of Women in the Churches* (1951) and *We the People* (1963).

MARGARETH BRANCH, A.A.P.S.W., is General Secretary of the National Association of Gifted Children. After training at Liverpool University she worked as a Personnel Manager and after the War was in U.N.R.A. for two years. On her return she took a diploma in Mental Health and has since worked at various hospitals. For some years Head P.S.W. at a London teaching hospital her interest in Gifted Children arose in the course of her work.

JOHN BURROWS is Her Majesty's Chief Inspector for Primary and Secondary Education. He was educated at the King Edward VI School, Southampton and at Gonville and Caius College Cambridge where he studied Modern Languages then spending a year in the University's Department of Education. He taught in Secondary and Junior Boarding and Day Schools in the West Country and the Home Counties. He became an H.M.I. in 1946 when he served in East Anglia, the North and London, becoming Divisional Inspector for the Metropolitan Division in 1960 and Chief Inspector in 1966. His special interests are the Middle School, socially and culturally deprived children and the links between secondary and further education.

LORD BUTLER OF SAFFRON WALDEN, P.C., C.H., M.A., has been Master of Trinity College, Cambridge since 1965: he is also Chancellor of the University of Essex and Sheffield University.

He was educated at Marlborough and Pembroke College, Cambridge where he was President of the Union. He entered Parliament as Member for Saffron Walden in 1929 and held the position of Under Secretary of State for the India Office from 1932–37. He was Parliamentary Secretary to the Ministry of Labour, 1937–38, Under Secretary of State for Foreign Affairs 1938–41, Minister of Education 1941–45, Chancellor of the Exchequer 1951–55, Lord Privy Seal 1955–59, Leader of the House of Commons 1955–61, Home Secretary 1957–62, First Secretary of State July 1962–October 1963 and Deputy Prime Minister and Minister in Charge of Central African Office for the same period, Secretary of State for Foreign Affairs 1963–64, Chairman of the Conservative Party organisation 1959–61, Chairman of the Conservative Research Department 1945–46, and Chairman of the Conservative Party's Advisory Committee of Policy 1950–64. He was created a Life Peer in 1965 on his retirement from politics.

He is President of the Royal Society of Literature, of the National Association for Mental Health and of the Council of National Union of Conservative Associations. He is High Steward of Cambridge University and of the City of Cambridge and a Freeman of Saffron Walden.

He holds Honorary Doctorates of Law from Cambridge, Nottingham, Bristol, Sheffield, St. Andrews and Glasgow, and an Honorary

Doctorate of Civil Law from Oxford. He holds Doctor of Literature degrees from both Oxford and Cambridge and he is an Honorary Fellow of Pembroke College, and Corpus Christi College, Cambridge and St. Anthony's College Oxford.

ANTHONY CHENEVIX-TRENCH, M.A., is Head Master of Eton College. He was educated at Shrewsbury School and Christ Church, Oxford where he was a Classical Scholar where he gained 1st. Class Hon. Mods, and the De Paravicini Scholarship. He joined the Royal Artillery in 1939 and was seconded to the Indian Artillery (4th Hazara Mountain Battery, Frontier Force) in 1940. He served in Malaya was captured and was a P.O.W. in Singapore from 1942 to 1945. He gained 1st Class Lit. Hum., and Prox. acc. Craven and Ireland Scholarships in 1948 and in the same year became an assistent Master at Shrewsbury. In 1951 he became a Tutor in Classics at Christ Church and returned to Shrewsbury as House Master of School House in 1952. In 1955 he was appointed Headmaster of Bradfield College where he remained until 1963 when he went to Eton as Head Master. He was a member of the Robbins Committee on Higher Education in 1961.

EDWARD S. CONWAY is Headmaster of the J.F.S. Comprehensive School in North London. He was educated in Llanelly, at the University College of Swansea and at the Universities of Liverpool where he gained his M.A. and London (L.S.E.) where he received his Ph.D. He taught in Liverpool schools from 1936 until 1951 becoming Headmaster of the Liverpool Hebrew All-Age School in 1944. He was Principal of the Jewish Orphanage from 1951 until 1958 when he took up his present appointment.

His publications include *Post-War Employment* (1943) and many articles.

DAVID DONNISON is Professor of Social Administration, University of London at the London School of Economics. He was educated at Marlborough College and at Magdalene College Oxford. He was an Assistant Lecturer and then Lecturer at Manchester University from 1950 to 1953 and from then until 1955 Lecturer at Toronto. In 1956 he became Reader at the London School of Economics which position he held until 1961 when he became Professor. He is Vice-Chairman of the Public Schools Commission.

His publications include *The Neglected Child and Social Services* (1954), *Welfare Services in a Canadian Community* (1958),

Housing since the Rent Act (1961), *Social Policy and Administration* (1965) and *The Government of Housing* (1967).

SIR RONALD GOULD is General Secretary of the National Union of Teachers, First President of the World Confederation of Organisations of the Teaching Profession, and Deputy Chairman of the I.T.A. He was educated at the Shepton Mallet Grammar School and Westminster Training College. He was an assistant Master at Radstock Council School from 1924 to 1941, Headmaster of Welton County School from 1941 to 1946, and Chairman of the North Radstock U.D.C. from 1936 until 1946. He was President of the National Union of Teachers from 1943 to 1944, becoming General Secretary in 1947.

He is an Hon. Fellow of the Educational Institute of Scotland and the College of Preceptors, a Governor of the Commonwealth Institute and holds an Hon. M.A. from Bristol and Honorary Doctorates of Law from British Columbia and McGill Universities. He is an Honorary Life Member of the National Education Association of the U.S.A., and he has their distinguished service citation, and is a member of the U.K. Commission of U.N.E.S.C.O.

T. R. HENN, C.B.E., M.A., is a Fellow of St. Catherine's College, Cambridge and University Reader in Anglo-Irish Literature. He was educated at Aldenham School and St. Catherine's College Cambridge where he was a Modern Languages Scholar and where he gained a Class 1 Tripos in 1922, and where he was Charles Oldham Shakespeare Scholar and Members' English Prizeman the following year. He was an assistant with the Burmah Oil Company (1923–1925) and in the following year was elected a Fellow of St. Catherine's. He became Praelector in 1927, Tutor in 1934, Special Pro-Proctor (1934–1939) and Senior Tutor (1945–1957). He was Chairman of the Faculty Board of Fine Arts (1952–1963) and Chairman of the Faculty Board of English (1947–1951 and 1961–1965). He is a Governor of Aldenham School. He was Seatonian Prizeman in 1957 and Donnellan Lecturer and Warton Lecturer, British Academy in 1965. During the Second World War he served as Brigadier, General Staff, and was awarded the C.B.E. (Mil) and the U.S. Legion of Merit and was twice mentioned in despatches. He is Director of the Yeats Summer School at Sligo.

His publications include, *Longinus and English Criticism* (1934), *Field Sports in Shakespeare* (1934), *The Lonely Tower* (1950 and 1965), *Practical Fly-Tying* (1950), *The Apple and the Spectroscope*

(1951 and 1963), *The Harvest of Tragedy* (1956), *Science in Writing* (1960), *Passages for Divine Reading* (1963), *Synge's Plays and Poems* (editor 1963), and *Poems* (1964).

The Rev. ROY HERBERT is Secretary of the Church of England Youth Council. He was educated at St. David's College Lampeter. Jesus College Oxford, and Wells Theological College. He was a curate in Cirencester from 1950 to 1954, the Bishop's Chaplain in the Diocese of Gloucester from 1955 until 1961, the Training Tutor of the Church of England Youth Council from 1961 until he became its Secretary in 1964. In 1962 his *Introducing Anglican Belief* was published.

LORD JAMES OF RUSHOLME is Vice-Chancellor of the University of York. He was educated at Taunton's School, Southampton and Queen's College Oxford (where he was an Exhibitioner and Hon. Scholar in 1927, and becoming an Hon. Fellow in 1959). He was Goldsmith's Exhibitioner in 1929, received his B.A. (1st Class Hons., Chemistry) and B.Sc. in 1931 and his M.A. and D.Phil in 1933. He was an assistant Master at Winchester College from 1933 until 1945 when he became High Master of Manchester Grammar School. He remained there until he became Vice-Chancellor of the University of York in 1962. He was a member of the University Grants Committee for ten years from 1949 on and was Chairman of the Headmasters' Conference 1953–54. He was a member of the Central Advisory Council on Education from 1957 until 1961 and a member of the Standing Commission on Museums and Galleries from 1958 until 1961. He holds an Honorary Doctorate of Law from McGill University, is a Fellow of Winchester College and has been a member of the Press Council since 1963.

His publications include (in part) *Elements of Physical Chemistry*, (in part) *Science and Education, An Essay on the Content of Education*, and *Education and Leadership*.

WALTER JAMES is Editor of the Times Educational Supplement. He was educated at Uckfield Grammar School and Keble College Oxford where he was a scholar and where he gained a first class Modern History degree as well as being Liddon Student and the Arnold Essay Prizeman. He was Senior Demy of Magdalen College in 1935 and in the same year was a Scholar in Medieval Studies at the British School in Rome. He was on the Editorial staff of the Manchester Guardian from 1937 to 1946 as well as being in the

National Fire Service for the duration of the War. In 1945 he contented Bury in Lancashire for the Liberal Party and was Deputy Editor of the Times Educational Supplement from 1947 until 1951. He was appointed Editor in 1952 and was a member of the B.B.C. General Advisory Council (1956–64) and of the Council of Industrial Design in 1961. He was elected to the Council of the Royal Society of Arts and was appointed to the Committee of British-American Associates in 1964. He was editor of *Technology* from 1957–60.

His publications include (Ed) *Temples and Faiths* (1958), *The Teacher and his World* (1962), *The Christian in Politics* (1962) and *A Middle Class Parent's Guide to Education* (1964).

BRUCE KEMBLE has been Universities and Education Reporter of the Daily Express since 1964. He was educated at Dulwich College and Downing College, Cambridge.

JAMES LUMSDEN is Senior Lecturer in the Education of Physically Handicapped Children at the University of London Institute of Education. He was educated at the High School, Dundee and Edinburgh University where he gained an M.A. (Hons) in English Literature and Language in 1926. He trained as a teacher at Murray House Edinburgh and graduated with a B.Ed. degree in 1928. He received a scholarship from Columbia University New York where he studied comparative education and educational psychology for a year. He returned to Scotland where he taught at Murray House School for a year and then became an H.M.I. with a special interest for the handicapped and Special schools. In 1945 he became Staff Inspector in charge of Special Education and Treatment until he retired in 1965. He then went to the Institute of Education as Senior Lecturer.

SIR ROBERT MAYER, LL.D., is the founder of the Robert Mayer Children's concerts which were started in 1923, of Youth and Music in 1956, and of the Transatlantic Foundation Anglo-American Scholarships. He is a member of the executive of the London Symphony Orchestra, the National Music Council, the English Chamber Orchestra, the Wind Music Society, the Council for Christians and Jews, the Anglo-Israel Association, and Morley College. He is Chairman of the First British American Corporation and of Colin Smythe Ltd. He received an Hon. LL.D. from the University of Leeds last year.

His publications include *Young People in Trouble* and *Crescendo*.

SIR JOHN NEWSOM, C.B.E., is Chairman of the Public Schools Commission and a Joint Managing Director of Longmanns, Green & Co. Ltd. He was educated at the Imperial Service College and The Queen's College, Oxford where he was a Scholar. He had varied experience in education, social work and licenced victualling from 1931 to 1940 when he became County Education Officer to the Hertfordshire County Council where he remained until 1957. He was Chairman of the Central Advisory Council for Education (England) from 1961 till 1963 and he has been its Deputy Chairman since then.

He was Chairman of the Committee set up to report of Secondary Education and whose report *Half Our Future* was published in 1963.

He has been Chairman of the Educational Advisory Council of the I.T.A. since 1964 and is Chairman of the Harlow Development Corporation.

His publications include *On the Other Side* (1930), *Out of the Pit* (1936), *Willingly to School* (1944), *Education of Girls* (1948), *Child at School* (1950), *Galloway Gamble* (1951), *Rogues Yarn* (1953), (as Marius Rose) *The Intelligent Teacher's Guide to Preferment* (1954), *A.D. History Newsheets* (1955).

E. PARKINSON, H.M.I., is a Staff Inspector in Further Education with the Department of Education and Science with a special interest in the liberal education of everyone above the school-leaving age, including those in penal establishments. He taught classics in northern Grammar Schools before the last War and, after serving in the R.A.F. and the Army, became County Inspector of Schools to the Devon L.E.A. and subsequently Assistant Education Officer with the Hampshire L.E.A.

RICHMOND POSTGATE, M.A., is Controller, Educational Broadcasting at the B.B.C. He was educated at St. Georges School, Harpenden, Herts and Clare College Cambridge. He was on on the editorial staff of the Manchester Guardian, a teacher, and then went in for County L.E.A. administration. He was Head of School Broadcasting and then became Director General of the Nigerian Broadcasting Corporation from 1959 to 1961. In 1963 he became Assistant Controller of Educational Broadcasting and then in 1965 Controller.

Biographies

SIR HERBERT READ, D.S.O., M.C., M.A., was educated at Crossley's School, Halifax and at the University of Leeds. He was Commissioned in 1915 rising to Captain in 1917. He fought in France and Belgium from 1915 to 1918 with the Yorkshire Regiment when he received the M.C., D.S.O. and was mentioned in despatches. After the War he became Assistant Principal, H.M. Treasury (1919–1922), Assistant Keeper, Victoria and Albert Museum (1922–1931), Watson Gordon Professor of Fine Art in the University of Edinburgh (1931–1933), Sydney Jones Lecturer in Art, and University of Liverpool (1935–1936). He was Editor of the Burlington Magazine from 1933 to 1939 and was Leon Fellow, University of London (1940–1942), Charles Eliot Norton Professor of Poetry, University of Harvard (1953–1954), A.W. Mellon Lecturer in Fine Arts, Washington (1954). He became Senior Fellow at the Royal College of Art in 1962 and holds a Doctorate in Fine Arts from the University of Buffalo and an Honorary Litt. D. from the University of Boston, Mass. He is President of the Society for Education through Art, the Institute of Contemporary Arts, the British Society of Aesthetics and the Yorkshire Philosophical Society. He holds distinctions from numerous foreign academic bodies and societies.

His publications include *English Prose Style* (1928), *Wordsworth* (Clerk Lectures 1930), *The Meaning of Art* (1931), *Art & Industry* (1934), *The Green Child* (1935), *Art & Society* (1936), *Collected Essays* (1938), *Education through Art* (1945), *A Coat of Many Colours* (1945), *Collected Poems* (1946), *The Philosophy of Modern Art* (1952), *The True Voice of Feeling* (1953), *Icon & Idea* (1955), *Art & Sculpture* (1956), *A Concise History of Modern Painting* (1959), *The Forms of Things Unknown* (1960), *The Contrary Experience* (1963), *A Concise History of Modern Sculpture* (1964), *The Origins of Form in Art* (1965), and *Henry Moore: Life & Works* (1965).

LORD ROBBINS OF CLARE MARKET, C.H., C.B., F.B.A., B.Sc., has been Chairman of the Financial Times and Chairman of the Committee on Higher Education since 1961. Educated at Southall County School, University College London and the London School of Economics, he served in the First World War. Between the Wars he held various positions at the London School of Economics and at New College Oxford. In 1941 he became Director of the Economic Section of Offices of the War Cabinet which position he held until the end of the War. He was President of the

Royal Economic Society 1954–55, has been a Trustee of the National Gallery almost continuously from 1952 to the present day and similarly at Trustee of the Tate Gallery from 1953 to 1967. He was created a Life Peer in 1959. He holds honorary Doctorates from Durham, Exeter, Strathclyde, York, Sheffield, Heriot-Watt, Columbia, Cambridge, Leicester, Strasbourg, London and California, and Honorary Fellowships of University College, London, and the Manchester College of Science and Technology, London School of Economics and the London Graduate School of Business Studies.

Lord Robbins' publications since the War include *The Economic Problem in Peace and War* (1947), *The Theory of Economic Policy in English Classical Political Economy* (1952), *The Economist in the Twentieth Century and other Lectures in Political Economy* (1954), *Robert Torrens and the Evolution of Classical Economics* (1963), *Politics and Economics* (1963) and *The University and the Modern World* (1966).

The Rt. Rev. A. J. TRILLO, M.TH., BISHOP OF HERTFORD was translated from the Diocese of Bedford at the beginning of this year. He was educated at The Quintin School and King's College, University of London. From 1931 he was in business in the film industry for five years, during the latter part of this period he was having theological training at King's College at evening classes. In 1936 he gained an exhibition which enabled him to study full time and in 1938 he graduated with a 1st Class Hons. B.D. and a 1st Class Hons A.K.C., gaining his M.Th. in 1943. From 1938 to 1941 he was assistant curate at Christ Church Fulham, and from then until 1945 he was Assistant Curate at St. Gabriels' Cricklewood where he was in charge of St. Michaels. From 1945 until 1950 he was North Eastern Secretary for the S.C.M. in schools and from then until 1955 he was Rector of Friern Barnet and Lecturer in New Testament Greek at King's College, London. In 1955 he was appointed Principal of Bishop's College, Cheshunt. In 1963 he was consecrated Suffragan Bishop of Bedford. He is a Fellow of King's College London.

MONICA WINGATE, M.A., has just retired as Principal of Balls Park College, Cambridge Institute of Education. She was educated at St. Paul's Girls School and Newnham College Cambridge where she was an exhibitioner and gained a 1st Class degree. She taught at Talbot Heath School, Bournemouth, Roedean and Dartford County School. In 1942 she became Headmistress of Gordon County School Maidenhead and in 1947 she was appointed the first Principal of Balls Park. Miss Wingate is a member of the Christian Frontier Council and an Associate of the British Parliamentary Group of World Development.

T. R. YOUNG is H.M. District Inspector for Leeds. He was educated at the Tynemouth High School and from there he gained an exhibition to Queen's College, Cambridge. He received his teaching qualification (Dip. Ed.) from London, and for twelve years he was in the Colonial Service in East Africa, where he was a Headmaster, and then a Lecturer at a Teachers' Training College. He made the first experiment in adult literacy in East Africa. In 1960 he returned to England and was appointed an H.M.I. first in the North Riding of Yorkshire until 1965 and then with the Schools Council helping to produce Working Paper No. 11 (Society and the Young School Leaver) which was published in 1966. In the same year he was appointed District Inspector.

His lecture *A Basis for Religious Education* was published last year.

THE EDITOR

Peter Bander is a Senior Lecturer at Wall Hall College, (Cambridge Institute of Education). His wide experience in teaching combined with his positive and constructive outlook and interest in education on all levels qualified him eminently to edit a symposium such as this. Since undertaking his editorial task, Mr. Bander has been in close contact with the contributors, discussing with them the problems and possibilities which arose and also conducting the interviews with Lord Butler, Lord Robbins, Lord James and Sir John Newsom.

As author of ONE FOR THE ROAD and TWO FOR THE IOAD, Peter Bander is already well known in many secondary schools.